KT-198-519

PLANTS, PEOPLE & PLACES

The Plant Lover's Companion

JULIA BRITTAIN

D&C

David and Charles

TYNNWYD O STOC
WITHDRAWN
FROM STOCK

A David & Charles Book

Copyright © David & Charles Limited 2006

David & Charles is an F+W Publications Inc. Company
4700 East Galbraith Road Cincinnati, OH 45236
First published in the UK in 2006

All rights reserved. No part of this publication may be reproduced, stored
in a retrieval system, or transmitted in any form or by any means, electronic
or mechanical, by photocopying, recording or otherwise, without prior
permission in writing from the publisher.

A catalogue record for this book is available from the British Library.
ISBN-13: 978-0-7153-24121-9
ISBN-10: 0-7153-2421-7

Printed in Singapore by KHL Pte Ltd
for David & Charles
Brunel House   Newton Abbot   Devon

Produced for David & Charles by
Outhouse Publishing
Winchester   Hampshire SO22 5DS

Consultant Editors Jennifer Harmer, Jane Sterndale-Bennett

For OutHouse Publishing:
Editor Sue Gordon   **Designer** Robin Whitecross
Proofreader Lindsey Brown   **Maps** Caroline Wollen

For David & Charles:
Commissioning Editor Mic Cady   **Head of Design** Prudence Rogers
Production Roger Lane

Visit our website at www.davidandcharles.co.uk

David& Charles books are available from all good bookshops;
alternatively you can contact our Orderline on 0870 9908222 or write to us
at FREEPOST EX2 110, D&C Direct, Newton Abbot TQ12 4ZZ
(no stamp required UK mainland); US customers call
800-289-0963 and Canadian customers call 800-840-5220.

NOTE FROM THE PUBLISHERS

The very broad subject area of *Plants, People & Places* carries with it considerable potential for error. Information has been gathered from many different sources, and it has not always been possible to check facts at first hand. While every effort has been made to give correct information, the publishers cannot accept responsibility for mistakes or their consequences. David & Charles would be happy to hear from readers should they find any inaccuracies, and will make every effort to put things right in any future edition.

Contents

Hibiscus syriacus

Foreword

We are so fortunate today that we have such a wonderful range of hardy plants at our disposal. However, it is hard to believe that the majority of the ornamental trees and shrubs that we grow in our gardens now have only been introduced into cultivation in the past 200 years.

In the early days of this exciting era in garden history, plant hunters collected on behalf of wealthy garden owners and, sometimes, nurseries. New plant introductions were jealously guarded by those who sponsored their discovery and then grew them in cultivation. Growing up in the hardy plant and nursery world, I was surrounded by plant treasures acquired by my grandfather Edwin Lawrence Hillier and my father, Harold Hillier. I remember hearing how they were invited to Caerhays, in Cornwall, by the Williams family to collect propagation material. Caerhays sponsored George Forrest for many years, so it was a garden with a wealth of rare and choice plants. These great Cornish gardens were the bastion of plant introductions. Remember that new plants were often introduced as seed: this might have been collected and distributed to several gardens in the same area, but we can be sure that every head gardener would claim that his garden had the finest form!

The owners of these great gardens and their head gardeners were all fanatical plantsmen and did not readily welcome the 'trade' into their world. However, my grandfather and my father were plant nuts too and spoke their language, so they sometimes gained access to this exclusive world. Certainly the desire to protect cherished plant possessions – and keep them out of the hands of commercial nurserymen – delayed their availability for quite some time. In many cases it is only recently that the general public has been able to acquire these plants.

Some might regard conifers as rather dull but my grandfather was a great enthusiast. His interest probably grew out of his love of forestry, and he was a keen member of the Royal Forestry Society. In the early 1920s he took my father, a very young man at the time, on a trip to Scotland with the society. On their visit to Glamis Castle my father was introduced to the young Lady Elizabeth Bowes-Lyon, who later became Her Majesty Queen Elizabeth The Queen Mother. They shared a love of plants and gardening that lasted throughout their lives.

Because of my grandfather's work with conifers, and in recognition of his contribution to the horticultural world, my father was presented with a specimen of *Metasequoia glyptostroboides*, the dawn redwood. This deciduous conifer exists in fossils, but it was only in 1941 that it was discovered growing in central China.

Harold Hillier with propagator Vic Polovsky in the 1950s

It was introduced to the West in 1944. Imagine how excited my father was when he received one of those first plants. I felt similar excitement when I saw this tree naturalized by the hundreds of thousands in Sichuan, in the late 1990s.

Now that world travel has become easier and remote areas of the world are more accessible, we are fortunate to be able to see plants in their native habitats as well as growing in our gardens at home. Plants are a passion for so many people, and understanding where they came from and reading the stories behind their introduction only fires that passion.

John Hillier VMH

Top: Hillier & Sons letterhead from 1931
Above: Some Hillier employees in the early 1930s

Introduction

How did plants reach our gardens? There are probably as many answers to that question as there are plants. Gathering together a miscellany of this information, *Plants, People and Places* gives a context to botanical names by identifying some of the people and places whose names are scattered across the plant world.

PLANTS, PEOPLE AND GARDENS

Many garden plants are so familiar to us that it is easy to forget they are foreign imports. From earliest times, travellers from all walks of life – doctors, missionaries, scientists, soldiers and diplomats – have been fascinated by unknown flowers, whether wild species or 'improved' garden versions, and have brought home seeds and plants. Later, professional plant collectors were sponsored by botanic gardens, wealthy garden owners and commercial nurseries hoping to display the newest discoveries. Plant hunters thrived on the challenge, enduring unimaginable hardships in order to obtain rare plant treasures. Through them, the number of plants in gardens and nursery catalogues grew exponentially, especially in the 18th and 19th centuries. Nurserymen and amateur breeders traditionally 'improved' this bounty: certain plant groups, such as roses, rhododendrons, hostas, irises and daylilies, attracted their attention at different times, resulting in even more kinds of plant (and even more names).

PLANTS ON THE MOVE

There is often confusion over the introduction of plants into cultivation, and it can be hard to be certain who introduced a particular plant, where it came from, and when. Identifying new plants was a hit-and-miss affair, far removed from today's DNA techniques and without even the help of photography. Transporting live plants from distant countries, on boats that took months to reach home, was a risky business, so plants were usually introduced as dried, pressed herbarium specimens, with or without seeds from which they could be propagated: most early plant collectors were more concerned with botany than horticulture. The role of the botanical artist was paramount in recording the appearance of living plants at different seasons (such as in flower and in fruit),

	Pierre Belon	Mathias de l'Obel		John Gerard	Carolus Clusius
William Turner	Leonhart Fuchs	Ogier Ghiselin de Busbecq			Jean Robin
1530	1540	1550	1560	1570	1580	1590	1600	1610
	Padua: Orto Botanico				Leiden Botanical Garden

so painters such as Bauer and Aubriet were key members of expeditions.

Only with the 1830s invention of the portable greenhouses called 'Wardian cases' did it become easier to ship live plants. But this did not end uncertainty, for the same plant could be introduced into different countries (or even the same country) by different collectors. Newly collected plants went unrecorded or were misidentified. Some failed to thrive, or met with accidents (pirates, earthquakes and shipwreck were all in a day's work for many plant hunters). It often took several attempts before an introduction was secure.

Conservation was not a priority for the plant hunters of the past, but accelerating habitat loss now makes it a central concern. Since the Convention on Biological Diversity of 1993, plant collecting throughout the world has been strictly regulated, and the proper consents are essential.

PLANTS AND THEIR NAMES

Plant names often commemorate an individual. This may be the person who discovered the plant in the wild, or introduced it into cultivation. It may be the nurseryman who bred a hybrid or selected a cultivar, or his relative, friend or mentor. Equally, it may be none of these: the genus *Fuchsia*, for example, is named to commemorate Leonhart Fuchs, who lived nearly 200 years too early even to see his namesake plant. Many plants are named after the place where they were raised – perhaps a village, a garden or a nursery – but the precise connection can be hard to determine: for example, a nursery may have raised, or introduced, or simply sold the plant.

ABOUT THIS BOOK

The background to plants and their names draws on a huge fund of information belonging to history, geography, botany, and the remarkable stories of individual lives. *Plants, People and Places* is deliberately confined to the discovery and development of the plants found in temperate gardens, but even this is such a vast subject that it is impossible to give more than a taster in a book of this size. Regrettably, much of interest has had to be omitted, but more information on many topics will be found in the books listed on pages 10–11.

Hosta sieboldiana, named in 1888 after Philipp von Siebold

Note: Semi-bold type denotes a cross-reference to another entry in the book.

About plant names

Most of the people and places featured in this book are here because there are plants named after them. This traditional way of linking a plant with a person or place can take one or more of several forms.

Modern botanical nomenclature is now standardized internationally, thanks largely to the 18th-century Swedish naturalist Carl Linnaeus. He proposed a universal binomial system, distinguishing between thousands of plants by giving each one a genus name and a species name or specific epithet.

The **genus** name (which has an initial capital letter) is applied to every member of a group of closely related plants of similar structure, for example *Fuchsia* or *Rudbeckia*.

A **species** name – more 'specific' – applies to a particular, uniquely identifiable plant found in the wild, for example *Fuchsia magellanica* or *Rudbeckia laciniata*.

Sometimes a species is subdivided. The abbreviations 'subsp.' (subspecies), 'var.' (varietas) or 'f.' (forma) are used when this occurs, indicating recognized, naturally occurring variants of a plant, as in *Pieris formosa* var. *forrestii*, a variety of

Pieris formosa distinguished by bright red young shoots.

Hybrids are indicated by a multiplication sign in their name. They can occasionally be intergeneric hybrids, for example × *Cupressocyparis leylandii* (a hybrid between *Cupressus macrocarpa* and *Chamaecyparis nootkatensis*), or, more commonly, hybrids between two species in the same genus, for example *Magnolia* × *loebneri*, a hybrid between *Magnolia stellata* and *Magnolia kobus*.

More often encountered in garden plants are **cultivar** names, which appear in inverted commas as, for example *Magnolia* × *loebneri* 'Leonard Messel'. Cultivars are variants selected for cultivation, originating as chance seedlings in a garden or in the wild, or as a particular form of a simple or complex hybrid deliberately raised in a nursery. Cultivar names are always accompanied by a genus name. They sometimes have a species name, as above, and sometimes not, as in *Magnolia* 'Felix Jury'. The same cross or hybrid may give rise to a number of different cultivars.

The latest addition to the plant name lexicon is the **trade designation** or selling name. This is a more attractive

Engelbert Kaempfer	Hans Sloane	Philip Miller		Pierre d'Incarville	John Bartram
Joseph Pitton de Tournefort	Mark Catesby			Georg Steller	Carl Linnaeus

1690	1700	1710	1720	1730	1740	1750	1760	1770
Brompton Park Nursery				Kew	Vilmorin		Loddiges	
			Späth Nursery			Vineyard Nursery		

> *'The plant-collector's job is to uncover the hidden beauties of the world, so that others may share his joy.'*
>
> Frank Kingdon Ward (1924)

or easily remembered name, used for marketing purposes in conjunction with certain 'nonsense' cultivar names that are adopted by some growers to indicate a plant's origin, usually linked with Plant Breeders' Rights. For example, in the name of *Clematis* Wisley ('Evipo001'), the cultivar name itself is a kind of code (in which 'Evi' identifies the breeder, Raymond Evison). In *Rosa* Gertrude Jekyll ('Ausbord') the cultivar name similarly reveals that David Austin is the breeder. For selling purposes these plants assume the more user-friendly trade designations Wisley and Gertrude Jekyll, which are distinguished typographically from the rest of the name.

As these examples show, any component of a plant's name can be commemorative. Sometimes the names of two or even three people appear in a single plant name, as in *Tolmiea menziesii* 'Taff's Gold', commemorating William Tolmie, Archibald Menzies and Stephen Taffler. The pages that follow tell something of the people honoured in the examples above and of many others.

Some of the place names that gardeners and plantsmen may come

MISLEADING NAMES

Places referred to in a plant's name can often be a clue to the native origin of the plant, but many are misleading, to say the least. *Hibiscus syriacus* comes from India and China, not Syria. *Argyranthemum maderense* is native to Lanzarote and Fuerteventura rather than nearby Madeira, while the Guernsey lily *Nerine sarniensis*, whose Latin and English names both suggest a link with the Channel Islands, actually hails from South Africa. *Scilla peruviana*? From the Mediterranean!

Scilla peruviana

NATIONAL COLLECTIONS

Founded in 1978, the National Council for the Conservation of Plants and Gardens (NCCPG) coordinates this successful volunteer scheme to conserve and document a wide range of species and cultivars of garden plants. Over 600 plant groups are protected in this way, in a range of nurseries, private gardens and institutions.

across are also explained. Species names often indicate a plant's origin – perhaps the country or region where it occurs in the wild. Cultivar names may feature the garden where the plant was found or the nursery where it was raised.

Carl Thunberg	*William Curtis*			*Nathaniel Wallich*		*James Tweedie*	*Sir William Hooker*	
Sir Joseph Banks		*Archibald Menzies*		*Thomas Nuttall*		*David Douglas*	*Robert Fortune*	
1770	1780	1790	1800	1810	1820	1830	1840	1850
	Pennells		*Glasnevin*	*Suttons Seeds*		*Westonbirt Arboretum*		
	Malmaison		*Longwood*	*Veitch*			*Tresco Abbey Gardens*	

Further reading

Below are listed a number of publications that contain more information on plant hunters, nurserymen, gardeners and the general background to plants and their names. For more detail on individuals, look for biographies and memoirs of gardeners and plant hunters, and the writings of key figures such as Tournefort, Kingdon Ward, Jekyll and many others.

Baren, Maurice *How it all Began in the Garden* (1994)

Bean, W.J. *Trees and Shrubs Hardy in the British Isles* (1988)

Bloom, Alan *A Plantsman's Perspective* (1987)

Bretschneider, E. *A History of European Botanical Discoveries in China* (1898)

Brickell, Christopher (ed.) *The Royal Horticultural Society A–Z Encyclopedia of Garden Plants* (2003)

Brown, Jane *Eminent Gardeners* (1990)

Brown, Jane *The Pursuit of Paradise* (1999)

Brummitt, R.K. and Powell, C.E. *Authors of Plant Names* (1992)

Campbell-Culver, Maggie *The Origin of Plants* (2001)

Coats, Alice M. *Flowers and their Histories* (1956)

Coats, Alice M. *Garden Shrubs and their Histories* (1963)

Coats, Alice M. *The Quest for Plants: A History of the Horticultural Explorers* (1969)

Coombes, Allen J. *Dictionary of Plant Names* (1994)

Desmond, Ray *A Dictionary of British and Irish Botanists and Horticulturists* (1994)

Druse, Ken *The Collector's Garden* (1996)

Elliott, Brent *Treasures of the Royal Horticultural Society* (1994)

Elliott, Brent *Victoria Medal of Honour 1897–1997* (1997)

Fogg, H.G. Witham *History of Popular Garden Plants* (1976)

Grimshaw, John *The Gardener's Atlas* (1998)

Hadfield, Miles *A History of British Gardening* (1960)

Hadfield, Miles *Pioneers in Gardening* (1955)

Hadfield, Miles, Harling, Robert and Highton, Leonie *British Gardeners: A Biographical Dictionary* (1980)

Harvey, John *Early Nurserymen* (1974)

Fritillaria thunbergii

Louis Van Houtte	Carl Maximowicz	William Robinson		Gertrude Jekyll		George Forrest
Sir Joseph Hooker	Armand David		Augustine Henry	Ellen Willmott		Luther Burbank
1850	1860	1870	1880	1890	1900	1910	1920	1930
Kelways	Hillier	Bodnant	Gravetye Manor		Wisley			
Sunningdale Nursery		Arnold Arboretum				Bees	Hidcote	Loddon Nursery

Hillier, John and Coombes, Allen (eds) *Hillier Manual of Trees and Shrubs* (2002)

Hobhouse, Penelope *Plants in Garden History* (1992)

Hobhouse, Penelope *The Story of Gardening* (2002)

Huxley, Anthony and Griffiths, Mark (eds) *New RHS Dictionary of Gardening* (1999)

Isely, Duane *One Hundred and One Botanists* (1994)

Jellicoe, G. and S. et al. *The Oxford Companion to Gardens* (2001)

Kelly, John *The National Plant Collection* (1993)

King, Peter and Lambert, Katherine (ed.) *The Good Gardens Guide* (2005)

Lamb, Christian *From the Ends of the Earth* (2004)

Lancaster, Roy *Travels in China* (1989)

Lloyd, Christopher (with Bennett, Tom) *Clematis* (1989)

Lord, Tony (ed.) *RHS Plant Finder* (published annually)

Marinelli, Janet (ed.) *Plant* (2004)

Musgrave, Toby; Gardner, Chris; Musgrave, Will *The Plant Hunters* (1998)

Pankhurst, Alex *Who does your Garden Grow?* (1992)

Pavord, Anna *The Naming of Names* (2005)

Richardson, Tim (ed.) *The Garden Book* (2000)

Wisteria sinensis

Stafleu, F.A. and Cowan, R.S. *Taxonomic Literature* (1987)

Stearn, William T. *Botanical Latin* (2004)

Stearn, William T. *Dictionary of Plant Names for Gardeners* (2002)

Stuart, David *The Plants that Shaped our Gardens* (2002)

Taylor, Patrick *The Gardens of Britain and Ireland* (2004)

Thomas, Graham Stuart *Recollections of Great Gardeners* (2003)

Trehane, Piers (ed.) *Index Hortensis* Volume 1: Perennials (1989)

Ward, Bobby J. *The Plant Hunter's Garden* (2004)

Willson, E.J. *Nurserymen to the World* (1989)

Periodicals
The Garden
Journal of the Royal Horticultural Society

Prunus armeniaca

The Plantsman and *The New Plantsman*

1930	1940	1950	1960	1970	1980	1990	2000	2010

Karl Foerster · Graham Stuart Thomas · Roy Lancaster · Dan Hinkley
Frank Kingdon Ward · Margery Fish · David Austin · Beth Chatto · Piet Oudolf · Barry Yinger

Sissinghurst · Blooms · Rosemoor · Great Dixter · Wave Hill · Crûg Farm
Waterperry · The Garden House · Barnsley House · Hadspen · Eden Project

Abbotsbury Subtropical Gardens, Dorset

Its location close to the Dorset coast gives Abbotsbury a temperate, humid climate in which a range of exotic plants can thrive, especially here where a historic walled garden and a woodland microclimate combine to give added protection to the many botanical treasures. The bold, dramatic foliage of palm trees, gunneras, bananas, tree ferns and cannas lends a jungle-like quality to much of the garden, while tender specimens of a different kind thrive in the Mediterranean garden. The collections include many rarities from the southern hemisphere, and there is a National Collection of *Hoheria*. Plants associated with the garden include *Pittosporum tenuifolium* 'Abbotsbury Gold'.

Abbotswood, Gloucestershire

A classic early 20th-century English garden set on a Cotswold hillside near Stow-on-the-Wold, Abbotswood was created by respected plantsman Mark Fenwick, its owner until 1945. It was later the home of Harry Ferguson, of tractor fame. Woodland planting with spring bulbs and shrubs complements the herbaceous borders, lawns and rose beds of the formal terraces. Several plants are named after the garden: *Potentilla fruticosa* 'Abbotswood' and 'Abbotswood Silver', *Rosa* 'Abbotswood' and *Lychnis* × *walkeri* 'Abbotswood Rose'. Another well-known plant from here, introduced to the British nursery trade by Mark Fenwick around 1930, is the charming compact pink *Clematis* 'Etoile Rose'.

Abel, Clarke (1780–1826)

This English surgeon and naturalist accompanied Lord Amherst on an ambassadorial visit to the Chinese emperor in 1816 and collected plants in various areas of **China**. *Abelia chinensis*, introduced to England in 1844, is named after him.

Aberconway see Bodnant

Acorn Bank Garden, Cumbria

The herb garden here, set in the former kitchen garden, is stocked with many kinds of culinary, medicinal or otherwise useful plants, including *Origanum vulgare* 'Acorn Bank'. Here in the Pennines, near Penrith, the climate can be harsh but the high garden walls of this National Trust property shelter a fine collection of herbaceous plants, roses and other shrubs. Drifts of bulbs in spring complement the blossom on a variety of fruit trees.

Adanson, Michel (1727–1806)

The genus *Adansonia*, which contains the extraordinary baobab tree, *Adansonia digitata*, is named after this French botanist who studied under Bernard de **Jussieu** and spent five years as a rather eccentric early plant hunter in tropical west **Africa**.

Africa see pages 14–15

Aiton, William (1731–1793) and William Townsend (1766–1849)

Both the Aitons, father and son, were key figures in horticulture because of their important role in the development of what was eventually to become the Royal Botanic Gardens at **Kew**. Aiton senior arrived at Kew in 1759, having moved to London from his native Scotland five years previously to work for **Philip Miller** at the **Chelsea Physic Garden**. As Kew's first head gardener, he combined the skills of practical horticulture with an aptitude for botanical observation and accuracy. He spent many years, helped by other botanists, in compiling *Hortus Kewensis*, a formidable list of all the plants grown at Kew at the time, with the dates of their introduction into Britain – information that has been valuable to botanists and gardeners ever since.

William Aiton had two sons: John, who became a royal gardener at Windsor, and William Townsend, who progressed from helping his father at Kew to designing gardens for distinguished clients. He returned to Kew to succeed his father in 1793 and, in 1804, became one of the founder members of the **RHS**. For many years Aiton remained devoted to Kew – not only when the gardens continued to prosper with **Sir Joseph Banks** at the helm, but also after Banks became elderly and less active, and as horticulture fell from favour – a victim first of changing fashions and then of political unrest and war. Support for Kew was not forthcoming until the time of Queen Victoria and the appointment of **Sir William Hooker** as director in 1841. The survival of Kew's important botanical collection through the difficult intervening period was largely due to the work of William Townsend Aiton.

Alcazar, Spain

Kniphofia 'Alcazar' and *Iris* 'Alcazar' are named after the great palace of the kings of Seville. The Moors had departed from the city in 1248 and their palace was rebuilt by later monarchs, beginning with the conquering Christian king Pedro I. The resulting royal residence and its extensive gardens (Jardines de las Reales Alcazares) retain many Islamic features, pioneering the style that became known as Mudejar (from the Arabic for 'allowed to remain').

Alhambra, Spain

The terraces and courtyards of the Alhambra and neighbouring Generalife, palaces on a hillside above the city of Granada, are among the most visited and spectacular gardens in the world. They are splendid survivors of the Moorish culture that prevailed in Granada for almost 500 years until 1492. Today crowds of visitors make it difficult to recreate the peace and seclusion that was so important in making these gardens a haven of pleasure. However, it is still possible to appreciate the sheer artistry of the buildings and their detailing, the cooling effect of fountains, pools and rills, the exquisite play of light and shade, and the fragrant planting that was such an important part of the Islamic tradition in which these gardens have their roots. There is a cultivar of myrtle called *Myrtus communis* 'Alhambra', and a number of plants are named after Granada, including a begonia, a camellia and an iris.

A

Africa

The first plant-hunting expedition ever recorded began in Africa. It was ordered by the female pharaoh Queen Hatshepsut (believed by some to be the biblical Queen of Sheba), who ruled Egypt around 1500BC. A fleet of five ships, with 30 oarsmen each, sailed from Kosseir, on the Red Sea, to the Land of Punt – generally thought to be in the area where Somalia is today, but located by some authorities in Lebanon or Palestine. They returned with valuable woods such as ebony, saplings of

Pelargonium zonale

myrrh (transported in the first recorded clay pots), frankincense (*Boswellia*), and other plants and fragrant resins that the Egyptians used in rituals, as cosmetics and for embalming. Some of these finds are described and depicted with remarkable accuracy on the walls of Hatshepsut's temple near Luxor.

Expeditions ordered by later Egyptian rulers are believed to have reached what is now South Africa, and by 600BC Phoenician sailors sent from Egypt travelled from the Red Sea right round the coast of Africa, returning via the Mediterranean. This was the first recorded circumnavigation of the continent, and was not repeated until nearly two millennia later, when Vasco da Gama sailed from the west round the Cape of Good Hope.

The Cape has a special place in the gardening history of the world. It was a vital stopping place on the routes of early navigators and explorers, and news of southern Africa's exceptionally rich flora spread quickly. The fynbos scrubland

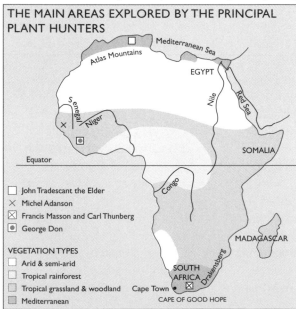

THE MAIN AREAS EXPLORED BY THE PRINCIPAL PLANT HUNTERS

Mediterranean Sea
Atlas Mountains
EGYPT
Senegal
Niger
Nile
Red Sea
SOMALIA
Equator
Congo
MADAGASCAR
Drakensberg
SOUTH AFRICA
Cape Town
CAPE OF GOOD HOPE

☐ John Tradescant the Elder
✕ Michel Adanson
☒ Francis Masson and Carl Thunberg
◉ George Don

VEGETATION TYPES
☐ Arid & semi-arid
☐ Tropical rainforest
☐ Tropical grassland & woodland
▨ Mediterranean

of the south and south-western Cape is one of the world's most botanically diverse places, with a species total approaching 9,000 plants, of which some two-thirds are found nowhere else. Like the **Atlas Mountains** of North Africa, the Cape enjoys a Mediterranean climate with small areas of mountain country qualifying as temperate. This means that at least some of the wild plants are hardy or nearly so. Among those that have

Kirstenbosch

South Africa's National Botanical Garden of Kirstenbosch is unrivalled as a place to experience the infinite variety of the Cape's native flora. Only a tiny area is cultivated, the rest being devoted to protecting threatened habitats such as coastal forest and species-rich fynbos. The conservation role of Kirstenbosch is paramount as more and more species become threatened in the wild. Cultivated plants that bear the name include *Salvia aurea* 'Kirstenbosch' and *Strelitzia reginae* 'Kirstenbosch Gold'.

found a place in temperate gardens are species or cultivars of *Agapanthus* (one of the first to reach Europe), *Kniphofia*, *Gladiolus*, *Lobelia*, *Nerine*, *Restio*, *Eucomis*, *Phygelius* and *Zantedeschia*. South African natives more likely to be seen in the conservatory or glasshouse, or perhaps outdoors in summer, include *Amaryllis*, *Pelargonium* and *Plumbago*, as well as succulent plants of the desert-like karoo, such as some kinds of *Aloe*, *Euphorbia* and *Lithops*. The 1770s and 1780s saw the near-contemporaries **Masson** and **Thunberg** sharing hair-raising adventures on long plant-hunting treks into the often inhospitable interior of southern Africa. Although very different, the two men were united by a common passion for new plants, and their successes were considerable.

Much of the rest of Africa, like **South America**, falls within the tropics, so its plants are suited to a warmer climate and a more constant day length than temperate gardens can provide. Tropical Africa's presence in those gardens has mainly been in the form of exotic plants such as tender *Impatiens*, *Nymphaea* and *Saintpaulia,* grown under cover or used as summer bedding.

Plant hunters everywhere needed to possess unusual fortitude, but more than ever in Africa, where malaria and dysentery, hippos and crocodiles, piracy and native wars added to the usual risks. Nevertheless, a few intrepid botanists and gardeners, including **Michel Adanson** and **George Don**, did explore equatorial Africa, travelling up major rivers such as the Congo, the Nile or the Niger. For most, however, success was rare, for even if they returned alive and well, the results of their collecting often fell victim to disasters ranging from battles to loss in transit, or simply cold weather on the way home.

Eucomis comosa

Phygelius capensis

SOME LATIN TERMS ASSOCIATED WITH AFRICA

aethiopicus, aethiopis from Ethiopia (also used to mean from southern Africa)
africanus; afer (afra, afrum) from Africa
atlanticus from the Atlas Mountains
capensis from the Cape
congolanus from the Congo
madagascariensis from Madagascar
numidicus from Algeria
zuluensis from the former kingdom of Zululand in southern Africa

Allegheny Mountains
This mountain range in the south-eastern United States is associated with the specific epithet *alleghaniensis* (*Betula alleghaniensis* is the grey or yellow birch native to the region). The range is also known as the home of an important rhododendron species, *Rhododendron catawbiense*, which, because of its hardiness, revolutionized breeding programmes after **John Fraser** introduced it to Europe in 1809.

Allen, James (1832–1906)
An amateur gardener and plantsman from Shepton Mallet, in Somerset, Allen was known especially as a breeder of snowdrops. Among the plants named for him is *Galanthus* × *allenii,* found in a parcel of bulbs he received from a nursery in Austria. Another is the beautiful blue spring bulb × *Chionoscilla allenii*, a hybrid between *Chionodoxa* and *Scilla*. Other Allen plants are *Anemone nemorosa* 'Allenii' and *Corydalis* × *allenii*. Snowdrop enthusiasts are also indebted to him for the fine cultivars 'Magnet' and 'Merlin'.

Allioni, Carlo (1728–1804)
This Italian physician, a friend of **Linnaeus**, was professor of botany at Turin. *Primula allionii*, which has many named cultivars, is named after him, as is the succulent *Jovibarba allionii*.

Alnwick Garden, Northumberland
A **David Austin** rose is named after Alnwick Castle which, set in its Capability Brown landscape, has been familiar to generations of visitors. The Alnwick Garden is an ambitious new development within the 18th-century walled garden. Opened in 2001, the multi-million-pound, 12-acre formal garden features Britain's largest collection of European plants, an elaborate 21-weir grand cascade, a huge tree-house and a 'poison garden' with toxic plants from all over the world.

Alströmer, Claus von (1736–1794)
This Swedish naturalist was a pupil of **Linnaeus**, who named the genus *Alstroemeria* for him after Alströmer found *Alstroemeria pelegrina* on a trip to Spain. He sent seeds of it to Linnaeus, who later recommended another of his students, **Anders Dahl**, to work for Alströmer in his private botanic garden and museum near Gothenburg.

Altai Mountains
This range in southern Siberia and Kazakhstan is known for its rich meadow and alpine flora, and is the origin of the epithet *altaicus*, as in *Anemone altaica* and *Daphne altaica*.

America see North America; South America

American Horticultural Society
The AHS was established in 1922 and is the principal organization for gardeners in the USA. It promotes horticultural education and environmentally responsible gardening, encourages excellence through an awards scheme and maintains demonstration gardens at River Farm (its headquarters on the Potomac River in Alexandria, Virginia, on land that belonged to **George Washington**).

Amherst, Alicia (1865–1941)

The Hon. Alicia Amherst is known chiefly as a gardening writer. Her first and most well-known book, *A History of Gardening in England*, was published under her maiden name in 1896, but later works appeared after her name changed, first on her marriage in 1898 when she became the Hon. Mrs Evelyn Cecil, and later when her husband was knighted and she became Lady Rockley. She travelled widely with him, and was also involved in the campaign to rescue the **Chelsea Physic Garden**. *Hebe* 'Alicia Amherst' is named after her.

Amherst, Sarah (1762–1838)

Lady Amherst was married to the Earl of Amherst, who became Governor General of India in 1823. She and her daughter had a keen interest in plants, collecting and sending home seeds of choice species that they found, notably on a long trip to the remote hill station of Simla in the Himalayas in 1826. *Clematis montana* and *Anemone vitifolia* are two plants that were introduced to European gardens in this way. The spectacular Burmese tree *Amherstia nobilis* was named for Lady Amherst by **Nathaniel Wallich** of Calcutta Botanic Garden. Its long-awaited introduction into Britain eventually proved something of a disappointment, as its new owners did not appreciate just how infrequently it flowers.

Anderson, Edward Bertram (1885–1971)

A widely respected and knowledgeable plantsman and horticultural author,

Bertram Anderson

Bertram Anderson moved around the British Isles during his career as a research chemist, making several gardens at different times in his life. A specialist in alpines, he was a founder member of the Alpine Garden Society. He exchanged choice plants with fellow enthusiasts in many countries, and travelled abroad in search of new plants until shortly before his death at the age of 85. He had built up a fine collection of plants, some of which came into the horticultural trade through his friendship with **Joe Elliott**, whose nursery business was not far from Anderson's last home, a cottage at Lower Slaughter in the Cotswolds. *Sedum* 'Bertram Anderson' and *Thymus pulegioides* 'Bertram Anderson' are probably the most widely known of several very good plants named after him, but others are *Galanthus* 'Bertram Anderson' and *Pulmonaria longifolia* 'Bertram Anderson', while *Oxalis* 'Beatrice Anderson' is named for his wife. His books include *Dwarf Bulbs for the Rock Garden* (1959) and *Rock Gardens* (1964), both classic works on their subject.

André, Edouard (1840–1911)

The well-known *Clematis* 'Madame Edouard André', dating from 1892, commemorates the wife of this internationally known French designer of gardens and parks. His name also appears in *Cytisus scoparius* f. *andreanus*, a broom he found growing wild in Normandy, where he had a nursery garden at La Croix. (*Prunus* × *blireana* was named by him after the nearby village of Blire.) Unlike many landscape designers, André had a keen interest in botany, having trained in horticulture, and was editor of the *Revue Horticole*. He also collected exotic plants on two trips to **South America**, returning with more than 3,000 specimens.

Anglesey Abbey, Cambridgeshire

Galanthus nivalis 'Anglesey Abbey' is a fitting plant to be named after this plantsman's garden at Lode, near Cambridge. Beautifully maintained, and on a huge scale, the garden is spectacular in every season, but is especially noted for its contemporary winter walk and for the generous drifts of snowdrops and other small bulbs in early spring. The garden was established in the 1930s by its owner, the 1st Lord Fairhaven, who also conceived the ambitious formal layout. The garden is now owned by the National Trust.

Apple Court, Hampshire

Apple Court is a delightful semi-formal walled garden near Lymington. This was formerly the home of hosta specialist Diana Grenfell and her husband, Roger Grounds, an expert on grasses, and the planting, like the stock in the adjacent nursery, owes much to their expertise. The name *Hemerocallis* 'Apple Court Ruby' is a clue to the garden's third

Hemerocallis middendorffii

speciality: a large area is planted as a display garden for many varieties of daylily, some of them bred here. They are planted with ornamental grasses.

Arboretum des Barres see Vilmorin

Arboretum Kalmthout see Kalmthout

Archibald, Jim and Jenny

Their long experience of seed collecting in many countries underpins the Archibalds' mail-order business, JJA Seeds, in Llandysul, Wales. Specializing in unusual non-woody species, they supply nurseries and adventurous gardeners from a list that includes many rarities. They previously ran The Plantsmen, a Dorset nursery where Jim Archibald was in partnership with **Eric Smith** until 1975.

Ardtornish Gardens, Argyll

The parents of the present owner **Faith Raven** came here in 1930, adding to the wide range of shrubs and trees. Many of the most celebrated finds of the great plant hunters are to be found here: dozens of choice rhododendrons, eucryphias, hydrangeas, katsuras (*Cercidiphyllum japonicum*), magnolias and enkianthus. Faith Raven's late husband **John Raven**, a respected plantsman and author, is commemorated by a memorial garden. There is also a primula garden, where many excellent candelabra and drumstick primulas grow alongside hostas, peonies and other plants that thrive here on Scotland's wild, wet but mild west coast.

Georg Arends (1863–1952)

Over his long career, the prolific German nurseryman Georg Arends made a huge impact on the world of garden plants through the dozens of hybrids and cultivars that he raised at his nursery in Ronsdorf-Wuppertal, near Cologne. Many well-known herbaceous perennials that have German cultivar names were bred by him (see panel).

Born in Essen, the young Georg learned from his nurseryman father, making his own herbarium and eventually deciding to train as a gardener. He then worked in the botanic garden at Breslau, and for a time in nurseries in London and Italy, before returning to Germany to set up his own nursery in 1888. The business grew rapidly in the years leading up to World War I, gaining an international reputation through the **RHS** London shows and recovering well after the difficulties of the war. Sadly, World War II was a different story. Initial staff shortages were followed by serious air-raid damage to the nursery. George Arends, by now an old man and deeply saddened by what he saw as the destruction of his life's work, never really recovered. However, his two sons, who worked with him, continued the business after his death, and have been succeeded in turn by his granddaughter, Ursula Maubach-Arends, and great-granddaughter Anja Maubach, who is also a landscape architect. Plants named in his honour include *Rosa* 'Georg Arends' and *Rhododendron* 'Georg Arends', while *Geum coccineum* 'Werner Arends' is named after his son.

PERENNIALS BRED BY GEORG ARENDS
Aconitum carmichaelii 'Arendsii'
Arabis × *arendsii*
Astilbe × *arendsii* (many cultivars)
Bergenia 'Abendglocken'
Bergenia 'Morgenröte'
Bergenia 'Silberlicht'
Erigeron 'Wuppertal'
Eryngium planum 'Blauer Zwerg'
Hosta sieboldiana var. *elegans*
Ligularia dentata 'Othello'
Phlox × *arendsii* (many cultivars)
Phlox subulata 'Maischnee'
Sedum 'Herbstfreude'

Arnold Arboretum, Massachusetts Founded in 1872, Harvard University's world-famous arboretum takes its name from its benefactor, a Massachusetts whaling trader named James Arnold. Under the terms of his legacy, the arboretum was to collect every kind of tree and shrub that would grow outdoors here. In 1873 the eminent dendrologist **Charles Sprague Sargent** became director, and it was he who steered the project through all the initial decisions and plans that set it on the road to becoming the world-class scientific establishment that it is today. He supervised the landscaping (by Frederick Law Olmsted), initiated the planting and the record-keeping system, set up research programmes, a library and herbarium, and encouraged and organized plant collectors such as **E.H. Wilson** (who was eventually to succeed Sargent as director) and **Joseph Rock**. Sargent's systems are still mostly in place today, as are several hundred of the original trees. (Many of the early plantings, however, were badly damaged during a hurricane in

1938.) The tradition of plant hunting also continues: a notable 20th-century discovery made with sponsorship from the Arnold Arboretum was the dawn redwood, *Metasequoia glyptostroboides*. Previously known only as a fossil, the tree was found growing in a remote valley in **China**, in 1941, and was later propagated successfully at the Arboretum. Garden shrubs raised here include *Hamamelis* × *intermedia* 'Arnold Promise', *Lonicera tatarica* 'Arnold Red' and *Forsythia* × *intermedia* 'Arnold Giant'.

Arnott, Samuel (1852–1930)

The fine scented snowdrop *Galanthus* 'S. Arnott' is named after Samuel Arnott, a provost of Maxwelltown, Dumfriesshire, and a keen amateur horticulturist and writer. His snowdrop was the flagship cultivar of the famous **Giant Snowdrop Company**. It won the RHS Award of Garden Merit in 1951, under the name 'Arnott's Seedling'.

Ashwood Nurseries, West Midlands

John Massey's long-established nursery near Kingswinford is widely known for its specialist breeding programme of special plants such as auriculas, hepaticas, hydrangeas and salvias and as a National Collection holder for lewisias and hardy cyclamens. Hellebores are a particular speciality associated with Ashwood, and plants named for the nursery include the renowned *Helleborus* × *hybridus* Ashwood Garden Hybrids, a number of lewisias, and the charmingly named golden-leaved *Salvia* × *jamensis* 'Moonlight over Ashwood'.

Aslet, Ken (1909–1980)

Superintendent of the rock garden at **RHS** Garden **Wisley** in the 1950s and 1960s, Ken Aslet was an expert plantsman and collector. *Tropaeolum tuberosum* var. *lineamaculatum* 'Ken Aslet' was named in his honour after his death, but Aslet himself discovered the choice rock garden plant *Anagallis tenella* 'Studland' and also *Verbascum* 'Letitia', which he named after his wife. *Clematis cirrhosa* 'Wisley Cream' was raised by the clematis specialist **Raymond Evison** from seed collected by Aslet. There is also a celandine named for him, *Ranunculus ficaria* 'Ken Aslet Double'.

Asturias

The early-flowering miniature daffodil *Narcissus asturiensis* is native to this province of north-west Spain.

Atkins, James (1802–1884)

One of the best of all garden snowdrops, the early and vigorous *Galanthus* 'Atkinsii', is named after James Atkins, a Northamptonshire nurseryman and plant collector who retired in 1871 to Painswick, in Gloucestershire, where he became a friend and mentor to **Henry Elwes**.

Atlas Mountains

The Atlas Mountains, stretching some 1,500 miles from Morocco and across northern Algeria to Tunisia, are one of the two small areas of **Africa**, at the northern and southern extremities of the continent, that enjoy a Mediterranean climate. Close to the Mediterranean itself, the Atlas range shares much of its plant life with other mountainous areas bordering the Mediterranean. The term *atlanticus* denotes a plant originating from the Atlas Mountains. Its most familiar use is in the name of the region's best-known tree, the Atlas cedar, *Cedrus atlantica*, an attractive conifer seen in parks and larger gardens, especially in its bluish-leaved form now known as *Cedrus atlantica* Glauca Group. The genus of perennial daisies called *Rhodanthemum* is also native to the area; one of its species is *Rhodanthemum atlanticum*. **Joseph Hooker** was the first major plant hunter to visit the area, in 1871, but his trip was difficult and unproductive and it was only after Morocco's annexation by France in 1912 that botanists had easier access.

Aubriet, Claude (1665–1742)

This French botanical illustrator from Châlons-sur-Marne was employed at the Jardin du Roi (later the Jardin des Plantes) in **Paris**. The genus *Aubrieta* (often misspelled '*Aubretia*' or '*Aubrietia*') is named after him. The distinguished French botanist **Joseph Pitton de Tournefort** commissioned Aubriet to illustrate his seminal work *Eléments de Botanique* (1694). On the strength of the precise and careful engravings that Aubriet produced, in 1700 Tournefort invited him to go with him on a two-year exploration of the

Aubrieta purpurea

Levant to record the plants they found. He returned home with numerous sketches, many of which he turned into finished paintings, using pressed plants gathered on the trip as reference material.

Austin, David

David Austin

One of the most successful plant breeders of his generation, David Austin has been breeding roses since the 1940s, introducing one of his most enduring cultivars, 'Constance Spry', in 1963. He founded David Austin Roses in 1969. The name has become synonymous with the so-called 'English roses', now available in many varieties and combining the old-fashioned beauty and fragrance of traditional roses with the longer flowering season of modern cultivars. Some of the best known are Graham Thomas ('Ausmas'), A Shropshire Lad ('Ausled') and Golden Celebration ('Ausgold').

Still a family business, the Shropshire nursery continues to raise new cultivars in its extensive breeding programme. The company name is known throughout the rose-growing world, and the catalogue includes nearly 1,000 rose varieties, of which more than 150 are English roses. David Austin has collected many awards, including the RHS Victoria Medal of Honour and the Dean Hole Medal of the Royal National Rose Society. The company has recently diversified into cut flowers, retailed alongside the garden roses.

Australia

The indigenous plant life of Australia numbers more than 20,000 species, of which about 17,000 occur nowhere else on earth. These riches have astonished outsiders since the early days of exploration: the pirate and adventurer **William Dampier** is believed to have brought the first Australian plants to Britain in 1699. However, before the momentous voyage of Captain

Olearia phlogopappa

James Cook in 1768–1771, the northern hemisphere knew little about Australia and its plants. It was on 17 April 1770 that the unknown land mass was sighted from the *Endeavour*, the ship carrying Cook and with him the botanist **Sir Joseph Banks** and several scientists. They sailed up the east coast of Australia, going ashore for the first time near what is now Sydney, at a place that became known as Botany Bay. By the time they left Australia, Banks and his team had gathered specimens of more than 300 plants that were previously unknown to science.

The 19th century saw several more British plant hunters in Australia. In the early 1800s **George Caley** explored the Hunter River area near Sydney. **Robert Brown** was sailing round the coast at the same time, collecting plants and doing research for the first major botanical treatise on Australia.

Next on the scene was **Allan Cunningham**, who travelled inland along the Nepean, Macquarie and Lachlan rivers of New South Wales and then around the coast. Areas of Western Australia were explored by **James Drummond**, mainly from the 1830s to the 1850s, and, from 1842, by the indefatigable Austrian

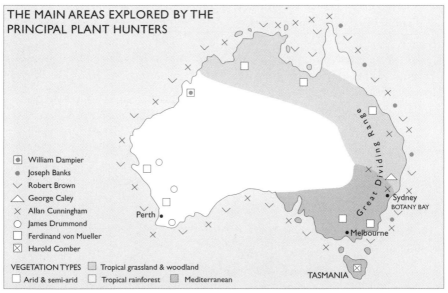

THE MAIN AREAS EXPLORED BY THE PRINCIPAL PLANT HUNTERS

- ⊙ William Dampier
- ● Joseph Banks
- ∨ Robert Brown
- △ George Caley
- ✕ Allan Cunningham
- ○ James Drummond
- ▢ Ferdinand von Mueller
- ⊠ Harold Comber

VEGETATION TYPES ▢ Tropical grassland & woodland
▢ Arid & semi-arid ▢ Tropical rainforest ▪ Mediterranean

Great Dividing Range

Perth

Sydney
BOTANY BAY

● Melbourne

TASMANIA

SOUTHERN, NOT AUSTRALIAN

The term *australis* in a plant name (such as *Baptisia australis* or *Cordyline australis*) does not necessarily indicate a plant native to Australia. It simply means 'southern'.

SOME GARDEN PLANTS FROM AUSTRALIA

Acacia dealbata
Callistemon species
Correa backhouseana
Dicksonia antarctica
Eucalyptus gunnii
Eucalyptus pauciflora
Grevillea rosmarinifolia
Leptospermum scoparium
Olearia phlogopappa
Ozothamnus rosmarinifolius
Prostanthera cuneata
Sollya heterophylla

AUSTRALIAN EXOTICS

In contrast to many species introduced from North America and the Far East, the plants of Australia were slow to make an impact in gardens. Sir Joseph Banks' plant collecting focused on botany rather than horticulture, and many Australian 18th- and 19th-century introductions proved unsuited to British winters. However, today's warming climate, and an increasing interest in exotic plants for both sheltered town gardens and conservatories, have brought more Australian species into the limelight. In 2004 the Chelsea Flower Show had its first-ever Australian show garden and in March 2005 an RHS seminar day on the plant life of Australia attracted wide interest.

botanist **Ferdinand von Mueller**, who settled in Australia, travelling extensively and naming thousands of new species. But there were still new discoveries to be made, and the 20th century saw the introduction into cultivation of *Ozothamnus ledifolius*, one of some 150 species brought from Tasmania by yet another plant hunter, **Harold Comber**. An even more recent arrival, from New South Wales, is the Wollemi pine (see panel).

Today many Australian plants are seriously threatened in the wild, and efforts are being made to conserve the country's extraordinary botanical heritage. Visitors can marvel at these plant treasures in the national parks and in botanical gardens such as the Australian National Botanic Gardens in Canberra, Kings Park and Botanic Garden in Perth, and the Royal Tasmanian Botanical Gardens in Hobart.

The Wollemi pine

In the 1770s, after Joseph Banks had returned, Australia gave gardeners some of the first 'must-have' plants, and recently it has produced the world's latest botanical novelty: the Wollemi pine. *Wollemia nobilis*, named for David Noble, who found it in 1994, is a relic of another age, resembling trees known only through fossil records from some 120 million years ago far more closely than it resembles any living species. Dangerously vulnerable in the wild, the tree has been successfully propagated for sale, and profits will help conserve the few remaining wild specimens. The Wollemi pine was seen at the 2005 Chelsea Flower Show, and its value as a botanical curiosity – or status symbol – became clear the following October, when the first batch of cultivated Wollemi pine saplings realized more than A$1million at auction in Sydney.

Backhouse, James (1794–1869)

In 1816, in partnership with his brother Thomas, the young Quaker James Backhouse established a nursery and ambitious alpine garden in York. In 1831 he went to **Australia** as a missionary, collecting plants and seeds of eucalyptus and other unfamiliar plants to send back to the nursery and also to **Sir William Hooker** at Glasgow Botanic Gardens. He travelled for ten years, returning via Mauritius and South Africa. The York business prospered, expanding to Leeds and securing not only plant sales but also, later, contracts to build alpine gardens, notably for the wealthy plantswoman **Ellen Willmott** at **Warley Place**, in Essex, for Frank Crisp at Friar Park near Henley on Thames (whose lavish rock garden famously contained a scale model of the Matterhorn, complete with 'snow') and at **Birmingham Botanical Gardens**. The nursery eventually closed in 1955, but the family name lives on in the heather *Erica carnea* 'James Backhouse' and the tender evergreen shrub *Correa backhouseana*, a native of Tasmania.

Backhouse, Robert Ormston (1854–1940)

Robert Ormston Backhouse shared an interest in plants and gardening with a number of his relatives. Born into a well-established northern banking family, he was the son of a pioneering daffodil breeder, William Backhouse (1807–1869), who had raised more than 200 named *Narcissus* cultivars. After William's death, his breeding stocks were acquired by Peter Barr of **Barr & Sons**, a leading nurseryman of the day, but his three sons continued his work with daffodils. Robert Ormston, the youngest, moved to Sutton Court, in Hereford, in 1886. Here he and his wife, Sarah (1857–1921), were both prolific breeders of daffodils, raising over 500 varieties. Some are no longer in commerce, but others, such as 'Little Witch' and 'Mrs R.O. Backhouse', are still popular. Lilies (Backhouse hybrids and 'Sutton Court'), colchicums and snowdrops (such as *Galanthus* 'Backhouse Spectacles') were also raised by Robert Ormston and his wife. Their son William Ormston Backhouse (1885–1962) continued the daffodil-breeding tradition but was the last in the line to carry the Backhouse name.

Baetica

This was an ancient Roman province in southern Spain, corresponding roughly to what is now Andalucia. It occurs in several plant names, such as *Aristolochia baetica* and *Myrtus communis* 'Baetica'.

Baggesen's Nursery, Kent

The classic compact, golden-leaved evergreen shrub *Lonicera nitida* 'Baggesen's Gold' was raised by the Danish nurseryman Niels Baggesen. He established a nursery near Cardiff after working at **Kew** when he first came to England in the early 1900s. He later moved to Pembury in Kent, where his sons Harald and John eventually joined him in the business. It was at this nursery that the Baggesens' other classic plant, *Chamaecyparis lawsoniana* 'Pembury Blue', was raised in the

1940s. Ironically, it was only after the nursery had closed down in the 1970s that these award-winning plants gained the wide popularity they enjoy today.

Baines, Chris

A pioneer of the movement towards gardening for wildlife and a champion of native plants, Chris Baines trained as a landscape architect and began his career as a contractor and lecturer. He was propelled to fame in 1985, when he not only created the Chelsea Flower Show's first-ever wildlife garden but also published his influential book *How to Make a Wildlife Garden* and made a successful BBC Television programme about wildlife gardening, *Bluetits and Bumblebees*. He has subsequently written many books and articles, made television programmes, and is a consultant and campaigner on environmental issues, with a particular interest in tree conservation.

Baker, Bill (1917–2001)

A professional dentist, Bill Baker was a widely respected and knowledgeable amateur plantsman who made numerous collecting trips abroad and grew many of the resulting plants in his garden at Old Rectory Cottage in Tidmarsh, Berkshire. He was particularly interested in breeding lilies, but had great enthusiasm for many other plant groups and was known for his generosity in passing his plants on to friends and fellow-gardeners. His expertise was recognized by the RHS when he was awarded the Veitch Memorial Medal in 1995. A number of plants are named after Bill Baker and his wife, Joan – for example *Phlox carolina* 'Bill Baker', *Geranium sylvaticum* f. *roseum* 'Baker's Pink', *Clematis* 'Joan Baker' and *Geranium phaeum* var. *lividum* 'Joan Baker'.

Balearic Islands

In common with that of many other island groups, the flora of the Balearic Islands, in the Mediterranean off the east coast of Spain, is both especially rich (with 1,450 plant species, of which 180 are found nowhere else) and especially threatened. A new botanic garden, the Jardí Botànic de Sóller, on the island of Mallorca, is dedicated to the conservation of endemic and endangered native plants. Garden plants named after the islands include *Buxus balearica*, *Ilex* × *altaclerensis* 'Balearica' and the well-known winter-flowering *Clematis cirrhosa* var. *balearica*.

Balfour, Betty (1867–1942)

A popular and vigorous late-flowering blue clematis is named for Lady Betty Balfour, whose garden near Woking was designed by Gertrude Jekyll.

Balfour, Isaac Bayley (1853–1922)

In his role as professor of botany and Regius keeper of the Royal Botanic Garden Edinburgh, from 1888 until his death, this proficient and energetic Scottish botanist made a big impact on the garden's development at an important time for new plant introductions and new gardening ideas. He grew and named many plants introduced from China by George Forrest, and is remembered in *Rhododendron balfourianum*.

Baljuan, Tajikistan
This region of central Asia (also Boldzhuan) is the home of the so-called mile-a-minute plant or Russian vine, *Fallopia baldschuanica*, which was discovered there in 1883.

Ballard, Ernest (1870–1952)
This gardener and plant breeder from Colwall, Herefordshire, was known

Ernest Ballard

for a lifetime of breeding Michaelmas daisies. He raised many cultivars, more reliable than their predecessors and with a wider colour range, showing them from 1907 at the RHS, where he won many awards. A number of cultivars of *Aster novi-belgii* are named for members of his family, including **Helen Ballard**, his daughter-in-law (see below). She is the Ballard usually associated with hellebores, but in fact the earliest hellebore to carry the name referred to Ernest Ballard. This was the coveted, very dark but now elusive *Helleborus* 'Ballard's Black'. Ernest Ballard bought the original plant at an RHS show.

Ballard, Helen (1909–1995)
One of the key names among hellebore breeders, Helen Ballard raised these sought-after plants in her Worcestershire garden, devoting some 30 years to producing ever more desirable new varieties in a wide range of colours. Hellebores have been the subject of many name changes and, of the numerous forms bred by Helen Ballard, several have been named after her at one time or another. *Helleborus* × *ballardiae*, which she first raised in the early 1970s, is a hybrid between *Helleborus lividus* and *Helleborus niger*, while *Helleborus* 'Ballard's Group' belongs to the orientalis hybrids.

Ballawley, Dublin
Desmond Shaw Smith ran a famous alpine nursery at Ballawley Park, Dublin, for more than 20 years until the early 1950s. It survives in the names of several bergenias and in *Saxifraga* 'Ballawley Guardsman'.

Balls, Edward Kent (1892–1984)
A lifelong plantsman, E.K. Balls worked with Clarence Elliott at **Six Hills Nursery**, building rock gardens for prestigious clients such as Lionel de Rothschild, at **Exbury**. He subsequently became a full-time collector and lecturer, travelling in South America in search of rare plants and seeds, and working as a horticulturist at the Rancho Santa Ana Botanic Garden. Plants named after him include *Sisyrinchium* 'E.K. Balls', *Gaultheria pumila* 'E.K. Balls', *Sempervivum atlanticum* 'Edward Balls' and *Sempervivum ballsii*.

Banat
Crocus banaticus, *Echinops bannaticus* and *Paeonia officinalis* subsp. *banatica* are named for the region of Banat, today shared between Romania, Hungary and Serbia-Montenegro.

Joseph Banks (1743–1820)

A key figure in the history of garden plants, the eminent botanist Sir Joseph Banks was a dynamic force in the early days of plant hunting, co-ordinating and making possible the efforts of many other characters in the story. A plant hunter himself, as a young Oxford graduate he explored Newfoundland and Labrador in 1766, collecting plants and producing navigational charts. More famously, he accompanied Captain Cook on his round-the-world voyage of 1768–1771. Family wealth, and the death of his father when he was 18, had made Banks one of England's richest young men, and he paid a staggering £10,000 to secure places on Cook's voyage for himself and his nine-strong team of scientists and staff. He returned with specimens or seeds of more than 1,000 new plants – the basis for a private herbarium that grew into a collection of international importance, now in London's Natural History Museum.

Over the next 50 years Banks became increasingly well respected and influential, with a wide knowledge of all things botanical and a circle of contacts at home and abroad who kept him in touch with the latest discoveries and developments. A founder member of the Linnean Society (see **Linnaeus**) and the **RHS**, he became King George III's scientific adviser in 1772, and president of the Royal Society in 1778 – a post he was to hold for the rest of his life. One of his main spheres of influence was as unofficial director of the Royal Gardens at **Kew**, arranging and sponsoring expeditions for important plant hunters, including **Francis Masson** and **Allan Cunningham**, and organizing the plants they brought home. His prodigious knowledge and networking skills meant that it was Banks who initially established Kew's reputation as one of the world's foremost botanic gardens.

Banks is commemorated in the names of a South Pacific Island group, a **New Zealand** peninsula and many different plants, including the Australian genus *Banksia*, *Hydrangea macrophylla* 'Joseph Banks', *Astelia banksii* and *Cordyline banksii*. *Rosa banksiae* is named in honour of his wife, Lady Dorothea.

Bancroft, Ruth

Fashioned from her family's former walnut grove, Ruth Bancroft's contemporary garden at Walnut Creek, near San Francisco, is known for its large collection of xerophytes – desert plants and succulents adapted to dry conditions. Agaves, aloes and many kinds of cactus fill the 4-acre garden, which captured the imagination of the distinguished plantsman **Frank Cabot** when he visited in 1989 and became the flagship project in his founding of the Garden Conservancy. Visitors to the garden have long marvelled at its pioneering design and planting ideas, and it has influenced many recent gardens planned with global warming in mind.

Agave americana

Banister, John (1650–1692)

This English clergyman and scientist emigrated to Virginia as a missionary and published accounts of the area's natural history. In 1688 he contributed 'A Catalogue of Plants observed by me in Virginia' to **John Ray's** book *Historia Plantarum*. Plants collected and sent home by Banister include *Magnolia virginiana* and *Rhododendron viscosum*.

Baoxing, China

This city in Sichuan, formerly known as Mupin, is represented as *moupinensis* in plant names, for example *Primula moupinensis*, *Cotoneaster moupinensis* and *Salix moupinensis*.

Barlow, Nora (1885–1989)

The granddaughter of **Charles Darwin**, Nora Barlow was the much-respected editor of his writings. A well-known aquilegia cultivar is named after her.

Barlow, Sam (1825–1888)

A dark-centred, double white pink, an old favourite, was named for this Lancashire grower who spent many years breeding connoisseurs' plants such as auriculas, polyanthus and tulips in his much-admired garden at Stakehill House, Castleton, near Rochdale.

Barnhaven, Oregon

This name is synonymous with special primulas. Barnhaven was the home of Florence Bellis (née Hurtig), who began hand-pollinating and selecting primulas of English origin to achieve the superior colours and habit she wanted. She first published a nursery list in 1939 and continued breeding the plants until her retirement, in 1966, when her collection passed to England and then, in 1990, to Brittany. Here, at Plestin les Grèves, seeds of a wide range of these connoisseurs' plants (still hand-pollinated) continue to be produced and sold, by Lynne and David Lawson.

Barnsdale Gardens, Rutland

Barnsdale Gardens came to fame in the long-running BBC Television series *Gardeners' World* when it was presented by the late **Geoff Hamilton** in the 1980s and 1990s. The show gardens created for the series – such as a cottage garden, an allotment and a paradise garden – have made Barnsdale and its nursery a very popular public attraction, now managed by Geoff Hamilton's son Nick and his wife. The garden features in cultivar names such as *Viola* 'Barnsdale Gem'.

Barnsley House, Gloucestershire

One of the great English gardens of the 20th century, Barnsley was the creation of the distinguished garden designer, plantswoman and author **Rosemary Verey**, who came here in 1951 after her marriage to David Verey, and cared for the garden for the next 50 years, until her death. Barnsley's combination of disciplined design and informal planting for all-year interest is a classic that has been the inspiration for many other gardens. Now belonging to a private hotel, the garden is open only to guests, but it lives on in Rosemary Verey's books and in plants associated with it, such as the popular *Lavatera* × *clementii* 'Barnsley' and *Geranium sanguineum* 'Barnsley'.

Baron-Veillard, France

This Orléans clematis breeder contributed to the late 19th-century boom in new varieties with cultivars like *Clematis* 'Madame Edouard André' (named for the wife of the *Revue Horticole*'s editor), and the late-flowering 'Madame Baron Veillard'.

Barr & Sons

This well-known former London nursery was established in Covent Garden in 1882 by Peter Barr (1826–1909) and continued by succeeding generations of his family until 1956, when George Barr co-founded Wallace & Barr at Tunbridge Wells. Barr & Sons had nurseries in Tooting until 1888, then moved out of London to Long Ditton, in Surrey, and in 1911 to Taplow, in Buckinghamshire (where *Echinops bannaticus* 'Taplow Blue' was raised). They also had a daffodil nursery at Gulval, in Cornwall. Their name survives in a number of bulbs and herbaceous plants: *Crocus tommasinianus* 'Barr's Purple' remains the most well-known of many crocuses they raised, including also *Crocus chrysanthus* 'Goldilocks' (1950) and *Crocus speciosus* 'Oxonian'. They are remembered in several of their cultivars of *Aster novae-angliae* ('Barr's Blue', 'Barr's Pink' etc.), *Fuchsia* 'George Barr' and *Penstemon procumbens* 'Claude Barr'.

Bartonia aurea

Barry, Patrick (1816–1890)

This Irish-born teacher emigrated to America in 1836 and became a nurseryman, working in partnership with another newly arrived immigrant, the German **George Ellwanger,** to found **Mount Hope Nurseries** in Rochester, in 1840.

Bartholomeus Anglicus

This 13th-century English Franciscan monk was the author of a remarkable early scientific encyclopaedia. Botany is the subject of just one of its 19 books, which range from astronomy to mineralogy.

Barton, Benjamin Smith (1766–1815)

A doctor, botanist and scientific author from Pennsylvania, Barton inspired, encouraged and later sponsored the young English plant collector **Thomas Nuttall**. The familiar yellow annual from California now correctly known as *Mentzelia lindleyi* is much better known by its former name, *Bartonia aurea*.

Bartram, John (1699–1777)

A Quaker farmer from Philadelphia, Bartram was a key figure in the discovery and distribution of plants from the developing colonies of eastern **North America**. **Linnaeus** described him as the greatest natural botanist in the world. Bartram collected plants on his extensive travels in North America over a period of some 30 years – often exploring wild regions unvisited by white settlers – and propagated many of them in the nursery garden he established. They included *Magnolia grandiflora*, which he found in South Carolina. Visitors to his Philadelphia garden today can see the collection he built up there, which also includes many specimens sent to him from botanists all over the world. He listed the plants he grew in his catalogue of 1773. Bartram corresponded with European plant enthusiasts including **Philip Miller** at the **Chelsea Physic Garden** and Peter Collinson. The latter, a London businessman, was instrumental in finding patrons for Bartram, and in his appointment as Botanist Royal in America by King George III. In all, Bartram is thought to have introduced as many as 200 plants into Europe, including rhododendrons, familiar garden perennials such as *Phlox divaricata*, *Monarda didyma*, *Lilium superbum*, *Actaea simplex* and the ostrich fern, *Matteuccia struthiopteris*. One of his sons, William Bartram (1739–1823), was a noted traveller, naturalist and artist.

Battandier, Jules (1848–1922)

A French pharmacist and botanist, Battandier compiled a complete flora of Algeria. The broom *Cytisus battandieri* is named after him.

Batsford Arboretum, Gloucestershire

Magnolias, acers, oaks and a National Collection of Japanese flowering cherries are some of the highlights of this informal but well-labelled tree garden in the Cotswolds. The house was built for a British diplomat who served in **Japan**, and the influence of the Far East is evident in the choice of plants, which include many bamboos and Japanese maples, and in the Japanese garden. A recent development has been the 'swampery', where stumps of old trees that had to be felled have been incorporated into a wildlife-friendly bog garden planted with damp-loving exotic foliage plants to create a jungle effect.

Bauer, Ferdinand (1760–1826)

The Austrian Bauer, a friend of **Joseph Banks**, was a gifted illustrator of plants and animals. He sailed to **Australia** in 1801 with Matthew Flinders on the *Investigator*, working as a botanical artist with the naturalist **Robert Brown**. Bauer had also travelled to Greece with the English botanist **John Sibthorp** and illustrated his book *Flora Graeca*. Subsequently he illustrated a monograph on foxgloves by **John Lindley**. *Bauera*, a genus of annuals, is named for him and his brother Franz (1758–1840), who was also a botanical artist.

Beales, Peter

This leading rose breeder is owner of the renowned rose nursery at Attleborough, Norfolk. One of their roses is named in his honour (though he did not raise it).

Bean, W.J. (1863–1947)

Based at **Kew** for much of his life, eventually becoming curator there, Bean was an expert in woody plants. His four-volume *Trees and Shrubs Hardy in the British Isles* is still the classic reference work on the subject. A holly is named after him: *Ilex* × *altaclerensis* 'W.J. Bean'.

Bedgebury National Pinetum and Forest Gardens, Kent

Owned by the Forestry Commission, Bedgebury has been described as the best place in the world to see and identify conifers. What began as one of many fashionable Victorian pinetums has now been developed into an outstanding reference collection of these plants, with nearly 500 species and more than 1,500 cultivars. Several National Collections can be found here, including *Taxus*, *Juniperus* and *Chamaecyparis lawsoniana*, and certain areas have geographical groupings of plants, such as the Japanese glade and the Chinese glade.

Begonia rex

Bees Nursery, Cheshire

A. Bee & Co. was the name of the nursery company begun in 1904 by **Arthur Bulley** in his garden at **Ness**, which was much later to become the botanic garden of the University of Liverpool. Bulley chose the name as a play on his initials, 'A.B.'. The nursery grew out of his passion for plants, which led him to sponsor some of the great plant hunters on their expeditions to the Far East, in order to obtain seeds and plants for his garden and bring new plants to public attention. In 1911 the nursery and seed firm, by then known as Bees Ltd, moved to Sealand, and Bees remained a prominent name in UK horticulture for much of the 20th century. Bees' plants include: *Armeria* Bees' hybrids, *Primula beesiana*, *Clematis* 'Bees' Jubilee', *Lobelia cardinalis* 'Bees' Flame', *Kniphofia* 'Bees' Lemon' and 'Bees' Sunset', and *Tanacetum coccineum* 'Bees' Jubilee'.

Bégon, Michel (1638–1710)

Bégon was a French colonial administrator who served in Canada and the Caribbean at the time of Louis XIV. A keen amateur botanist, he organized the 1688 scientific expedition to the West Indies on which begonias were first collected. They were named in his honour.

Belon, Pierre (1517–1564)

A French doctor and botanist, Belon had an insatiable curiosity for the natural world and for medicinal plants in particular. He travelled extensively, studying and describing new plants from a wide area around the Mediterranean, from Italy to the Lebanon and from **Turkey** to Egypt. Two pirate raids put paid to many of the plants he had collected, but memoirs of his travels survived, recording many remarkable new discoveries whose introduction would later transform gardens, landscapes and lives: holm oak, cork oak and oriental plane; garden plants such as *Cistus ladanifer*, *Helleborus niger* and *Prunus laurocerasus* and exotics like bananas, papyrus and sugar cane. Belon's patron was the Bishop of Le Mans, in whose garden at Savigné l'Evêque Belon was able to try out some of his new plants after his return. However, almost a century later, many of them were only just acquiring public recognition, in the newly established Jardin du Roi (later the Jardin des Plantes) in **Paris**.

Belsay Hall, Northumberland

A romantic garden in the Victorian tradition was created here by amateur plantsmen Sir Charles Monck and his grandson Sir Arthur, who successively owned the property throughout the 19th century and planted many exotic and newly discovered rarities here. Rhododendrons, ferns, magnolias and other ornamental trees are among the highlights. *Fuchsia* 'Belsay Beauty' and the comfreys *Symphytum* 'Belsay' and 'Belsay Gold' are named after the garden.

Benenden see Ingram, Collingwood

Benmore Botanic Garden, Argyll

One of the three Scottish regional gardens linked to the Royal Botanic Garden **Edinburgh**, Benmore, near Dunoon, offers a spectacular mountainside home to some of the finest introductions of the great plant hunters. Conditions here, on the mild, damp west coast of Scotland, suit many species that would struggle in colder, drier areas. Begun in the 1820s and acquired by RBGE in 1929, the garden is known for its collections of magnolias and rhododendrons (these include a *Rhododendron montroseanum* 'Benmore'). There is also a towering avenue of giant redwoods (*Sequoiadendron giganteum*) dating from 1863. Other plantings replicate a Chilean forest and a glade with species from **Bhutan**.

Benton End see Morris, Cedric

Bergen, Karl August von (1704–1760)

The ground-cover perennial *Bergenia* is named for this German botanist.

Bertoloni, Antonio (1775–1869)

One of Italy's foremost botanists and the author of the ten-volume *Flora Italica*, Bertoloni was professor of botany at Bologna from 1816 until his death. *Aquilegia bertolonii* is named in his honour.

Beth Chatto Gardens see Chatto, Beth

Bhutan

This remote independent mountain kingdom in the eastern Himalayas is recognized as one of the world's great botanical hotspots, with an enormous variety of plants including many endemic species. Bhutan was relatively unexplored until the 20th century (when plant hunters there included **Frank Kingdon Ward, George Forrest** and **George Sherriff**), because of the difficulty of access, both physical and political. Garden plants associated with Bhutan include *Rhododendron bhutanense* and *Malus bhutanica*.

Bicton College, Devon

An impressive variety of planting, including an arboretum, an avenue of monkey-puzzle trees and National Collections of *Agapanthus* and *Pittosporum*, is a feature of the gardens of this college of agriculture and horticulture near Budleigh Salterton.

Adjacent Bicton Park Gardens, the other half of the original estate, has a very early domed glasshouse and an American garden, created in the 18th century to display newly arrived plants from **North America**. *Agapanthus* 'Bicton Bell' and *Gazania* 'Bicton Cream' and 'Bicton Orange' are named for the gardens.

Biddulph Grange, Staffordshire

A lavish monument to the twin Victorian passions for garden design and plant collecting, Biddulph was the creation of James Bateman (1811–1897), a wealthy and cultured amateur orchid collector and botanical author, and his wife Maria. Different areas are devoted to the garden styles of other cultures – **China**, Egypt, Italy – and the planting fashions of the day are displayed in features such as the pinetum, the rose garden, the stumpery and the parterres. The National Trust has owned the garden since 1988 and has carried out a major and highly successful restoration of the landscaping and planting. There is a rose named after the garden, *Rosa* Biddulph Grange ('Frydarkeye').

Bignon, Abbé (1662–1743)

Librarian to Louis XIV of France, Bignon is commemorated in the name of the subtropical climber *Bignonia* and indirectly in the tree species named after it, and more familiar to gardeners, *Catalpa bignonioides*.

Catalpa bignonioides

Birmingham Botanical Gardens

This is one of two botanical gardens in the Edgbaston district of Birmingham (the other is the university's). Established in 1829, these gardens were initially owned and run by a private society whose enthusiasm and subscriptions ensured the rapid acquisition of plants, many of which represented the latest discoveries of the time. After five years the catalogue numbered 9,000 plants. Later additions included a rock garden, several glasshouses, a National Collection of bonsai and a garden planted with the discoveries of **E.H. Wilson**, who was a young employee here.

Bithynia

This ancient province of Asia Minor covered an area on the southern shores of the Black Sea, north of present-day Ankara and east of **Istanbul**. It is the source of the specific epithet *bithynicus*, as in *Fritillaria bithynica* and *Scilla bithynica*.

Blackmore & Langdon, Bristol

Founded in 1901, the name of this traditional nursery is synonymous with delphiniums and begonias, of which impressive displays still appear every year at the Chelsea Flower Show. The breeding of these plants goes back to the firm's earliest days. The company is still owned by the same family. The award-winning *Delphinium* 'Langdon's Royal Flush' is one that preserves the name.

Blooms of Bressingham, Norfolk

Alan Bloom

One of the key names in contemporary horticulture, Blooms began in 1946 when Alan Bloom (1907–2005) bought Bressingham Hall near Diss. He was to become the much-respected founder and father figure of a family nursery and gardening business that spans three generations and is known and respected throughout the horticultural world. He was also a founder member of the Hardy Plant Society, in 1958.

Alan's sons Robert and Adrian joined the business as young men and took it over in 1970, and Adrian's sons in turn are now involved in the nursery. The family have dozens of very successful garden plants to their credit. Many of them bear the name Bressingham, or those of members of the family (see panel), but there are numerous equally famous plants raised by Blooms – such as *Achillea* 'Moonshine' and *Crocosmia* 'Lucifer' – that do not.

As well as breeding many favourite garden perennials, Alan Bloom was renowned as the creator of the 'island-bed' style of garden layout, exemplified in the Dell Garden, which he began to make at Bressingham Hall in the 1950s. It grew into one of Britain's largest collections of hardy garden plants, with over 5,000 different cultivars. Adrian's garden, Foggy Bottom, also became famous, concentrating on year-round colour and focusing on his special interests, conifers and heathers.

SOME BLOOMS PLANTS

Aconitum 'Bressingham Spire'
Bergenia 'Bressingham White'
Clematis tubulosa Alan Bloom ('Alblo')
Dicentra 'Adrian Bloom'
Echinacea purpurea 'Robert Bloom'
Geranium psilostemon 'Bressingham Flair'
× *Heucherella alba* 'Bridget Bloom'
Hosta 'Bressingham Blue'
Kniphofia 'Jenny Bloom'
Thymus 'Alan Bloom'

Blackthorn Nursery, Hampshire

Robin White's nursery in Kilmeston, near Alresford, is known especially for its hellebores, which attract enthusiasts to the annual hellebore open days each February. The nursery also specializes in daphnes and choice perennials such as epimediums, hardy geraniums and a range of alpines. There are a number of 'Blackthorn' plants, including several hellebore seed strains, *Daphne cneorum* 'Blackthorn Triumph' and the popular *Diascia barberae* 'Blackthorn Apricot'.

Blaikie, Thomas (1751–1838)

This Scottish gardener and plant hunter made significant collections of alpines and other hardy plants on an expedition to the Alps and the Jura Mountains in 1775, when the first rock gardens were beginning to appear.

Blanchard, Pierre Louis (1700s)

Blanchard is thought to have been responsible for the first lasting introduction of the chrysanthemum into Europe, in 1789. He was a ship's captain travelling regularly between the Far East and Marseilles, and is recorded as bringing three chrysanthemums from **China**, including one formerly called 'Old Purple', which reached England in 1795.

Bobart, Jacob (1599–1680)

The first superintendent of **Oxford University Botanic Garden,** Bobart presided over the garden from 1642. He was succeeded by his son, another Jacob, who was there until 1719 and was also a professor of botany at the university. It was he who began circulating lists of seeds collected in the garden – the start of a valuable seed exchange programme. This practice was adopted by botanic gardens all over the world and continues today.

Bodinier, Emile (1842–1901)

Callicarpa bodinieri is a familiar garden plant named after this French plant hunter and missionary, whose collection of dried plant specimens from **China** added significantly to the growing knowledge of Chinese plants in the late 19th century.

Bohemia

This former region of central Europe, corresponding roughly to the western half of what is now the Czech Republic, is centred on Prague and is bounded by mountain ranges. Plants named after it include *Geranium bohemicum* and *Fallopia* × *bohemica* 'Spectabilis'.

Boisselot, Auguste (1800s)

This French clematis breeder in Nantes raised several well-known cultivars in

Bodnant Garden, Conwy

Bodnant's magnificent site, on the side of the Conwy Valley, north Wales, with the mountains of Snowdonia as a backdrop, was chosen by the wealthy industrialist Henry Pochin in 1875. He rebuilt the house and shaped the garden by making lawns and planting trees, many of which are still in place. Three subsequent generations of his family have contributed to the garden of today, as have their head gardeners, who came from three generations of the Puddle family. A notable figure in the garden's development was Pochin's grandson, who became the 2nd Lord Aberconway in 1934. He took the helm in the garden from the turn of the century until he gave Bodnant to the National Trust in 1949. He not only created some of Bodnant's most significant design features, including the terraces and lily pond, but also followed up his grandfather's work by sponsoring plant-hunting expeditions and ensuring that the garden kept up with new arrivals in the plant world. Bodnant still has four National Collections, and remarkable displays of camellias, magnolias, rhododendrons, primulas and gentians – all thriving in the climatic conditions of north Wales. Several rhododendrons and other plants are named after Bodnant, the most familiar being *Viburnum* × *bodnantense, Carpenteria californica* 'Bodnant' and *Anemone hupehensis* var. *japonica* 'Bodnant Burgundy'.

Boskoop, The Netherlands

The nursery capital of The Netherlands, Boskoop has given its name to a number of plants, including a favourite grape vine and a well-known blackcurrant. Boskoop is a village in the fertile fenlands. The land around it was drained and cultivated in the customary Dutch manner some 500 years ago, and in the mid-18th century there began what has become a unique nursery cooperative, where some 1,000 small nursery businesses of many kinds thrive alongside one another. In the early days Boskoop's principal crop was strawberries. This successful enterprise was extended to all kinds of fruit, and today the nurseries have diversified into ornamental plants, with trees, hedging and shrubs a speciality. Traditional nursery skills such as grafting are nurtured, and the nurserymen operate a system that commits them to help one another in times of crisis such as illness or a death in the family. The nursery exchange is an official weekly bartering session to enable the small businesses to overcome shortfalls or to use surplus produce to help fill the orders of their fellow traders. There is a thriving export market: more than three-quarters of the produce goes abroad. The Boskoop Agricultural Research Station supports the growers through its important role in the development and trialling of new plants.

> ### SOME BOSKOOP PLANTS
> *Acer palmatum* 'Boskoop Glory'
> *Calluna vulgaris* 'Boskoop'
> *Chamaecyparis lawsoniana* 'Triomf van Boskoop'
> *Clematis* 'Boskoop Beauty'
> *Cytisus* 'Boskoop Ruby'
> *Hedera helix* 'Boskoop'
> *Malus domestica* (apple) 'Belle de Boskoop'
> *Ribes nigrum* (blackcurrant) 'Boskoop Giant'
> *Vitis* 'Boskoop Glory'
> *Weigela* 'Boskoop Glory'

the 1880s, including *Clematis* 'Mevrouw Le Coultre', 'Belle Nantaise' and 'Marie Boisselot' (named for his daughter).

Bonpland, Aimé (1773–1858)

Bonpland was a French doctor, naturalist and explorer who travelled with **Alexander von Humboldt** to Central and **South America**. He collected thousands of new plants, returning with them to Paris, where he published several botanical works and was head gardener at **Malmaison**. He returned to South America in 1816 to teach natural sciences. He soon began exploring again, but was arrested in Paraguay on suspicion of spying and spent ten years in jail.

Boothman, Stuart (1906–1976)

Phlox douglasii 'Boothman's Variety' and *Dicentra* 'Stuart Boothman' are two award-winning plants that commemorate this knowledgeable nurseryman who moved from his native Lancashire to work with **Walter Ingwersen** in Sussex. Boothman set up his own business, Nightingale Nursery, at Furze Platt, near Maidenhead in Berkshire, in 1933. There are other dicentras, two primulas and a juniper named for him.

E.A. Bowles (1865–1954)

Bowles was a well-loved English amateur plantsman and author, whose garden at **Myddelton House**, in Enfield, north London, provided material for his three classic books, *My Garden in Spring, My Garden in Summer* and *My Garden in Autumn and Winter.* With their detailed accounts of Bowles' gardening successes and failures, the books have remained favourites with several generations of gardeners. Many plants are named after him: *Erysimum* 'Bowles' Mauve', *Crocus chrysanthus* 'E.A. Bowles' and *Viola* 'Bowles' Black', as well as Bowles' golden grass (*Milium effusum* 'Aureum') and Bowles' golden sedge (*Carex elata* 'Aurea'). The crocus 'E.P. Bowles' is thought to have been named for Eustace Parker, who adopted the family name when he married Bowles' niece.

Borde Hill Garden, West Sussex

This privately owned 300-acre garden is a fine place to see many of the discoveries of the great plant collectors. Camellias, rhododendrons and magnolias are especially abundant, many of them the result of sponsorship of the plant-hunting expeditions of the day by the garden's creator, Colonel Stephenson Clarke, who bought the property in 1892. He was a keen hybridizer, and was responsible for the justifiably popular *Camellia* × *williamsii* 'Donation'. Other plants with links to the garden include *Camellia sasanqua* Borde Hill form, *Skimmia laureola* 'Borde Hill', *Rhododendron glaucophyllum* Borde Hill form and *Hoheria* 'Borde Hill'.

Boris, King of Bulgaria (1894–1943)

King of Bulgaria from 1918, Boris was an enthusiastic amateur plantsman who made botanical expeditions in the Alps and the Balkans. Plants named for him range from the King Boris fir, *Abies borisii-regis*, a native conifer of Bulgaria and northern Greece, to tiny sempervivums and saxifrages, and the well-known orange herbaceous perennial *Geum* 'Borisii'.

Bougainville, Louis-Antoine de (1729–1811)

The first Frenchman to circumnavigate the world, in 1766–1769, Bougainville was a distinguished military and naval commander. He visited many islands in the Pacific, of which one is now named after him, as were several French naval ships and the subtropical climber *Bougainvillea*.

Bougainvillea

Boughton see Finnis, Valerie

Bourbon, Ile see Réunion

Bradenham Hall, Norfolk

Unmissable for tree lovers, Bradenham Hall has one of Britain's best privately owned tree collections. Begun in the 1950s, it now numbers some 800 species and cultivars, all identified. There are especially large collections of *Acer*, *Quercus* and *Prunus*.

Bradshaw, Mrs John (d.1928)

The scarlet *Geum* 'Mrs J. Bradshaw' was found in the early 1900s in two boxes of seedlings that were sent as a gift by **Amos Perry** to John Bradshaw of The Grange, Southgate, London. Bradshaw's gardener, Mr Whitelegg, selected this one, named for his employer's wife.

Bramdean House, Hampshire

Nepeta grandiflora 'Bramdean' and *Daphne* × *napolitana* 'Bramdean' are named after this 18th-century house and its beautifully planted garden, which is known in particular for its spring bulbs and cleverly designed mirror-image herbaceous borders.

Branklyn Garden, Perthshire

A rather special Scottish garden with many plant treasures, Branklyn was made and cared for between 1922 and 1966 by amateur plantsmen John and Dorothy Renton. On an unlikely 2-acre site in suburban Perth they created a home-from-home for the alpines and ericaceous plants that fascinated them, sensitively building a beautiful, purpose-made landscape of rock gardens, pools and scree where their charges would thrive. Now cared for by the National Trust for Scotland, the garden remains a tribute to their enthusiasm and remarkable plant knowledge. Plants named after the garden include a form of *Meconopsis* and the prostrate form of eastern hemlock *Tsuga canadensis* 'Branklyn'.

Bremner, Alan

Orkney is the home of this farmer, gardener and accomplished plant breeder who is known especially for hybridizing hardy geraniums. He is responsible for more than 40 cultivars, notably *Geranium* 'Nora Bremner' (named after his mother), 'Chantilly', 'Orkney Pink' and 'Patricia'.

Bressingham see Blooms

Bretschneider, Emil (1833–1901)

Like many plant collectors, Latvian-born Bretschneider was a doctor working abroad. Keen to introduce new woody plants into the world's gardens, he spent time while working at the Russian Legation in Beijing collecting seeds, plants and dried specimens in the region. These he sent to the foremost botanical institutions of the day: **Kew**, the **Arnold Arboretum**, the Jardin des Plantes in **Paris** and the botanic garden in St Petersburg. He also became an authority on plant hunters in **China**, and wrote a book on the subject, published in 1898. His name appears in the forms of *Hydrangea heteromalla* known officially as Bretschneideri Group.

Brewer, William (1828–1910)

A scientist from Poughkeepsie, New York State, who studied at Yale and in Germany, Brewer developed special interests in botany and agriculture, and spent several years in California where he was responsible for botanical work involved in the geological survey there in the 1860s. Other botanical expeditions took him to Alaska, Greenland, Switzerland and Colorado. The Brewer spruce, *Picea breweriana*, is named in his honour.

Brickell, Christopher

The eminent horticulturist and author Christopher Brickell began his long career with the **RHS** in 1958, culminating in the office of director-general from 1985 until his retirement in 1993. He has led many botanical expeditions, lectured widely, and written or edited many important books, including the indispensable *RHS A–Z Encyclopedia of Garden Plants*, of which he is editor-in-chief. His many awards include the CBE and the RHS Victoria Medal of Honour. A cultivar of osteospermum is named after him.

Bristol University Botanic Garden

A recent move – to the fourth site in its 120-year history – has given the university's plant collections a new home at The Holmes, Stoke Bishop. Four themed exhibitions form the basis of the new garden: useful plants (such as medicinal herbs, and economic plants like cereals, rubber and coffee); plants of the five Mediterranean climate regions of the world; local and rare native plants (with special displays of aquatic species, and of plants from the nearby Avon Gorge); and plant evolution. Many of the plants for these collections have been moved from the garden's former site, with additional material from other botanic gardens such as **Kew** and **Edinburgh**. New

glasshouses accommodate less hardy specimens in four different climatic zones from tropical to cool temperate.

Broadleigh Gardens, Somerset

This well-respected mail order nursery and 5-acre garden near Taunton have been owned since 1972 by the eminent bulb expert Lady Skelmersdale and her husband. Broadleigh had previously been run for some 30 years by narcissus breeder Alec Gray, who was known especially for his miniature daffodils, such as the popular *Narcissus* 'Tête-à-tête'. Gray's hybrids form a National Collection still maintained here. Today the nursery propagates and sells a wide range of small bulbs and choice woodland and foliage plants, specializing also in agapanthus. A range of Pacific Coast iris hybrids and *Cyclamen coum* 'Broadleigh Silver' are named for Broadleigh, while *Iris* 'Broadleigh Joyce' and *Euphorbia characias* 'Joyce's Giant' are dedicated to Lady Skelmersdale's mother.

Brodick Castle, Isle of Arran

By no means all of the treasures discovered and brought home by plant hunters have thrived in cultivation. Sited on south-facing slopes, sheltered from west winds and soothed by the tempering Gulf Stream, the garden at Brodick Castle provides one of Britain's best opportunities to see splendid specimens of some of the plants that were not hardy enough to succeed elsewhere. The garden was restored between the wars by the Duchess of Montrose. Plants came from the similarly favoured

Tresco Abbey Gardens in the Isles of Scilly, from the wonderful collection of Himalayan plants at **Muncaster Castle**, in Cumbria, and from the last generation of Himalayan plant hunters such as **George Forrest** and **Frank Kingdon Ward**. The woodland garden offers walks among countless very special shrubs and trees, some of them, such as *Rhododendron sinogrande*, now specimens of enormous size. Primulas and ferns are among other highlights. The castle and garden have been in the care of the National Trust for Scotland since 1958. Brodick cultivars include *Griselinia littoralis* 'Brodick Gold' and *Narcissus* 'Brodick'.

Brodie, James (1744–1824)

The genus *Brodiaea* was named after this Scottish botanist – strangely, since *Brodiaea* are corms, and Brodie was noted for special expertise in algae, mosses and ferns.

Brogdale, Kent

The Brogdale Horticultural Trust is guardian of the largest fruit collection in the world, cultivating several thousand varieties – both historic and new – of fruit, nuts and vines in 150 acres of orchards near Faversham, in the heart of the county known as the Garden of England. The collection is of international scientific and historical importance: a living archive of temperate fruit plants and a gene bank for future breeding. The collections were owned and managed by the **RHS** until the 1950s, when they were moved to Brogdale. They were saved from threatened closure in 1990,

and today aspects of their ownership, management and development are shared between the Department for Environment, Food and Rural Affairs (DEFRA), the Brogdale Horticultural Trust and Imperial College, University of London. A plant centre sells a wide variety of fruit trees and bushes, and the Trust runs an identification service.

Brompton Park Nursery, London

An important London nursery founded in 1681, Brompton Park played a part in the creation of many of the great early gardens. With numerous customers among the nobility and the wealthy, the Kensington nursery became the largest in the country, and was instrumental in training garden designers of the day such as Charles Bridgeman and Stephen Switzer, who served apprenticeships there under Brompton's owners George London (d.1714) and Henry Wise (1653–1738). London and Wise were themselves successful designers as well as nurserymen, with royalty among their clients and leading gardens such as Hampton Court Palace to their credit. Plants named after the nursery include Brompton stocks, a well-known and highly fragrant strain bred here by Henry Wise.

Brooklyn Botanic Garden, New York

Established in 1910 under the directorship of Charles Stuart Gager, the garden's 52 acres include a range of themed areas developed over the years. One of the first was the Japanese hill-and-pond garden, created in 1915;

others are the Shakespeare garden, planted with species mentioned in the playwright's works, and the fragrance garden. Plant highlights include the rose garden (with some 1,200 varieties), a bonsai collection, and the cherry esplanade, whose rows of flowering cherries are the focus of a spring festival each year. Successful garden plants developed at Brooklyn Botanic Garden include *Malus × scheideckeri* 'Red Jade' (1956) and the first yellow magnolia, *Magnolia* 'Elizabeth' (1977). Other plants associated with the garden are *Magnolia × brooklynensis* and *Papaver orientale* 'Brooklyn'.

Browall, Johan (1707–1755)

This Swedish professor of physics later became Bishop of Abo. He was honoured by **Linnaeus** in the name of the genus *Browallia* – most familiar as annuals for summer bedding.

Brown, Bob see Cotswold Garden Flowers

Brown, Robert (1773–1858)

A Scottish botanist who travelled with Matthew Flinders on his mission to circumnavigate **Australia** in the *Investigator*, Brown collected hundreds of plants from unexplored areas in Western Australia, the Northern Territory and Tasmania. He brought back nearly 4,000 new plant specimens. His book,

Robert Brown

Prodromus Florae Novae Hollandiae, was a key work in early Australian botany. It was illustrated by **Ferdinand Bauer**, a botanical artist who had accompanied Brown and Flinders on the voyage.

Brunner, Samuel (1790–1844)

The genus *Brunnera* is named after this Swiss botanist, who travelled as a plant collector, with a special interest in the plants of Italy, West **Africa** and the Crimea.

Buchanan, John (1819–1898)

A Scotsman associated with the plants of **New Zealand**, Buchanan emigrated there in 1851 and travelled as a gold prospector. These expeditions inspired him to collect plants to send home. His drawing skills and his increasing knowledge of plants soon gained him invitations to join official expeditions in various parts of New Zealand, where he recorded his new surroundings in maps, watercolours, journals and botanical drawings. The author and illustrator of a three-volume work on New Zealand grasses, he is commemorated in the names of several New Zealand plants, among them *Carex buchananii*, *Hebe buchananii* and *Pittosporum buchananii*.

Buckland Monachorum see Garden House

Buddle, Adam (1660–1715)

Linnaeus named the genus *Buddleja* after this amateur botanist and taxonomist who was born in

Lincolnshire and became vicar of Great Farmbridge in Essex. He published an English flora in 1708.

Buenos Aires see South America

Bukhara (also Bokhara)
This historic city and region of the former Persian Empire now falls within Uzbekistan. The early-flowering red *Tulipa praestans* and *Tulipa linifolia* are among the plants native to Bukhara, and it is associated with the specific epithet *bucharicus*, as in *Iris bucharica*, *Fritillaria bucharica* and *Nepeta bucharica*.

Bulley, Arthur (1861–1942)
Ness Botanic Gardens, in Cheshire, began life as the private garden of this wealthy Liverpool cotton trader whose keen interest in horticulture led him to subscribe to the famous plant-hunting expeditions of the day. In his new garden he planted many of the recent arrivals introduced from **China** by plant hunters such as **George Forrest** and **Frank Kingdon**

Ward. He was especially interested in the primulas from the Himalayas, and one of the most familiar – *Primula bulleyana* – bears his name. Less familiar plants named for him include *Adenophora bulleyana*, *Iris bulleyana* and *Salvia bulleyana*. Such was Bulley's enthusiasm for plants that he also founded the historic Cheshire nursery and seed supplier, **Bees**.

Bunge, Alexander von (1803–1890)
An eminent botanist of German extraction, Bunge was born in Kiev, in the Ukraine, but spent much of his life in Estonia, where he was a student and, later, professor of botany, at the German-speaking university in Dorpat (now Tartu). When he was in his 20s, he spent two years at a mission in Beijing, collecting many new plants in the countryside around the city, including *Jasminum nudiflorum* and *Pinus bungeana*. Later plant-collecting trips took him to Mongolia, Siberia and the north of **China**. Other plants that commemorate von Bunge include

Luther Burbank (1849–1926)

A key figure in the development of American horticulture, Burbank was a prolific experimental plant breeder. Born in Massachusetts, he moved to California, where he worked from his home and garden in Santa Rosa and his farm, Gold Ridge, near Sebastopol. He had a particular interest in producing food plants of better quality, with the aim of increasing the world's food supply. He worked on vegetables, cereals and fruits, and also raised new garden flowers including Shasta daisies (*Leucanthemum*), which he launched in 1901 and named after Mount **Shasta** in northern California. Among the many ornamental plants he 'improved' for garden use are *Gladiolus* and *Crinum*, and there is a large-flowered violet-blue clematis cultivar named after him. He also developed the first thornless blackberry – just one of some 800 new plant varieties that he introduced.

Catalpa bungei, Clerodendrum bungei and *Euonymus bungeanus.*

Bunyard, George (1841–1919)

George Bunyard was born into a Kent nursery family who had a leading fruit-growing business, founded in 1796, which moved from Maidstone to nearby Allington in 1889. Royal Nurseries was the home of the apple 'Allington Pippin'. Bunyard was one of the original recipients of the RHS Victoria Medal of Honour, instituted in 1897 to celebrate the Diamond Jubilee of Queen Victoria. The broad bean 'Bunyard's Exhibition', a favourite with Victorian gardeners, is still a reliable and popular variety. Edward Ashdown Bunyard (1878–1939), George's son, wrote several books on fruit, as well as *Old Garden Roses* (1936). Frances, his daughter, was a talented illustrator.

Burbidge, Frederick W. (1847–1905)

This English naturalist, gardener, plant collector and botanical author-illustrator specialized in narcissi, orchids and chrysanthemums. A gardener at **Kew** as a young man, he visited Borneo in 1877, collecting for the **Veitch** nurseries, and returning with the giant pitcher plant *Nepenthes rajah*. He later became curator of the garden at Trinity College Dublin.

Burford House, Worcestershire

Owned by the Burford Garden Company since 2002, this garden and nursery in Tenbury Wells have long been synonymous with clematis. This is still the home of the National Collection of *Clematis*, established

in the 1950s by the much-respected nurseryman John Treasure, who made the garden and founded an important clematis nursery here. After Treasure's death, the garden designer and author Charles Chesshire became the owner of Burford House, restoring the garden and maintaining the collection, which now numbers some 500 varieties. Among other highlights of the garden is a large specimen of *Wisteria* 'Burford' – one of a number of plants, including several clematis, named after the house. *Clematis* 'Burford White', for example, was raised by one of the nursery's customers.

Burke, David (1854–1897)

Burke was a plant collector who worked for the **Veitch** nurseries in South America and the Far East.

Burkwood, Arthur (1888–1951) and Albert (b.1890)

As young men, the Burkwood brothers trained with established nurseries such as **Veitch** and Dickson's, going on to found their own nursery at Kingston upon Thames, with G.R. Skipwith, around 1928. Their speciality was breeding improved forms of various garden shrubs, and they prided themselves, especially, on their brooms and evergreen ceanothus. Many hybrid shrubs they raised are named after them, such as *Ceanothus* 'Burkwoodii', *Cytisus* 'Burkwoodii', *Daphne* × *burkwoodii* (which has a cultivar 'Albert Burkwood', named after its breeder), and *Osmanthus* × *burkwoodii*. *Viburnum* × *burkwoodii* 'Park Farm Hybrid' is named after their nursery.

Burle Marx, Roberto (1909–1994)

A world-renowned Brazilian landscape designer, Burle Marx's distinctive style was strongly influenced by his empathy for native plants. It was only in Berlin, as a young man visiting the glasshouses of the Dahlem Botanical Gardens, that Burle Marx first encountered the richness of Brazil's flora. At that time the colonial gardens that he had known in his home country were full of European plants – seen (as alien plants have nearly always been) as more prestigious than native species. After he returned to Brazil in 1930, the indigenous plant life inspired his designs for public parks and gardens over many years as he developed his trademark style of organic, fluid shapes and massed planting in swathes of exciting colour, with plant combinations that were ecologically correct – a revolutionary idea at the time. When he purchased an estate in 1949 he began to build up the enormous private plant collection that helped inform his work: 100 acres of tropical luxuriance with some 3,500 plants, some of which he collected on botanical trips to the wild interior of Brazil. He donated his home, garden and plants to the Brazilian state in 1985 – a fitting memorial to a great plantsman and designer. Just as appropriately, a plant named in his honour belongs to one of the genera he championed: *Begonia* 'Burle Marx'.

Burncoose Nurseries, Cornwall

Familiar to gardeners all over Britain from exhibits at **RHS** shows, Burncoose is known for its huge range of trees and shrubs, which includes many rarities.

The nursery belongs to the Caerhays Estate, and propagates many special varieties from the famous garden at **Caerhays Castle**. It has its own 30-acre garden, where many of the plants can be seen. Those named for the nursery include two cultivars of *Camellia* × *williamsii*, a magnolia, and *Viola* 'Burncoose Yellow'.

Burpee, W. Atlee (1858–1915)

A cousin of **Luther Burbank**, Burpee was an American seedsman and plant breeder whose name is still found in many varieties of vegetable and ornamental bedding plant. Burpee, whose name was Americanized from the French Canadian Beaupé, was interested in genetics and selective breeding even as a teenager, when he began to breed poultry, then farm animals and dogs. He soon added flower and vegetable seeds to his repertoire, widening his range by collecting seed in Europe and employing selective breeding to produce varieties that were adapted to the American climate. He prided himself on the quality of his seeds and on his magnificent annual catalogue. By the time he was 40, his company had become the largest seed supplier in the world. After he died, it was run for many years by his son David. A recent Burpee acquisition was Heronswood, the successful Washington nursery of master plantsman **Dan Hinkley**.

Busbecq, Ogier Ghiselin de (1522–1592)

An important early go-between linking East and West, Busbecq, a

Fleming, was sent by the imperial Viennese court as an ambassador to Constantinople at the time of Sultan Süleyman the Magnificent in the mid-16th century. The legendary wealth and opulence of Süleyman's city and the wonderful paradise gardens of the Turks made a profound impression on Busbecq, and over the eight years he spent in Constantinople he made the most of the opportunity to send back to Vienna some of the sumptuous plants that filled these gardens. Most important were the first cultivated tulips, hyacinths and crown imperials (*Fritillaria imperialis*), lilac, philadelphus and hibiscus, and the horse chestnut tree – all exotics that had long been known in the East but were unfamiliar to Europeans. A Busbecq find of a different kind during his time in Constantinople was an ancient manuscript that turned out to be an important medical work of classical times, *De Materia Medica*, by the Greek soldier and doctor **Dioscorides**.

Hyacinthus orientalis

Butt, Walter (1880–1953)

Walter Butt moved in 1940 from the 7-acre garden he had created at Hyde Lodge, Chalford, in Gloucestershire, (later to become the home of the **Giant Snowdrop Company**). His new home was Bales Mead, Porlock, in Somerset, where he made another garden, next door to that of the great plantsman **Norman Hadden**. In 1947, ill health forced Butt to move again and Bales Mead became the home of **E.B. Anderson**, another distinguished gardener. Anderson found a rather special early-flowering *Iris unguicularis* in his new garden and named it 'Walter Butt' after the previous owner.

Buxton, Edmund Charles (1838–1925)

Two highly successful classic herbaceous plants, *Anthemis tinctoria* 'E.C. Buxton' and *Geranium wallichianum* 'Buxton's Variety', are named after this London-born plantsman. He settled in north Wales, where he had a famed garden, Coed Drew, at Betws-y-Coed.

Bygrave Nurseries, Hertfordshire

Adopting an idea imported from the USA and Australia, the family firm of the little-known but influential nurseryman Dennis Bygrave shaped the course of gardening by pioneering pot-grown plants at their nursery at London Colney in the early 1960s. The 'cash-and-carry' concept of garden centres was unthinkable before the advent of plants in containers, which enabled customers to be enticed by plants in flower and buy them throughout the year rather than only in the dormant season.

Byzantium see Istanbul

Cabot, Frank

A leading contemporary American gardener and plant collector, Cabot was the visionary founder, in 1989, of the Garden Conservancy, a successful organization set up to help preserve some of the best private gardens in **North America**. He and his wife, Anne, were also instrumental in the campaign to restore the 16th-century garden of Aberglasney, in Wales. Cabot has made two gardens himself: Stonecrop Gardens at Cold Spring, New York, which incorporates a school of practical horticulture, and the exceptional Les Quatre Vents, the Cabots' home in Quebec, hailed as one of the great gardens of the world. It is the subject of Frank Cabot's book *The Greater Perfection*.

Caley, George (1770–1829)

Caley was an English plant collector in **Australia** in the early 19th century.

Although he had no formal qualifications and was reputed to be a difficult man, he was sponsored for several years by **Sir Joseph Banks** of Kew. A champion of the infamous Captain Bligh of the *Bounty*, Caley left Australia in 1810 and eventually settled in St Vincent in the West Indies, where he was in charge of the botanic garden.

Cambessedes, Jacques (1799–1863)

Paeonia cambessedesii, introduced from Mallorca in 1895, is named after this French plant hunter who worked in the **Balearic Islands** and was noted for his unorthodox use of a shotgun to detach tenacious plant specimens from the islands' rocky cliffs.

Cambridge University Botanic Garden

The original botanic garden in Cambridge was begun in 1762 on 5 acres of land donated by Trinity

Caerhays Castle, Cornwall

A handsome house, designed by John Nash, in a wonderful setting on the south coast of Cornwall, Caerhays is also an outstanding plantsman's garden. The estate has been in the Williams family since 1854. In the great plant-hunting era of the early 20th century it belonged to **John Charles Williams**, grandson of the original owner and a great plant enthusiast. His subscriptions to the Far East expeditions of collectors such as **George Forrest**, **Frank Kingdon Ward** and **Reginald Farrer** resulted in many of the wonderful mature shrubs and trees to be seen at Caerhays today. The four National Collections here include *Magnolia*, with 'Caerhays Belle' and 'Caerhays Surprise' among many named forms. Already by 1917 the garden contained more than 250 kinds of rhododendron, whose offspring include several cultivars named after Caerhays. The third shrub genus that plays a major role here is *Camellia*. Some of the best were raised by J.C. Williams himself: his very successful hybrid *Camellia* × *williamsii* has around 100 named cultivars. Caerhays' plant-breeding tradition continues today at **Burncoose Nurseries**, near Redruth, which is owned by the Caerhays Estate.

College. Its first curator was Charles Miller (1739–1817), son of **Philip Miller**, the respected curator of London's **Chelsea Physic Garden**, who helped Thomas Martyn, professor of botany at Cambridge at the time, with the garden's design. Cambridge has remained one of Britain's principal botanic gardens. The present garden, opened in 1846, covers 40 acres and the total number of plant species is over 10,000, with an outstanding collection of trees, a renowned winter garden and nine National Collections, including fritillaries, hardy geraniums and species tulips.

Cambridge features in quite a large number of plant names, in one form or another. Sometimes it takes the Latin form *cantabrigiensis*, for example *Rosa* 'Cantabrigiensis', *Geranium* × *cantabrigiense* (of which there is a cultivar called 'Cambridge') and *Prunus pseudocerasus* 'Cantabrigiensis'. There are also several cultivars with the abbreviated name 'Cantab', such as the reticulata iris called *Iris* 'Cantab' and a grape hyacinth, *Muscari armeniacum* 'Cantab'. 'Cambridge Favourite' is a well-known variety of strawberry and 'Cambridge Gage' an equally popular plum, while *Monarda* 'Cambridge Scarlet' is one of the most familiar varieties of bergamot for the herbaceous border. Cambridge is also associated with 'Cambridge blue', and this is reflected in *Campanula cochlearifolia* 'Cambridge Blue' and *Salvia patens* 'Cambridge Blue', among others.

Canterbury Plains see New Zealand

Cappadocia

This ancient province of Asia Minor is now in central **Turkey**. Several plants carry the epithet *cappadocicus*, for example *Acer cappadocicum* and *Omphalodes cappadocica*.

Caria

The fig, *Ficus carica*, is named after this ancient region in the

Ficus carica

mountainous far south-west of Asia Minor. It is now part of **Turkey**, close to the Greek islands of Rhodes and **Kos**.

Carles, William (1867–1900)

A British consul and plant collector in **China**, Carles found *Viburnum carlesii* in Chemulpo, Korea. The plant reached **Kew** via **Japan** in 1902.

Carniola

The Latin term *carniolicus* refers to this former region in what is now Slovenia, and is found in several plant names, including *Astrantia carniolica*, *Primula carniolica* and *Saxifraga* 'Carniolica'.

Carpathian Mountains

Campanula carpatica is the most familiar of several plants named after this range, which forms an arc through Slovakia, the western Ukraine and Romania.

Carpenter, William (1811–1848)

The lovely shrub *Carpenteria californica*, a rare woodland native of California and a favourite for sunny gardens, is named after this Louisiana physician.

Carrière, Elie Abel (1816–1896)

An important figure in horticulture in Paris at a time when many new plants and seeds were being sent home by French missionaries such as **Armand David**, Carrière was editor of the *Revue Horticole* and head gardener at the nursery of the Muséum d'Histoire Naturelle in **Paris**, where many of the new finds were grown and named. A familiar garden tree that bears his name is the excellent ornamental hawthorn *Crataegus × lavalleei* 'Carrierei', and there are cultivars of begonia, weigela and pelargonium called 'Abel Carrière'.

Castle of Mey, Caithness

This 16th-century fortified house on the far north coast of Scotland was from 1952 the holiday home of the late Queen Elizabeth The Queen Mother. A keen plantswoman, she had the walled garden beside the castle restored and laid out to protect a surprising variety of plants from the harsh, windy conditions. Those named after the castle include *Agapanthus* 'Castle of Mey', *Rosa* Castle of Mey ('Coclucid') and *Rhododendron* 'Castle of Mey'.

Castlewellan: National Arboretum, County Down

The golden Leyland cypress × *Cupressocyparis leylandii* 'Castlewellan' and the cherry laurel *Prunus laurocerasus* 'Castlewellan' are the most widely known plants named after the National Arboretum of Northern Ireland, but others include a juniper, a eucryphia and a dierama. The 1,000-acre Castlewellan Forest Park

is now government-owned, but the impressive arboretum and the Annesley Garden were planted by several generations of the Annesley family from the mid-19th century onwards. The large collection features many rare conifers, and a number of trees here are the largest or the oldest specimens of their type in cultivation.

Catesby, Mark (1682–1749)

A pioneering naturalist and collector from Essex, Catesby went to America twice, discovering and recording American plants and birds. *Cornus florida* was among his finds. He subsequently corresponded with like-minded contacts across the Atlantic. All this provided the material for his series of 220 magnificent paintings, published between 1730 and 1747 as *The Natural History of Carolina, Georgia, Florida and the Bahama Islands*. Catesby is credited with the introduction to Britain of the first *Stewartia* and several other trees and shrubs; *Trillium catesbyi* and *Sarracenia × catesbyi* are named after him.

Cornus florida

Catt, Peter

This contemporary nurseryman has raised many popular shrub cultivars at his wholesale nursery, Liss Forest Nursery, in Hampshire. They include the golden Mexican orange blossoms *Choisya ternata* Sundance ('Lich') and *Choisya* Goldfingers ('Limo'), as well as *Spiraea japonica* 'Candlelight' and 'Firelight', improved versions of the well-known 'Goldflame'. *Penstemon barbatus*

Caucasus

This botanically rich area – one of the world's officially designated biodiversity hotspots – lies between the Black Sea and the Caspian Sea. Named after the Greater and Lesser Caucasus mountain ranges in its midst, the hotspot takes in parts of **Russia**, Georgia, Azerbaijan, Armenia and **Turkey**. The Caucasus is very varied in topography and climate, and has more than 6,000 plant species, of which about a quarter are found only here. Many of the region's plants and animals are endangered, especially in lowland areas. A huge range of familiar garden plants and choice ornamental trees are among the native species of the Caucasus, including *Paeonia mlokosewitschii*, *Colchicum speciosum*, *Crambe cordifolia*, *Parrotia persica* and *Zelkova carpinifolia*. A large number of plants carry the species epithet *caucasicus*, for example *Artemisia caucasica*, *Scabiosa caucasica*, *Symphytum caucasicum* and *Arabis alpina* subsp. *caucasica*.

Scabiosa caucasica

'Peter Catt' is named after him, while *Ceratostigma willmottianum* Forest Blue ('Lice') is named for the nursery.

Cecil family, Earls and Marquesses of Salisbury see Hatfield House

Chalcedon
Now part of **Istanbul**, this ancient town in **Bithynia** in Asia Minor is recalled in the name *Lychnis chalcedonica*. There is also a plant called *Lilium chalcedonicum*.

Chatham Islands
Astelia chathamica is one of nearly 50 plant species that are found only in this tiny island group some 500 miles east of **New Zealand**. Another, prized by gardeners, is the Chatham Island forget-me-not, *Myosotidium hortensia*, a beautiful but tender perennial with large fleshy leaves and blue forget-me-not flowers. It grows on the coasts of the islands. Other garden plants from

the Chatham Islands include *Hebe chathamica* and *Carex chathamica*, and also *Olearia chathamica* and *Olearia* 'Henry Travers', which were both collected in 1910 by Captain A. Dorrien-Smith of **Tresco Abbey Gardens** in the Isles of Scilly.

Chatsworth, Derbyshire
Historic seat of the Cavendish family, Dukes of Devonshire, Chatsworth has been famous for its huge and splendid garden for well over three centuries. It has links with many great names in gardening, from George London and Henry Wise of **Brompton Park Nursery**, who carried out lavish improvements in 1688, to Joseph Paxton, who, as head gardener from 1826, made Chatsworth one of the leading gardens of Europe. Today the garden is a blend of design features from every age including the present, which is represented by a new kitchen garden and a cottage

Beth Chatto

Now firmly placed in the front rank of contemporary plantswomen, Beth Chatto began her garden and nursery at Elmstead Market near Colchester in the early 1960s. The site was not an easy one, with sun-baked, free-draining gravel in one area and a boggy hollow in another – but Beth Chatto's choice of plants was strongly influenced and inspired by her husband Andrew, a knowledgeable ecologist whose understanding of the habitats of wild plants shaped his wife's gardening philosophy. She pioneered an ecological approach to planting, and brought many significant plants, especially ones with good foliage, to a far wider public. Beth Chatto first became known through the unusual plants she introduced at her lectures to the postwar 'flower clubs' of England, gaining wider fame through her nursery's series of innovative and hugely influential Gold medal-winning exhibits at the Chelsea Flower Show in the 1970s and 1980s. Her garden and nursery have developed over 45 years and continue to attract many visitors and customers, and she has written a number of books informed by her wealth of first-hand experience, particularly of using the right plants to transform problem areas. Two recent projects at the Beth Chatto Gardens – the Gravel Garden and the Woodland Garden – have each been the subject of a book by her, and her earlier books *The Dry Garden* and *The Damp Garden* are classics. She was awarded the RHS Victoria Medal of Honour in 1987. Plants named for her include *Geranium maculatum* 'Beth Chatto' and *Pulmonaria* 'Beth's Blue' and 'Beth's Pink'. The variegated *Pulmonaria rubra* 'David Ward' was named for the propagation manager at the nursery, who spotted it in the garden there.

garden. Plants named after Chatsworth include *Camellia* 'Chatsworth Belle', *Rosa* Chatsworth ('Tanotax') and *Heliotropium arborescens* 'Chatsworth'. There is also a pelargonium named for the Duchess of Devonshire, and an apple and a peony named for the Duke.

Chelsea Physic Garden, London

Perhaps the best and most interesting historic garden in central London, the Chelsea Physic Garden dates from 1673, when it was leased by the Worshipful Society of Apothecaries as

an aid to the study of medicinal plants. The freehold was later purchased by the wealthy society doctor, **Sir Hans Sloane,** who had the garden restored and leased it back to the apothecaries at a generous annual rent of £5 – still the same today. His statue presides over the garden. Already in 1685 **John Evelyn** had described the garden's 'innumerable rarities', but its reputation grew under the curatorship of the distinguished gardener **Philip Miller**, who arrived in 1722, and soon the garden was considered the finest in Europe. Today it can boast the oldest rockery in Britain, built from 1774 under the direction of **William Forsyth** – a hugely ambitious project incorporating stone from the

Chelsea Physic Garden, with Sir Hans Sloane's statue

Tower of London and Icelandic lava brought back as ballast by **Sir Joseph Banks** in Captain Cook's ship. Some of the oldest trees here also date from the 18th century: a black mulberry, a pomegranate and an olive (there is an olive cultivar called 'Chelsea Physic Garden'). Special displays include the finds of various plant hunters and curators, as well as medicinal and other useful plants in the Garden of World Medicine.

Chenault, Leon (1853–1930)
A nurseryman in Orléans, France, Chenault was responsible for the arrival in gardens of many of the new hardy shrubs and trees that had been discovered by the French missionaries of the day in **China**. The privet *Ligustrum compactum* was formerly named after him as *Ligustrum chenaultii*.

Chiloé
Fragaria chiloensis and *Grindelia chiloensis* are named after this island just off the west coast of Chile. It was on the route of early travellers, including **Charles Darwin**.

China see pages 52–53

China see pages 52–53

Chollipo Arboretum, South Korea

C

Euonymus japonicus 'Chollipo' and *Corylopsis glabrescens* var. *gotoana* 'Chollipo' are named after this late 20th-century garden founded by the American-born Ferris Miller (d.2001). Magnolias in all their glory are the central (but by no means the only) attraction.

Christopher, Marina
A contemporary nurserywoman and botanist, and a partner for ten years in the widely respected Green Farm Plants of Bentley, in Hampshire, Marina Christopher is now owner of Phoenix Perennial Plants at nearby Medstead. Specialities among the wide range of unusual perennials and annuals include many verbascums. The nursery is managed with biodiversity as a high priority, and has many plants chosen to attract beautiful and beneficial insects.

Cilicia
Cilicia was an ancient region of Asia Minor along the Mediterranean coast, now part of southern **Turkey**. Fertile in the east, with wooded mountains in the west, it is represented by the Latin epithet *cilicicus*, found in a number of plant names, including *Thymus cilicicus*, *Cyclamen cilicicum*, *Colchicum cilicicum* and *Scilla cilicica*.

Claridge Druce, George see Druce

China

The great plant hunter **E.H. Wilson** described China as 'the mother of gardens'. This huge and varied land has contributed more than any other single country to the gardens of the temperate world – partly because

Paeonia suffruticosa

of its rich indigenous flora and partly because of Chinese garden tradition, which made an art form of the expert breeding and selection of just a few kinds of showy flowering plants, such as chrysanthemums, roses, hydrangeas, peonies and camellias. Depictions of gorgeous cultivated flowers like these reached other countries in Chinese art and ceramics, so these 'man-made' plants were the ones that the West coveted. Access to the interior of China was severely restricted, which meant that the first foreign plant collectors visited gardens and nurseries rather than the countryside. Many of the early introductions to the West and gardens were therefore cultivated stock, and most of China's native botanical wealth remained untapped.

China had long held a mysterious fascination for Westerners, but rapid colonization of other countries by western European powers such as England, Portugal and The Netherlands had made the Chinese mistrustful and unwilling to trade with these profiteering nations. A few Chinese plants had made their way west, with exports such as silk, along ancient overland trading routes, and others via interested Westerners (such as **John Reeves**) who worked for the East India Company in Guangzhou (then Canton). **Sir Joseph Banks** even managed to install his **Kew** gardener **William Kerr** there for eight years. Kerr made some significant plant introductions, but was not allowed to travel farther afield. This began to change in the 1840s, when Shanghai and several other Chinese ports opened to trade with

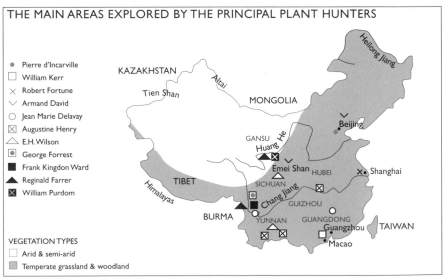

THE MAIN AREAS EXPLORED BY THE PRINCIPAL PLANT HUNTERS

- ● Pierre d'Incarville
- □ William Kerr
- ✕ Robert Fortune
- ∨ Armand David
- ○ Jean Marie Delavay
- ⊠ Augustine Henry
- △ E.H. Wilson
- ◉ George Forrest
- ■ Frank Kingdon Ward
- ▲ Reginald Farrer
- ⊠ William Purdom

KAZAKHSTAN

Altai

Tien Shan

MONGOLIA

Heilong Jiang

Beijing

GANSU

Huang He

Emei Shan   HUBEI

Shanghai

TIBET

SICHUAN

Himalayas

Chang Jiang

GUIZHOU

BURMA

YUNNAN

GUANGDONG

Guangzhou

TAIWAN

Macao

VEGETATION TYPES

- □ Arid & semi-arid
- ▨ Temperate grassland & woodland

Western nations at the end of the Opium Wars. This paved the way for the first of the major collectors, **Robert Fortune**, whose large legacy of introduced plants came mostly from gardens and nurseries in and around these treaty ports.

Little would have been known about China's native flora until the early 20th century, had it not been for a handful of French missionaries there, such as **d'Incarville**, in the mid-18th century, and, from the 1860s, **David** and **Delavay**. These were the first Europeans to tackle inland China. Thanks to them, a few wild Chinese plants were grown in Western gardens in the 19th century. They brought reports of hundreds more, whetting gardeners' appetites for all kinds of exotic plants that would suit temperate gardens, and setting the agenda for the famous plant hunters of the early 20th century: the intrepid **George Forrest**, **Frank Kingdon Ward**, **Reginald Farrer**, **E.H. Wilson** and others. Each returned with hair-raising stories of plant hunting in remote and inhospitable places, and with seeds and plants that were to transform Western gardens.

China continues to draw plantsmen and scientists. New discoveries continue to be made by botanists, nurserymen and plant hunters such as **Roy Lancaster**, the Wynn-Joneses of **Crûg Farm Plants**, and the American **Dan Hinkley**. Fortunately the large-scale collecting of the early 1900s has become a thing of the past. Modern collectors usually take only tiny quantities of seed, and a strict code of practice minimizes any conservation threat. Plants can be transported more efficiently, and micropropagation enables nurseries to use small amounts of plant material to yield many saleable plants in a short time, so there is no need to collect from the wild in large q uantities. Research programmes, local initiatives, and increased awareness of conservation issues, are starting to make an impact, and the hope is that these will all gather enough momentum for China's irreplaceable wild plant life to be saved before it is too late.

FROM THE WILD

Some wild species from China are now well-loved garden plants

Buddleja davidii
Davidia involucrata
Gentiana sino-ornata
Kolkwitzia amabilis
Lilium regale
Lonicera nitida
Meconopsis betonicifolia
Parthenocissus henryana
Pieris formosa var. *forrestii*
Viburnum farreri
Wisteria sinensis

CHINESE PROVINCES IN PLANT NAMES

hupehensis from Hubei
kansuensis from Gansu
kouytchensis from Guizhou
setchuenensis or *szechuanicus* from Sichuan
yunnanensis from Yunnan

CONSERVATION

Conservation used not to be a priority, but today China's wild places and their plant life are threatened as never before. Pressure from development, tourism and industrialization is one problem. Another is the harvesting of wild plants for use in traditional medicine. Rural communities are now more aware of the money to be made from harvesting wild plants for this purpose: a few roots of a rare native tree peony, for example, can bring in an average day's wage. To prevent these depredations, schemes are now in place to cultivate plants for pharmaceutical use; workers who grow such crops can make a good and more secure living.

Clark, William (1770–1838)

This American soldier was co-leader, with **Captain Meriwether Lewis**, of a historic expedition in the American West in 1804–1806. The genus of annuals called *Clarkia* was discovered by Lewis near the Clark River.

Clayton, John (1694–1773)

A plant collector in Virginia who had travelled there from England to join his father, an early settler, Clayton cultivated native species in his garden. He is an important figure in botanical history because of the specimens and descriptions of American plants that he sent to **Gronovius**, a Dutch botanist who worked with **Linnaeus**. The genus *Claytonia* is named for him.

Clusius, Carolus (1526–1609)

Clusius was the Latinized name of Charles de l'Ecluse, a remarkably well-travelled and widely educated Flemish scholar and botanist whose many talents and achievements included establishing the first botanic garden devoted to ornamental (rather than medicinal) plants. Located at **Leiden** in The Netherlands, and now restored, it was the *Hortus Academicus*, and was known, among other things, for the collection of tulips that Clusius assembled there, which became very important in the establishment of the Dutch bulb industry. Helped by his network of scholarly friends in many countries, he introduced new varieties of *Narcissus*, fritillaries and even scarlet runner beans, and was the first European to grow a potato. Plants named after this early polymath include *Tulipa clusiana*, *Gentiana clusii*, *Cistus clusii* and a recently introduced disease-resistant elm hybrid, *Ulmus glabra* 'Clusius'.

Colborn, Nigel

A well-known gardening lecturer, author and broadcaster, ex-farmer Nigel Colborn has long been a familiar figure in British gardening and in the **RHS**, serving on committees, as a show judge, and as a Council member.

Colchis

The genus *Colchicum* and the ivy *Hedera colchica* are the most common of several plants named after this region of the **Caucasus** on the eastern shore of the Black Sea, now part of western Georgia.

Colesbourne Park see Elwes, Henry

Coleton Fishacre, Devon

Crocosmia × *crocosmiiflora* 'Coleton Fishacre' is named after a 1920s home and garden, close to Dartmouth on the South Devon coast, now owned by the National Trust. It was built for Rupert D'Oyly Carte (son of Richard D'Oyly Carte, the 19th-century theatrical impresario) and his wife, owners of London's Savoy Hotel at the time.

Collinson, Peter (1694–1768)

Collinson was not a plant hunter, nor a botanist, nurseryman or traveller, but his great enthusiasm for plants led him to play a leading role in the story behind the arrival in European gardens of the great botanical riches of **North America**. As a draper based in London, he had business associates in America who put him in contact with the important Philadelphia plant collector **John Bartram**. The two men thus began an exchange of letters and drawings, seeds, plants and other natural history specimens. This was to last for more than 30 years, although they never met. Collinson acted as agent, negotiator and general facilitator, persuading the wealthy, influential and titled of the day to sponsor Bartram's collecting expeditions in exchange for a share in the exciting new plant material Bartram sent back from the other side of the Atlantic.

Columbia River see Douglas, David

Colvill, James (1746–1822)
Colvill founded his London nursery in the King's Road, Chelsea, in the 1780s and was in partnership with James Buchanan by about 1790. He was succeeded in the business by his son, also James Colvill (1777–1832).

Comber, Harold (1897–1969)
The son of James Comber, who was head gardener for the Messel family at **Nymans** in Sussex, Harold Comber grew up surrounded by the exotic trees and shrubs for which Nymans was famed. This may have inspired him to travel, especially at a time when plant hunters were becoming a rare breed. He went to **South America**, and introduced several connoisseurs' plants from Chile, including *Sophora macrocarpa*, the evergreen climbing shrub *Asteranthera ovata* and

Desfontainia spinosa 'Harold Comber'. In 1929, sponsored by a syndicate organized by Lord Rothschild, Comber went to Tasmania, returning with several new garden plants, including *Ozothamnus ledifolius*. Other plants named for Comber are *Fuchsia magellanica* 'Comber' and *Olearia phlogopappa* 'Comber's Blue' and 'Comber's Pink'.

Commelin, Caspar (1667–1731)
Commelina, a genus of mostly blue-flowered annuals and tender perennials, is named after this Dutch physician who was professor of botany at the University of Amsterdam and did much to improve the city's botanic garden.

Commelina coelestis

Commerson, Philibert (1727–1773)
This French botanist was renowned as a compulsive plant collector even as a young student at **Montpellier**. At last, aged 40, Commerson joined a westbound ship for the trip of a lifetime. In **South America** he marvelled at the tropical plant life, discovering drifts of the crocus-like white bulb *Zephyranthes candida* and an exotic flowering climber, which he named *Bougainvillea* after **Louis-Antoine de Bougainville**, captain of another ship on the same expedition. Commerson's ship accompanied that of Bougainville on the next leg of the journey, rounding Cape Horn and arriving in Tahiti, where Commerson caused a stir when it was revealed that his 'valet' on the trip

was, in fact, Jeanne Baret, his devoted French housekeeper, in disguise. Her loyalty was such that she stayed with Commerson when illness forced him to leave the expedition in December 1768. Eventually, though desperate to return to France, Commerson died on the island of **Réunion** (then the Ile Bourbon, a French colony). Jeanne subsequently returned to France with the plant material and information that Commerson had collected. In the process, she became the first woman to circumnavigate the world. Commerson was honoured posthumously; he is thought to have discovered up to 3,000 species new to science.

Compton, Henry (1632–1713)

Fulham Palace, seat of the bishops of London, had an extensive and famous garden, which reached its peak during the incumbency, from 1675, of Bishop Henry Compton, who was a passionate gardener and an early plantaholic. His involvement in the Church in the developing American colonies gave him every excuse to take an interest in the many new plants that were arriving from across the Atlantic in the 17th century. He was a patron of the **Tradescants** and a good customer of the leading London nurseries of the day, including **Brompton Park Nursery**, whose founder, George London, had been his gardener. Reputed to have a guilty conscience about the amount of money he spent on his garden, the bishop is said to have had a collection of more than 1,000 exotic plants, not to mention dozens of rare, newly introduced trees – many of which were

cut down by his successor in order to make room for growing vegetables.

Copton Ash, Kent

Euphorbia 'Copton Ash' is named for this plantsman's garden and specialist nursery at Faversham, owned and run by Tim and Gillian Ingram.

Corning, Betty (1912–1993)

Betty Corning was president of the Garden Club of America in the 1960s and wife of the mayor of Albany, New York. She had found the beautiful lavender-blue viticella clematis that is named after her in 1933, growing over a porch in Albany, and had grown it in her garden for many years before it was named *Clematis* 'Betty Corning' and made available in the nursery trade.

Cornubia

Cornubia ('Land of the Saints'), the Latin name for the Celtic kingdom that became Cornwall, occurs in some plant names such as *Cotoneaster frigidus* 'Cornubia', *Rhododendron* Cornubia group, and the fern *Polypodium interjectum* 'Cornubiense'.

Correia de Serra, José (1750–1823)

The Australian genus *Correa* is named after this Portuguese botanist and diplomat.

Correvon, Henri (1854–1939)

A houseleek and a primula are among the plants named after this Swiss alpine specialist in Geneva, author of *Les Plantes des Alpes*. The more well-known *Clematis* 'Madame Julia Correvon' was raised in the late 19th century by **Morel**.

Cory, Reginald (1871–1934)

A well-travelled horticulturist who was active in the **RHS**, Cory inherited the magnificent Dyffryn Estate near Cardiff, in Wales, from his father, the Victorian shipping and coal magnate Sir John Cory. The nurseryman-turned-landscape architect Thomas Mawson had been commissioned in 1906 to design the gardens, and Reginald Cory worked closely with him, choosing many of the trees and shrubs: he had himself made plant-hunting expeditions overseas, with **Collingwood Ingram**, and sponsored other plant hunters, including **E.H. Wilson**. Cory is remembered as a benefactor of **Cambridge University Botanic Garden** and in the Reginald Cory Memorial Cup, an RHS award for work with new garden hybrids. A huge Lottery-funded restoration programme in recent years has seen Dyffryn Gardens returning to their original Edwardian splendour.

Cosyra

The small island of Pantellaria, in the Mediterranean between Sicily and North **Africa**, was formerly called Cosyra and is recalled in the name of *Limonium cosyrense*.

Cotswold Garden Flowers, Worcestershire

Leading plantsman Bob Brown, who has a keen interest in hardy perennials, grows a huge and eclectic range of both unusual plants for connoisseurs and trouble-free garden stalwarts at his nursery in Evesham,

which he established in 1991. *Erysimum* 'Cotswold Gem' is one of the plants raised here and named for the nursery.

Coulter, Thomas (1793–1843)

Romneya coulteri is named after this Irish botanist and plant collector who was curator of the herbarium at Trinity College Dublin. He also spent some ten years in Mexico.

Courson, France

France's principal plant fair, the *Journées des Plantes de Courson*, is held every May and October in the grounds of this elegant 17th-century château south-west of Paris. From small beginnings with a handful of specialist nurseries in 1982, the fair now welcomes well over 200 exhibitors and runs a programme of lectures and conferences as well as awarding *mérites de Courson* for exceptional plants.

Cowichan, British Columbia

The Cowichan strain of primula, prized by connoisseurs, is unusual in that the plants lack the typical 'eye' of other primroses. The plant from which the various Cowichan colour groups were bred was found in a garden in Cowichan Station on Vancouver Island.

Bob Brown

Cox, Euan (1893–1977)

This Scottish plantsman and collector travelled in the Far East with **Reginald Farrer** and was with him on his final expedition in Burma in 1919–1920. Among the plants brought back from that trip was the Chinese coffin tree, subsequently named *Juniperus recurva* var. *coxii,* which was prized for its aromatic wood. Cox described the exploits of various plant hunters in his books including *Plant Hunting in China* and *Farrer's Last Journey.* Cox's son Peter and grandson Kenneth, also distinguished plant collectors and rhododendron specialists and breeders, have nurtured and expanded the nursery established by Euan Cox in 1954 at **Glendoick**, near Perth, in Scotland. It now has one of the best rhododendron collections in the world.

Craigieburn, Dumfries & Galloway

Euphorbia amygdaloides 'Craigieburn' is from Janet Wheatcroft's celebrated garden and specialist nursery near Moffat. She discovered the remarkable *Arisaema griffithii* 'Numbuq' in Nepal, as well as meconopsis that thrive here in the Scottish climate.

Crarae, Argyll

This important Scottish woodland garden combines an extraordinary collection of rare trees and shrubs with a rugged highland setting designed to resemble a Himalayan ravine. The garden and its planting were the vision of Sir George Campbell (1894–1967), whose family had owned the garden since 1825. He was the cousin of the great plant hunter **Reginald Farrer**, who visited Crarae in 1914, bringing seeds collected on his travels in **China**. Trees and shrubs from many temperate regions of the world make Crarae a very

varied garden, with a host of different deciduous trees as well as some 400 kinds of rhododendron and a National Collection of *Nothofagus*. A form of eucryphia is named after the garden.

Crete

This large and somewhat mountainous Greek island in the eastern Mediterranean has long been renowned for its wealth of flowering plants, including well over 100 endemic species. Specialist botanical tours still frequent the island to see wild orchids, tulips and other spring-flowering bulbs, and rare aromatic shrubs, following in the footsteps of the 16th-century traveller and botanist **Pierre Belon**. Robbed by pirates and abandoned close to Crete in 1547, he used the opportunity to acquaint himself with

A 19th-century botanists' map of Crete

the island's rich flora, discovering plants that would later be prized in cultivation, such as a white oleander and *Cistus ladanifer*. A later visitor was the eminent French botanist **Joseph Pitton de Tournefort**, who spent three months here in 1700. Plant names recalling the island include *Cistus creticus* and *Iris unguicularis* subsp. *cretensis*.

Crewe, Henry Harpur (1828–1883)

The beautifully scented, double golden wallflower *Erysimum cheiri* 'Harpur Crewe' is named after this Buckinghamshire cleric who was rector of Drayton Beauchamp. A keen gardener, he knew and grew many plants, and was immediately attracted by this rather special wallflower when he saw it in the grand Hampshire garden of his relative Lady Crewe, propagating it for posterity. It was named after him when it was first marketed by **Paul**'s nursery in 1896. Other plants bearing his name are the spring-flowering yellow daisy *Doronicum* × *excelsum* 'Harpur Crewe' and *Crocus biflorus* subsp. *crewei*, which was named after him by **Sir Joseph Hooker**.

Sue and Bleddyn Wynn-Jones

Cripps, Thomas & Sons, Kent

This nursery, founded in Tunbridge Wells by Thomas Cripps (1809–1888), was noted in the late 19th century for its ornamental trees, Japanese maples and clematis (including the well-known 'Star of India' and 'Gipsy Queen'). *Chamaecyparis obtusa* 'Crippsii', raised here, is still one of the best compact golden-leaved conifers.

Croftway Nursery, West Sussex

The nursery was established after World War I, on a government smallholding at Barnham, near Bognor Regis, by Frank Toynbee (whose house was called 'Croftway'). The respected plantsman **Ken Aslet** was manager of the nursery, and its lasting plant successes have included *Sidalcea* 'Croftway Red' and *Monarda* 'Croftway Pink'. There is also a conifer named after it, *Chamaecyparis lawsoniana* 'Croftway'. The nursery closed in 2003.

Crûg Farm Plants, Gwynedd

Bleddyn and Sue Wynn-Jones, owners of this highly respected specialist nursery, are in the front rank of contemporary plant hunters. The Crûg (pronounced 'Creeg') Farm list includes hundreds of plants the Wynn-Joneses have grown from seed that they have gathered themselves on their ambitious annual collecting trips, which over the years have taken in the Far East, Central America, and elsewhere. For some expeditions they have joined forces with other internationally known plantsmen, such as **Dan Hinkley**, often working closely with established botanical institutions. Crûg Farm specialities include a wide range of woodland perennials, rare collected shrubs and hardy geraniums, and the nursery holds National Collections of *Coriaria*, *Polygonatum* and *Paris*. Many of their introductions are named for the nursery, ranging from cranesbills, such as *Geranium* 'Sue Crûg', 'Bertie Crûg' (named after the Wynn-Joneses' terrier), Crûg strain and 'Dusky Crûg', to the highly scented *Jasminum officinale* 'Crûg's Collection' and the Boston ivy cultivar *Parthenocissus tricuspidata* 'Crûg Compact'.

Culpeper, Nicholas (1616–1654)

One of the most famous names among all the early herbalists, Culpeper was an apothecary in Spitalfields, London, and author of the *Complete Herbal* (originally *The English Physician*) of

C

1653, which has been reproduced in many later editions.

Cunningham, Allan (1791–1839)

An important early botanist and plant collector in **Australia**, Cunningham had trained at **Kew** and was one of the first plant hunters to be sent out after the Napoleonic Wars had called a temporary halt to plant hunting. He spent two years in Brazil before travelling on to New South Wales in 1816. Cunningham spent the next 15 years in Australia, exploring, for the first time, several river valleys to the west of the Blue Mountains, and also surveying the coast on several naval expeditions. This even took him, in 1830, to the remote penal colony of Norfolk Island. He returned to spend several years in England from 1831, but went back to Australia in 1837 as colonial botanist and director of the botanic garden at Parramatta, near Sydney. A number of plants are named after him – notably *Araucaria cunninghamii*, the Moreton Bay pine – but most are too tender for temperate gardens. He did, however, introduce the hardier evergreen flowering shrub *Grevillea rosmarinifolia*.

Cunningham, James (d.1709)

The first known amateur plant collector in **China**, Cunningham was a surgeon with the East India Company and first visited China in 1698. He spent time on the island of Zhoushan (Chusan), near Shanghai. The Chinese fir, *Cunninghamia lanceolata,* is named after him, but was introduced into Britain later, by **William Kerr**, in 1804.

Cupani, Francesco (1657–1711)

Cupani was an Italian monk, the author of a botanical book, *Hortus Catholicus* (published in 1697), and fêted for the discovery of sweet peas. He is said to have found the original bicoloured purple-and-maroon flowers on the island of Sicily in 1699, and to have sent them to the London schoolteacher and plantsman **Robert Uvedale**. *Lathyrus odoratus* 'Cupani' is the name of one of the most sweetly scented of these immensely popular flowers. Other plants named in his honour include the charming Mediterranean daisy, *Anthemis punctata* subsp. *cupaniana*, which flowers in late spring.

Curtis, Charles (1853–1928)

A plant collector for **Veitch** nurseries, Curtis spent several years plant hunting in the islands of Indonesia for orchids, pitcher plants and other exotics. Subsequently he became superintendent of the botanic gardens in Penang.

Curtis, William (1746–1799)

Curtis was an eminent naturalist who had his own botanic garden, but his chief claim to fame was as the producer of the long-lived gardening periodical *The Botanical Magazine*. The first issue appeared in 1787, and it is still published today, under the title *Curtis's Botanical Magazine.* High-quality, botanically accurate colour illustrations have always been a landmark feature of the periodical, which is now published by Blackwell on behalf of the Royal Botanic Gardens, **Kew**.

Dahl, Anders (1751–1789)
The genus *Dahlia* is named for this Swedish doctor, a one-time student of **Linnaeus** at the University of Uppsala.

Daisy Hill see Newry

Dammer, Carl (1860–1920)
Cotoneaster dammeri pays tribute to this botanist who worked at Berlin's botanical museum.

Dahlia coccinea

Dampier, William (1652–1715)
Stories of this Somerset-born early adventurer vary widely. Some portray him as a bloodthirsty buccaneer, others as a pragmatic explorer, amateur scientist and author who often found it expedient to travel on pirate vessels. Either way, he must have been a remarkable man. He circumnavigated the world three times, learning much about exotic flora and fauna as well as navigational techniques. His published journals, such as *A New Voyage Round the World* (1697) and *A Voyage to New Holland* (1703–1709), influenced great men from Captain Cook to **Charles Darwin**. Dampier's collection of plant specimens, including acacias and a lotus, is now part of Oxford University's herbarium. Impressed by the unique antipodean flora on his first voyage to **Australia** in 1688, Dampier was responsible for the arrival in Europe of the first Australian plants to be seen in the northern hemisphere. The Australian genus *Dampiera* and the elm *Ulmus × hollandica* 'Dampieri'

and its better-known cultivar 'Dampieri Aurea' are named after him.

Darke, Rick
Curator of plants at **Longwood Gardens** in Pennsylvania from 1986 to 1997, the American botanist, plantsman and author Rick Darke is an expert in ornamental grasses and plants native to North America. His books include *The American Woodland Garden* and several titles on grasses.

Dartington Hall, Devon
One of England's great 20th-century gardens was created here as a setting for the medieval manor where Dorothy and Leonard Elmhirst, who arrived in 1925, established their innovative arts college. The garden's design involved important names: Percy Cane, **Beatrix Farrand** and, later, Preben Jakobsen. Among several Dartington plants are *Dianthus* 'Dartington Laced', *Helichrysum italicum* 'Dartington' and *Saxifraga* 'Dartington Double'.

Darwin, Charles (1809–1882)
This great evolutionary scientist came from a scientific background: his grandfather, Erasmus Darwin, had been a physician and had edited translations of **Linnaeus**. As a young field naturalist, Charles travelled to many distant destinations, including South America and Australia (1831–1836), getting to know their wildlife, especially that of islands like the Falklands, the Galapagos and **Chiloé** (where he discovered *Berberis darwinii*). Other plants named in his honour

include the tender Australian shrub genus *Darwinia* as well as *Calceolaria darwinii* and *Hoya darwinii*. Darwin tulips were named after his death, with the permission of his son. The classic *Origin of Species* (1859) is only one of several books he wrote: his lifelong observation of plants provided subject matter for several others. Darwin's garden at his home of 40 years, Down House in Orpington, Kent, has been restored by English Heritage using the plants he wrote about. The garden served Darwin as an outdoor laboratory as well as a productive kitchen garden.

Davenport-Jones, Hilda see **Washfield Nursery**

David, Jean Pierre Armand (1826–1900)

The French monk Père David (as he is usually known) became a missionary and teacher in Beijing in 1862. He soon showed great zeal as a naturalist, collecting and carefully preserving many specimens of new plants to send home to France. Despite frequent illness, he spent 12 years on extensive and intrepid plant-collecting travels in remote regions of **China**, discovering species that are now familiar in gardens in many countries. Among these are *Rodgersia aesculifolia* and *Photinia davidiana*, many rhododendron species and the snakebark maple, *Acer davidii* (Père David's maple), which he found near **Baoxing** (Mupin) in Sichuan province, in 1869. Other well-known plants commemorating Père David include *Clematis armandii*, *Viburnum davidii*, the handkerchief tree *Davidia*

involucrata, and *Buddleja davidii.* The plants he discovered featured in his two-volume illustrated work, *Plantae Davidianae*, published in 1884 and 1888.

Davidson, Byard LeRoy (Roy) (1918–2000)

Pulmonaria 'Roy Davidson' and *Penstemon procerus* 'Roy Davidson' are named after this American plantsman and florist who was born in Idaho and settled in the Seattle area. A world expert on irises, he had a keen interest in many other plants and his books included one on the genus *Lewisia* and the first guide to penstemon cultivars.

Dawyck Botanic Garden, Borders

This is a regional offshoot, near Peebles, of the Royal Botanic Garden **Edinburgh**. It is especially well known for its collection of trees brought back from **North America** by **David Douglas**. Another American connection is with the **Arnold Arboretum** and its founder **Charles Sprague Sargent**, who passed on to Dawyck plant material from the Chinese expeditions of **E.H. Wilson**. The garden is associated with the fastigiate beeches *Fagus sylvatica* 'Dawyck', which originated here in the early 19th century.

Decaisne, Joseph (1807–1882)

Ultimately a respected botanist and director of the Muséum d'Histoire Naturelle in **Paris**, Decaisne had travelled to Paris from his native Brussels as a young man and began

Jean Marie Delavay (1834–1895)

One of the most productive of the renowned group of French missionary plant collectors working in late 19th-century **China**, Delavay went to Guangdong (Kwangtung) province in 1867 and later to north-west Yunnan, in the far west of the country. This was the area he knew best, spending much of his time there until his death after several years in poor health following a bout of bubonic plague. During his time in China he is said to have sent more than 200,000 dried plant specimens (1,500 of them were species new to science) from Yunnan to the Muséum d'Histoire Naturelle in **Paris**. Unfortunately, identifying and cataloguing them was such an enormous task that many remained neglected for a long time. However, some of Delavay's plants were successfully propagated for garden use; many more served as an inspiration to the next generation of plant hunters, who helped stock the legendary herbaceous borders of late Victorian and Edwardian times. He was the first (in 1886) to record the elusive blue poppy, *Meconopsis betonicifolia*, later introduced into cultivation by **Frank Kingdon Ward**. Delavay lives on in the names of many plants familiar to present-day gardeners, such as *Thalictrum delavayi*, *Paeonia delavayi* and *Incarvillea delavayi*.

AGAINST THE ODDS

Delavay is said to have sent the first seeds of the fragrant spring-flowering evergreen shrub *Osmanthus delavayi* from Yunnan to the **Vilmorin** nursery in France in 1890. Only one germinated, and a single plant was raised. It was then successfully propagated by grafting.

his career as a gardener there. Becoming an authority on plant naming, he specialized in the plants of **Japan** and **China** and named many of the new species that were arriving from there at the time. He was also associated with the naming of *Sequoia gigantea*, the giant sequoia or Wellingtonia, a new discovery from California that had caused high-profile taxonomic squabbles (it is now named *Sequoiadendron giganteum*). Decaisne is commemorated in the genus name of *Decaisnea fargesii,* an unusual shrub known for its long blue seedpods.

Delile, Alire (1778–1850)

Ceanothus × *delileanus* is named after this French botanist and physician who travelled to Egypt with Napoleon and later went to America. He was professor of botany at **Montpellier** from 1819 to 1850.

Denny, Vincent (1918–2001)

This nurseryman from Broughton in Lancashire bred many new clematis cultivars, including *Clematis* 'Broughton Star', 'Broughton Bride', 'Denny's Double', 'Vince Denny' and 'Samantha Denny'. The widely known *Clematis* 'Sylvia Denny' was named for his wife, who worked with him.

Desfontaines, René (1750–1833)

Desfontainia spinosa, an evergreen shrub from the Andes, is named after this botanist at the Muséum d'Histoire

D

Naturelle in **Paris**. His book on the flora of North **Africa** was published in 1798.

Deshima see Japan

Dickson, James (1738–1822)

The tree fern *Dicksonia* is named after this Scottish botanist, nurseryman and gardener who was one of the founder members of both the **RHS** and the Linnean Society (see **Linnaeus**). As a young man, Dickson moved from his native Peeblesshire to London, working as a nurseryman at Brompton, then for the British Museum as a gardener, before setting up his own seed and herb business in Covent Garden in 1772.

Dillon, Helen

Widely respected in horticultural circles all over the world, plantswoman and garden consultant Helen Dillon is known for her vibrant and inspirational Irish garden. She and her husband Val moved to Ranelagh, Dublin, in 1972 and gradually transformed their 1-acre garden into one of Ireland's best: a wonderfully balanced mixture of successful design and abundant rare plant treasures. Helen Dillon has lectured and collected plants in many countries and books such as *Garden Artistry* and *Helen Dillon on Gardening* have long been favourites among knowledgeable gardeners. She is also known in Ireland as a presenter of television gardening programmes and as a newspaper gardening columnist. She is honoured in several plant names including *Heuchera* 'Helen Dillon' and *Scabiosa* 'Helen Dillon'.

Dioscorides, Pedanios

Dioscorides

This ancient Greek herbalist was the author of *De Materia Medica*, an influential treatise on medicinal plants, which was used by physicians well into medieval times. He is commemorated in several botanical names: *Arum dioscoridis* and *Acanthus dioscoridis*, *Dioscorea* – a genus of mainly tropical climbers – and the plant family Dioscoreaceae.

Docwra's Manor Garden, Cambridgeshire

John and **Faith Raven** created this excitingly varied plantsman's garden at Shepreth, near Royston, after they moved here in 1954. Roses and clematis help give a cottage-garden feel to the borders, and there are many plants such as euphorbias, hellebores and cistus collected by the Ravens on their travels, especially in the Mediterranean area.

Dodoens, Rembert (1517–1585)

The writings of this Flemish botanist and herbalist were translated into English by **Henry Lyte** in 1578, and were subsequently used by **Gerard**. Dodoens' later work gained him fame as the first botanical author to produce a study of flowers as objects of beauty and pleasure, rather than simply as medicinal plants. He is commemorated in the name of a disease-resistant elm cultivar, *Ulmus* 'Dodoens', raised at **Wageningen**, in The Netherlands.

Dodson, Harry (1920–2005)

Harry Dodson was a traditional gardener of the 'old school' who, with horticultural consultant Peter Thoday, became well known and influential through BBC Television's *The Victorian Kitchen Garden*. In this inspired 1987 series, the walled garden at Chilton Foliat, in Berkshire, where Dodson had been head gardener for 54 years, was painstakingly restored to show exactly how it worked in its 19th- and early 20th-century heyday. The series was a precursor to other Victorian garden restorations, notably **Heligan**, and sparked wider interest in the rescue from extinction of heritage seed varieties threatened by modern legislation.

Dombey, Joseph (1742–1796)

Nothofagus dombeyi, *Salvia dombeyi* and the tropical genus *Dombeya* are named after this ill-fated Frenchman, who made a voyage to **South America** in 1777 on behalf of the Jardin des Plantes (then the Jardin du Roi) in **Paris**, where he was a botanist. He travelled with two inexperienced Spanish plant collectors, who took advantage of his generosity and greater learning throughout the eight-year trip but claimed credit for the expedition's finds. Shipwreck, war and a fire also took their toll. Dombey returned to Spain ahead of the others, only to have his precious remaining specimens and notes confiscated in Cadiz on the way home. Disillusioned with life and driven away by the French Revolution, he returned to the West Indies but was imprisoned as a suspected spy and died on the island of Montserrat.

Don, George (1798–1856)

Notable as the first plant collector commissioned by the **RHS**, Don was the son of a Scottish nurseryman, also George (1764–1814), who became superintendent of the botanic garden at **Edinburgh**. George himself was foreman at the **Chelsea Physic Garden** from 1816 to 1821. In January 1822 he joined an expedition on HMS *Iphegenia*, sailing down the west coast of **Africa**, where he collected plants in Sierra Leone, and returning via **South America** (where he discovered the Brazil nut), the West Indies and New York. Sadly, by the time the ship reached northern latitudes it was winter again. Few of Don's tropical plant specimens survived the cold, but the knowledge he gained informed his later writings, including a monograph on the genus *Allium*.

Don, Monty

Familiar as a contemporary gardener and television personality, Monty Don is known chiefly as the presenter of the BBC's *Gardeners' World* and for his books. *Pelargonium* 'Sarah Don' is named after his wife.

Doncaster, Amy (1894–1995)

This great 20th-century plantswoman, a member of the Baring banking family, gardened well into her 90s. Her Hampshire garden in Chandler's Ford contained many special plants and particularly reflected her interest in woodland plants such as hellebores and epimediums. Cultivars commemorating her include *Anemone nemorosa* 'Amy Doncaster' and *Geranium sylvaticum* 'Amy Doncaster'.

D

Doubleday, Henry (1808–1875)

The name of this Essex naturalist and Quaker became familiar through the organic movement and its flagship, the **Henry Doubleday Research Association** (Garden Organic).

Downie, John (d.1892)

One of the most popular crab apples, *Malus* 'John Downie', takes its name from this Edinburgh nurseryman, who also had a florist's shop in Princes Street. His nursery had its own palm house, and also a special begonia house.

Dropmore, Buckinghamshire

This estate in Beaconsfield was the home of William Grenville, prime minister from 1806 to 1807. The formal and woodland garden, at one time celebrated for its splendour, is the origin of several plant names: *Lonicera* × *brownii* 'Dropmore Scarlet', *Anchusa azurea* 'Dropmore', *Nepeta* 'Dropmore', *Kniphofia* 'Dropmore Apricot' and *Lythrum virgatum* 'Dropmore Purple'.

Druce, George Claridge (1850–1932)

A pharmacist and botanist from Northamptonshire who became mayor of Oxford in 1900, George Claridge Druce had a chemist's shop in Oxford. His book *The Flora of Oxfordshire* was published in 1886 and his collection of some 200,000 British plants still forms an important part of the university's herbarium. Today his name is also remembered in *Geranium* × *oxonianum* 'Claridge Druce'.

Drummond, James (c.1784–1863)

James Drummond was already well into his 40s when he went to **Australia**, but his previous experience as a nurseryman and then as curator of the botanic garden in Cork helped him in his designated task, which was to make a new botanic garden in Western Australia. This was to become Kings Park and Botanic Garden in Perth, still one of the world's leading botanic gardens. His career, however, was at the mercy of the financial ups and downs of the new colony and the prospects did not live up to expectations: he became the grand-sounding but rather poorly paid official government naturalist and, by 1835, was a farmer and an independent plant collector. However, he travelled far and wide, even into his 70s, continuing to send seeds of many new discoveries back to Britain. Sometimes his youngest son John, a keen ornithologist, accompanied him, but tragedy struck on their last expedition together, when John was murdered.

Drummond, Thomas (c.1790–1835)

Phlox drummondii is named after this brother of **James Drummond**, who took over the Forfar nursery of **George Don** senior after Don's death in 1814. Drummond later travelled in America, but died in Cuba following a long period of intermittent illness.

Phlox drummondii

Dyffryn Gardens see Cory, Reginald

David Douglas (1799–1834)

David Douglas's life was the shortest of all the great plant hunters, but it was also one of the most adventurous. His taste for the outdoors, and for garden plants, was nurtured during his childhood at Scone, near Perth, in Scotland. By the age of 11 he was apprenticed in the garden at Scone Palace, learning botany and gaining experience that equipped him for a post at the botanic gardens in Glasgow. Here he was discovered by the newly arrived professor, **William Hooker**, who became his mentor. Three years later, when the Horticultural Society of London asked Hooker to recommend a plant hunter for them, the enthusiastic and talented young Douglas seemed made for the job.

Limnanthes douglasii

Douglas's first trip, in 1823, took him to New York, from where he travelled to Lake Erie, visiting Niagara Falls and returning via Philadelphia. The Horticultural Society was delighted with his finds, which included seeds of new herbaceous plants and a number of new fruit varieties. A more ambitious trip, six months later, saw Douglas setting sail for Cape Horn and the American west coast. After stopping at Madeira, Rio de Janeiro and the Galapagos Islands, he finally reached the Columbia River (now the state boundary between Washington and Oregon) in April 1825. He spent more than two years on expeditions that were beset by mishaps, bad weather and hardships of every kind, travelling on foot or horseback, or by canoe, and trekking into the undiscovered Blue Mountains, the Rockies, and even as far as Hudson Bay.

The compensations for a plant hunter were great. Douglas was the first to collect seed of many huge coniferous trees that were to transform parks, gardens and forests and also of shrubs and flowering plants that have since become garden classics in many countries. He received a hero's welcome on his return home in October 1827, only to embark on a third trip to America two years later. This time he revisited the Columbia River and spent 18 months in California, where the milder climate introduced him to many more new plants, over 600 of which he sent back to England. Thwarted – and nearly losing his life – in an 1833 attempt to reach Alaska and travel home via Siberia, Douglas instead decided to sail to Hawaii, where he died in a dreadful accident, gored by a trapped bull. His memorial in the churchyard at Old Scone lists all the plants he introduced. Well-known plants commemorating him include *Limnanthes douglasii* and *Phlox douglasii*.

SOME DOUGLAS INTRODUCTIONS

Abies grandis
Abies nobilis
Abies procera
Camassia quamash
Clarkia elegans
Erythronium grandiflorum
Eschscholtzia californica
Garrya elliptica
Lupinus polyphyllus
Mahonia aquifolium
Penstemon species
Pinus radiata
Pseudotsuga menziesii
(Douglas fir)
Ribes sanguineum
Thuja plicata

East Lambrook Manor, Somerset

The garden here is packed with interesting and unusual plants – a tribute to the late **Margery Fish**, who bought the house in 1938 with her husband Walter, when they were both still working in London at the *Daily Mail* (of which Walter became editor).

Margery Fish at work in her garden

SOME EAST LAMBROOK PLANTS

Artemisia absinthium 'Lambrook Silver'
Euphorbia characias subsp. wulfenii 'Lambrook Gold'
Polemonium 'Lambrook Mauve'
Geranium × oxonianum 'Lambrook Gillian'
Santolina chamaecyparissus 'Lambrook Silver'
Symphytum 'Lambrook Sunrise'

They gradually restored the house and planted the garden, and after Walter's death Margery devoted herself entirely to gardening and writing here, becoming a much-loved and respected plantswoman and author in her own right. The garden and nursery at East Lambrook have been restored in recent years and are a place of pilgrimage for plant lovers from all over the world, with interest at every season.

East Malling, Kent

Although it is now an independent company, East Malling still has its roots in the research station that was established here in 1913, initially as a service to the local fruit-growing industry. During its long history East Malling has produced many leading varieties of plant, ranging from rootstocks for grafting fruit trees, to well-established favourite varieties of apple ('Fiesta'), pear ('Concorde'), black currant ('Wellington XXX'), raspberry ('Autumn Bliss'), gooseberry ('Invicta') and many more. Several raspberry varieties carry the Malling name ('Malling Jewel', 'Malling Admiral' etc.), as do the apple 'Malling Kent' and *Clematis* 'East Malling'.

Raspberry

'BLACK BEAUTY' AND 'BLACK LACE'

East Malling has traditionally been known for fruit, but in the 1980s it added shrubs to its breeding programme. The first big success with gardeners was the very dark purple-leaved ornamental elder 'Black Beauty', correctly known as *Sambucus nigra* f. *porphyrophylla* 'Gerda' (released in 1999). This was followed in 2003 by the similar, but even more desirable, cut-leaved cultivar 'Black Lace' (*Sambucus nigra* f. *porphyrophylla* 'Eva').

Eccleston Square, London

The rather special 3-acre garden in the centre of this Pimlico square was restored and replanted by the residents in a scheme coordinated by one of them, the plantsman, photographer and author **Roger Phillips**. The large collection of fascinating plants includes many camellias and roses (with some rarities), a *Davidia involucrata* (handkerchief tree) and a *Paulownia tomentosa* (foxglove tree), which are well suited to the London microclimate. There is even a National Collection of *Ceanothus*. The garden is occasionally open to the public.

Eden Project, Cornwall

Since it opened in 2001, the story of the Eden Project has become a legend of which few people can be unaware. Overcoming countless difficulties, Tim Smit and his team transformed a sterile china-clay pit into a 'living theatre of plants and people' – a world-class attraction that has drawn visitors in their millions and, with unbelievable success, has put into the spotlight the importance of plants and their relationship with humans. The basis of Eden was the construction of three climatically different environments for growing plants – known as biomes. Two are gigantic domed conservatories, housing plants from the humid tropics and Mediterranean zones respectively, while the third, outdoors, is a huge showcase for plants of the world's

Edinburgh: Royal Botanic Garden

The Royal Botanic Garden Edinburgh (RBGE) has long occupied a place at the heart of British and international botany and horticulture. The collection of plants in its care is now such that no other institution in the world, apart from **Kew**, can rival it in terms of botanical riches. RBGE has had connections with numerous important plant hunters and significant gardens. Apart from its Edinburgh headquarters, it has three Scottish satellite gardens: **Benmore**, **Dawyck** and **Logan**.

RBGE began in 1670 as a physic garden of medicinal herbs, within the grounds of Holyrood Palace, in the centre of Edinburgh. The garden moved to Leith, but the expanding collections necessitated a further move, involving many mature plants, to its current site in Inverleith, where it has been since 1820. This is home to a wide variety of specialist collections, from tropical plants and species of economic importance in the various glasshouses, to a world-famous rock garden, a woodland garden, and a Chinese hillside with the largest collection in cultivation of plants from **China**. Opened in 1997 and echoing the landscapes of Yunnan, this is a fitting setting for the many plants, including rhododendrons and primulas, that were introduced by legendary plant hunters of the past such as **George Forrest**, **Robert Fortune**, and many others whose exploits are described elsewhere in this book.

In addition to the living plant collections, RBGE has a herbarium of more than 2 million specimens, and a comprehensive library with botanical and horticultural books, periodicals, archives and pictures from all over the world.

A number of plant cultivars are named after RBGE's Edinburgh site, including *Gentiana* 'Inverleith', *Jasminum officinale* 'Inverleith', *Persicaria amplexicaulis* 'Inverleith' and *Pinus sylvestris* 'Inverleith'.

temperate zones. Operated as an educational charitable trust, Eden continues to grow and develop, with innovative and seemingly inexhaustible programmes of lectures, events, arts projects and exhibitions that continue to capture the public's imagination. In late 2005 it came first in a poll to find Britain's favourite modern building.

Edgeworth, Michael Pakenham (1812–1881)

Edgeworthia – a genus related to *Daphne* and found in the Himalayas and **China** – and *Rhododendron edgeworthii* are named after this Irish amateur botanist and author who worked for the East India Company and collected plants in India and the Middle East.

Edrom Nurseries, Berwickshire

Primula allionii 'Edrom' is named after this plantsman's nursery at Coldingham near Eyemouth. Now run by Catherine Davis and Terry Hunt, the nursery has an 80-year tradition of specializing in alpines, and offers a large range of connoisseurs' plants, including lilies, trilliums, arisaemas and hardy orchids. Its former owner, Jim Jermyn, now a frelance author and lecturer on plants and plant hunting, exhibited regularly at the **RHS** London shows.

Ehret, Georg (1708–1770)

The highly gifted Ehret was a leading botanical artist from Heidelberg in Germany. He spent much of his life in England, working at the **Chelsea Physic Garden** and the **Oxford University Botanic Garden**, as well as carrying out commissions for wealthy private clients.

Eichstätt, Germany

One of the most famous of all early gardens, the 'Hortus Eystettensis' – or Eichstätt Garden – at Willibaldsburg Castle, in Bavaria, was created by Basilius Besler, head gardener to Johann Konrad von Gemmingen, Prince-Bishop of Eichstätt. The early 17th-century garden was significant not only for its comprehensive plant collection, but also because Besler recorded its plants in a magnificent series of 367 coloured engravings, published in 1613. This remarkable work has guided the restoration of the garden since 1995. *Narcissus* 'Eystettensis' is named after the garden.

Elliott, Clarence see Six Hills Nursery

Elliott, Jack (1924–2004)

A knowledgeable plantsman and widely respected gardener, Dr Jack Elliott was president of the Alpine Garden Society and chairman of the Hardy Plant Society; he also served on the Council of the **RHS** and was a holder of their Victoria Medal of Honour. His garden was at Coldham, Little Chart Forstal, near Ashford, in Kent. He was the author of several books – not widely known, but revered by connoisseurs – including *The Smaller Perennials, The Woodland Garden* and *Bulbs for the Rock Garden*. Plants named after him include *Diascia vigilis* 'Jack Elliott', which he introduced from the Drakensberg Mountains of South **Africa** on one of his many plant-collecting trips abroad. *Agapanthus* 'Jack Elliott' is another of his plants, and there are cultivars of iris and trillium named after his elder brother, Roy Elliott, also an eminent plantsman, who was editor of the Alpine Garden Society's journal.

Elliott, Joe (1915–1998)

The son of Clarence Elliott of **Six Hills Nursery**, Joe Elliott trained at the Royal Botanic Garden **Edinburgh** and founded his own business, Broadwell Nursery, in the Cotswolds in 1946. *Campanula* 'Joe Elliott' is named after him, while *Campanula glomerata* 'Joan Elliott' and *Primula auricula* 'Joan Elliott' are named after his wife.

Ellwanger, George (1818–1906)

This German-born horticulturist arrived in the USA in 1835 and later founded **Mount Hope Nurseries** in Rochester with **Patrick Barry**. A garden of perennials planted by Ellwanger in Rochester has been restored as a memorial to him, and plants still in commerce that are named after him include *Crataegus ellwangeriana*, *Picea abies* 'Ellwangeriana' and *Thuja occidentalis* 'Ellwangeriana Aurea'.

Embley Park, Hampshire

The family home of Florence Nightingale, Embley Park has been a school since 1946 but retains some of the choice trees, rhododendrons and camellias planted when it was a fine private garden. Plants named after it include the well-known *Sorbus commixta* 'Embley' and *Juniperus recurva* 'Embley Park'.

Henry John Elwes (1846–1922)

The name of H.J. Elwes is known to snowdrop lovers through *Galanthus elwesii*, a species he found on a trip to western **Turkey** in 1874. Elwes was an inveterate traveller, visiting the Himalayas several times as well as the Crimea and Greece. He was just as interested in birds and insects as in plants, though as he grew older and took to gardening his enthusiasm for plant collecting increased. His garden at Colesbourne Park near Cheltenham, in Gloucestershire, became known for the collection of rare plant treasures he built up there, and he was one of the first recipients of the RHS Victoria Medal of Honour, in 1897. His writings include a monograph on lilies and, with **Augustine Henry** as co-author, the classic *The Trees of Great Britain and Ireland* (1906–1913). Colesbourne Park, still in the Elwes family, has recently undergone a restoration, and some 200 snowdrop varieties still have pride of place, attracting galanthophiles every winter.

Galanthus elwesii

Emei Shan see page 72

Endress, Philip (1806–1831)

Geranium endressii is named for this German plant collector who worked in Germany, France and Spain.

Emei Shan (Mount Omei), China

Renowned for its extraordinarily rich flora, this 10,167ft mountain in **China's** Sichuan province has long been a magnet for botanists and plant hunters. The number of plant species found on the mountain is thought to number about 3,000 (representing about 50 per cent more indigenous species than are found in the whole of the British Isles). Emei Shan is also one of China's four most sacred mountains and a place of pilgrimage, at one time studded with Buddhist temples, of which only a handful remain. The 29-mile route to the summit is known as the pilgrim's path.

The plant life of Emei Shan is associated with the great British plant hunter **E.H. Wilson**, who first came here in 1903 on one of his expeditions for the **Veitch** nurseries. **Roy Lancaster** gives a detailed account of his own 1980 visit to Emei Shan in his book *Travels in China*.

The list of species found here includes hundreds of names now familiar from gardens and nursery catalogues, among them: *Actinidia chinensis*, *Buddleja davidii*, *Clerodendrum bungei*, *Sorbus sargentiana*, *Rubus cockburnianus* and *Davidia involucrata*. Plants named for the mountain include *Impatiens omeiana*, *Aucuba omeiensis* and *Pittosporum omeiense*.

Engelmann, George (1809–1884)

The Engelmann spruce, *Picea engelmannii*, is named after this German-born doctor and botanist who emigrated to the USA in 1832 and eventually practised in St Louis. He travelled and collected plants in the south-western states, and corresponded with **Asa Gray**.

Escalon y Flores, Antonio José (1700s)

This 18th-century Spanish botanist discovered the evergreen shrub escallonia when he was in **South America**, in the service of the Viceroy of Colombia (then known as New Granada).

Eschscholtz, Johann von (1793–1831)

An Estonian ship's doctor who visited California on the same Russian ship as the botanist Adalbert von Chamisso, Eschscholtz was professor of anatomy and medicine at the German-speaking University of Dorpat (now Tartu), in Estonia. It was Chamisso who named the Californian poppy *Eschscholtzia californica* after him.

Euphorbius

The genus *Euphorbia* is named after this 1st-century AD Numidian physician who is known to have served Jubal II, King of Mauritania.

Evelyn, John (1620–1706)

Perhaps more familiar as a diarist than a gardener, John Evelyn was a man of wide interests and a founder member of the Royal Society, in 1660. He was knowledgeable about gardening, having designed parts of the garden at Wotton, his ancestral home in Surrey (which he eventually inherited aged

79). Sayes Court in Deptford, now in Greater London, was his wife's family home, and after he moved there in 1652 he completely overhauled the garden with a programme of ambitious design and planting. These experiences, together with travel in France and Italy, informed his writings on gardening and preparing food, which still find an audience today: his elaborately constructed 'salad calendar', for example, is a classic. He spent many years working on *Elysium Britannicum*, a weighty treatise on gardening. Unfinished when he died, this was published for the first time nearly 300 years later, in 2001. In contrast, his book *Sylva, or a Discourse of Forest Trees*, published in 1664, was the key work on the subject for many years.

Evison, Raymond

The Guernsey Clematis Nursery, founded by Raymond Evison in 1984, is one of the world's foremost clematis growers, marketing several million plants a year of some 200 species and cultivars. More than 70 of these have been either bred by Evison or introduced by him into the horticultural trade. Well-known Evison introductions include *Clematis viticella* 'Polish Spirit', *Clematis* 'Guernsey Cream' and the winter-flowering *Clematis cirrhosa* var. *purpurascens* 'Freckles'. Raymond Evison founded the International Clematis Society in 1984, having acquired considerable expertise in clematis breeding through working with John Treasure at **Burford House**, in Tenbury Wells. He is author of several books, notably *The Gardener's Guide to Growing Clematis*. He was awarded the RHS Victoria Medal of Honour in 1995 and the OBE in 2000.

Raymond Evison

Exbury Gardens, Hampshire

The Rothschild family's extensive gardens, in a favoured maritime setting beside the Beaulieu River and the Solent, hold one of Britain's great rhododendron collections. Lionel de Rothschild began to create the gardens in the 1920s, intending that they should contain as many different shrubs and trees as possible, so there are also magnolias, camellias, heathers, conifers and many more. A keen plantsman, he had an orchid house and a huge rock garden built. However, breeding rhododendrons was his passion, and several cultivars including *Rhododendron* 'Exbury Naomi' are named after Exbury. Among other plants raised here is *Cotoneaster frigidus* 'Cornubia', while *Cotoneaster salicifolius* 'Exburyensis' and 'Rothschildianus' also have clear Exbury connections.

Exeter, Devon

The Latin term *exoniensis* ('from Exeter') is generally associated with the famous 19th-century West Country nursery firms **Lucombe & Pince** or **Veitch**. It occurs in several plant names, such as *Escallonia* × *exoniensis*, *Passiflora* × *exoniensis* and *Ulmus glabra* 'Exoniensis'.

Fairchild, Thomas (1667–1729)

Lychnis coronaria

The **David Austin** rose named 'The Ingenious Mr Fairchild' (after the title of Michael Leapman's biography of Fairchild) celebrates this London gardener and nurseryman who carried out pioneering work in raising hybrid plants – a new idea, regarded by many with deep suspicion. His first cross – between a carnation and a Sweet William, produced in 1720 – was nicknamed 'Fairchild's mule'. His nursery was at Hoxton, in east London, and his book of 1722, *The City Gardener*, described the plants he considered appropriate for the gardens of his London clients, and for public spaces. One was *Lychnis coronaria*.

Farges, Paul (1844–1912)

One of the French Jesuit missionaries in **China**, Farges was a prolific plant collector in Sichuan province for several years. In 1897 he claimed a 'first' by bringing back to France seeds of the much sought-after handkerchief tree, *Davidia involucrata*, from which the **Vilmorin** nursery firm raised a single, precious specimen. Farges is particularly associated with rhododendrons, such as *Rhododendron oreodoxa* var. *fargesii*. Other plants bearing his name include *Abies fargesii*, *Decaisnea fargesii*, *Salix fargesii* and the bamboo genus *Fargesia*.

Farrand, Beatrix (1872–1959)

Forsythia 'Beatrix Farrand' is named for this American landscape gardener and designer whose work included Dumbarton Oaks in Washington DC, as well as gardens at the universities of Princeton and Yale.

Farrer, Reginald (1880–1920)

Farrer's passion for plants started in early childhood. Born in the Yorkshire Dales, he began by studying the flora of the local limestone fells, and made his first rock garden at the age of 14. After graduating from Oxford University, he began to write the first of several books, *My Rock Garden*, published in 1907 – a foretaste of his two-volume classic *The English Rock Garden*, which appeared 12 years later. He also established his own nursery, Craven Nursery, in Yorkshire, where he grew many rare alpines, always insisting that planting should look as natural as possible and deploring the Victorian fashion for rockeries that looked like 'almond puddings' or 'dogs' graves'. All through his short life, his taste for travel to places where he could see rare and beautiful plants never left him. He went to the Alps, the Dolomites, **Japan** and Canada and, despite poor health, later undertook plant-hunting trips to remote and dangerous parts of **China** and Burma, travelling first with **William Purdom** and then with **Euan Cox**. Farrer eventually fell ill and died, aged only 40, in Upper Burma, where he is buried with the epitaph 'He died for love and duty in search of rare plants'. Garden plants found by or named for him include *Daphne tangutica*, *Buddleja alternifolia*, *Viburnum farreri*, *Geranium farreri*, *Gentiana farreri* and *Nomocharis farreri*.

Ferdinand, King of Bulgaria (1861–1948)

Several plants including *Saxifraga ferdinandi-coburgi* and *Arabis ferdinandi-coburgi* (usually seen in its variegated form) are named after this cultured monarch who had a keen interest in botany.

Finnis, Valerie

Artemisia ludoviciana 'Valerie Finnis' and *Muscari armeniacum* 'Valerie Finnis' are two of several plants honouring this respected gardener, plantswoman and photographer who worked for nearly 30 years at **Waterperry** Horticultural School near Oxford. After her marriage in 1970 to Sir David Scott, she developed the garden at their home, The Dower House at Boughton House, near Kettering – the origin of the names of several plants she found or bred. Among these are *Artemisia stelleriana* 'Boughton Beauty', *Helleborus* × *sternii* 'Boughton Beauty', *Hebe recurva* 'Boughton Silver' and *Helianthemum* 'Boughton Double Primrose'. Lady Scott founded the Merlin Trust, which gives grants to British horticulturists. She was awarded the RHS Victoria Medal of Honour in 1975 and the Kew Medal in 2003.

Valerie Finnis

Fish, Margery (1892–1969)

A true plant connoisseur, Margery Fish documented her plants and garden at **East Lambrook Manor** in great detail in the eight books she wrote in the 1950s and 1960s. The tone of her writing is always diffident and modest, often with a dash of wry humour, but she was extremely knowledgeable, and her books were informed entirely by her own first-hand gardening experience. She championed the cottage garden at a time when it was rather unfashionable, and cherished rare forms of plants especially, propagating them and sharing them generously with fellow-gardeners to keep them in cultivation. Plants named after her include *Bergenia* 'Margery Fish', *Penstemon* 'Margery Fish' and *Pulmonaria* 'Margery Fish', and many other unusual cultivars owe their existence to her, for example *Astrantia major* subsp. *involucrata* 'Shaggy'.

Fisk, Jim (1912–2004)

Fisk was a master clematis breeder and enthusiast, and his marvellous displays at the Chelsea Flower Show in the 1960s and 1970s did much to reawaken interest in clematis. He first discovered clematis when he worked as a teenager at **Notcutts**, and founded his own clematis nursery at Westleton, Suffolk, in 1950. The many varieties Fisk introduced included excellent new cultivars from breeders abroad, such as Wladyslaw Noll (*Clematis* 'Niobe') and **Brother Stefan Franczak** (*Clematis* 'Warszawska Nike') in Poland; **Uno Kivistik** in Estonia; and **Alister Keay** in New Zealand (*Clematis* 'Allanah'). *Clematis macropetala* 'Westleton' is named after the village where Fisk had his nursery, and *Clematis* 'Alice Fisk' honours his mother, who worked with him. He wrote three books on clematis, and was awarded the MBE in 1997.

Karl Foerster (1874–1970)

Revered by many garden and landscape designers for his innovative and practical approach to planting schemes, this German nurseryman and designer set a trend for well-structured informality, stringently selecting perennials for robustness, good shape and texture, and a long season of interest. At his garden and nursery near Potsdam, where he moved in 1911, Foerster bred plants like this that suited his design philosophy, introducing as many as 650 new varieties during his long life. They included many grasses, achilleas, asters, heleniums and phlox. He also wrote more than 20 books and, in 1920, founded the influential magazine *Die Gartenschönheit* with Camillo Schneider, a dendrologist. Foerster's design practice closed after World War II, but the nursery continued under the new regime in East Germany, recovering from wartime difficulties and establishing new contacts with growers in **Russia** and Eastern Europe. His home and garden are now a designated historic monument. Plants named in his honour include two widely used grasses, *Calamagrostis* × *acutiflora* 'Karl Foerster' and *Molinia caerulea* subsp. *arundinacea* 'Karl Foerster', as well as *Erigeron* 'Foersters Liebling' and *Campanula carpatica* var. *turbinata* 'Foerster'. Some of the many award-winning Foerster cultivars are: *Aster amellus* 'Veilchenkönigin', *Erigeron* 'Dunkelste Aller', *Helenium* 'Feuersiegel', *Heliopsis helianthoides* var. *scabra* 'Goldgefieder' and 'Spitzentänzerin', and *Phlox paniculata* 'Prospero'.

Fletcher, Harold (1907–1978)

A prominent horticulturist and botanist, Fletcher was director of RHS Garden **Wisley** and, from 1956 to 1970, Regius keeper of the Royal Botanic Garden **Edinburgh**. *Chamaecyparis lawsoniana* 'Fletcheri' and *Rhododendron fletcherianum* are named after him.

Forsythia

Folkard, Oliver

The magenta-flowered *Geranium* 'Ann Folkard' was raised in 1973 by the Revd Folkard from Sleaford, in Lincolnshire, and named after his wife.

Forsyth, William (1737–1804)

The Dutch botanist Martin Vahl named *Forsythia* after this founder member of the RHS. Much of Forsyth's life was spent in prestigious gardening jobs: at Syon House, the Duke of Northumberland's west London home, then at the **Chelsea Physic Garden**, where he succeeded **Philip Miller**, and finally as gardener to King George III at Kensington and St James's Palace.

Fortune, Robert see page 78

Fothergill, John (1712–1780)

The North American shrub genus *Fothergilla* is named after this Quaker doctor from Wensleydale, Yorkshire, who was a friend of **Peter Collinson**. A successful London medical practice enabled him to sponsor plant-hunting

George Forrest (1873–1932)

The lives of most of the great plant hunters were punctuated by dangers, disasters and narrow escapes, but the adventures of George Forrest in the wilds of **China** perhaps produced the most hair-raising stories of all. From childhood, Forrest had loved the outdoor life, and a pharmaceutical training taught him about medicinal plants and herbarium techniques. By the age of 18 he had been to **Australia**, from where he returned to take a job at the Royal Botanic Garden **Edinburgh**. From here he was recommended to **Arthur Bulley**, who was looking for a plant collector to help him stock his new garden at **Ness**, in Cheshire.

This was Forrest's great opportunity, and in May 1904 he left for the high mountains of Yunnan on the first of the seven plant-hunting trips (all sponsored individually or jointly by garden owners and nurseries) that took up much of the rest of his life. Perhaps more than some of his fellow plant hunters, he engaged with the communities he encountered in China, living among them, learning their language and training teams of locals to help with collecting. Forrest's accounts of his exploits, sent back in letters and in articles for the *Gardeners' Chronicle*, describe not only the great beauty of the country and its plants but also many discomforts, setbacks and even atrocities: once, he was chased for nine days by a band of hostile Tibetans who brutally murdered the inhabitants of a nearby Christian mission and killed all but one of Forrest's 17 collectors and servants. He stood up to this gruelling life for 28 years but, perhaps finally exhausted by so many mental and physical ordeals, died suddenly in Yunnan, aged 59, at the end of his seventh expedition.

SOME FORREST INTRODUCTIONS

Abies forrestii
Acer forrestii
Camellia saluenensis
Gentiana sino-ornata
Iris forrestii
Pieris formosa var. forrestii
Primula bulleyana
Primula forrestii
Primula malacoides
Rhododendron sinogrande

---

trips in order to stock his fine private gardens in London and Cheshire.

Foxhollow, Surrey
John Letts built up an extensive heather collection at his nursery here, near Windlesham, collecting unknown varieties from elsewhere as well as raising new cultivars of his own. He became a leading authority on heathers and heaths, and wrote two books on the subject. The award-winning *Erica carnea* 'Foxhollow' remains a popular winter-flowering heath, and several others are named after the nursery. There is also a heather named after him: *Calluna vulgaris* 'John F. Letts'.

Franchet, Adrien (1834–1900)
Director of the Muséum d'Histoire Naturelle in **Paris**, and commemorated by *Cotoneaster franchetii*, this French botanist was an expert on Chinese and Japanese plants, so was invaluable at the time when French missionaries such as **David** and **Delavay** were sending plant

Robert Fortune (1812–1880)

Travelling to **China** in 1843, Robert Fortune was the first major plant collector there to make a significant impact on the gardens of the West. He was helped in this by a simple but clever recent invention, the Wardian case (see **Ward**). This enabled him to send home many of his important discoveries (estimated at 120 new species and varieties) as living specimens.

Saxifraga fortunei

Born in Berwickshire, the young Fortune worked for a time at the Royal Botanic Garden **Edinburgh** before moving to the Horticultural Society's garden at Chiswick in London. From there, he was chosen by the society (later the **RHS**) to go to China on their behalf to collect plants. His annual pay was to be £100 – poor recompense for three years of danger and discomfort. Almost everywhere he went, Fortune met with hostility. He was attacked, robbed, almost shipwrecked, and shot at by pirates, and sometimes had to disguise himself as a local. However, the botanical trophies he somehow managed to collect, mainly from gardens and nurseries, helped to compensate. Fortune returned to London and became curator of the **Chelsea Physic Garden**, but he was recruited by the East India Company in 1848 to investigate tea-growing. Back in China, he obtained thousands of tea plants, which were wanted in India for the infant tea industry there. Historians remember Fortune for his contribution to the tea industry, but to gardeners his legacy will always be the many familiar and beautiful ornamental plants that he gathered, both in China and on a trip to **Japan** in 1860–1862.

SOME FORTUNE PLANTS

Anemone hupehensis
Cryptomeria japonica
Dicentra spectabilis
Euonymus fortunei
Eupatorium fortunei
Hosta fortunei
Jasminum nudiflorum
Lilium auratum
Lonicera fragrantissima
Lysimachia fortunei
Mahonia japonica
Mahonia fortunei
Paulownia fortunei
Primula japonica
Prunus triloba
Rhododendron fortunei
Skimmia japonica subsp.
reevesiana 'Robert Fortune'
Trachelospermum jasminoides
Trachycarpus fortunei
Weigela florida

specimens by the thousand back to Paris from **China**. Sadly, this deluge of plants was too much for one man to cope with and many remained unidentified for years after Franchet's death.

Fraser, John (1750–1811)

Born near Inverness, in Scotland, Fraser moved to London in 1770 to make a career as a draper, but after becoming friends with **William Forsyth** the young Scotsman began to take an interest in plants, eventually establishing a nursery in Chelsea. By the age of 30, he was on the first of several plant-hunting trips to **North America** – a change of career that was to last for much of the rest of his life.

Brother Stefan Franczak

This remarkable Polish Jesuit monk, born in 1917, has devoted much of his life to breeding many clematis that have found a place in the world's gardens. Working in a monastery garden in Warsaw, he began by breeding irises and daylilies, but it is his excellent clematis cultivars, such as the award-winning *Clematis* 'Polish Spirit', that have made the greatest impact on gardeners and nurserymen. Brother Stefan's plants have become established internationally,

SOME FRANCZAK CLEMATIS CULTIVARS EXPLAINED

Clematis 'Blekitny Aniol': *'Blue Angel'*
Clematis 'Jan Pawel II': *Pope John Paul II*
Clematis 'Kardynal Wyszynski': *a Polish archbishop, later a cardinal, who was imprisoned in 1953*
Clematis 'Matka Teresa': *Mother Teresa*
Clematis 'Monte Cassino': *a World War II battle near Rome, in which Polish soldiers achieved a remarkable victory*
Clematis 'Warszawska Nike': *in Polish legend, a character akin to a mermaid, depicted in a Warsaw monument*

largely through enthusiasts and experts such as the late **Jim Fisk**, champion of several Franczak cultivars, and **Raymond Evison**, who first propagated 'Polish Spirit' under licence at his Guernsey nursery and introduced it in 1989.

He went to Newfoundland, then in 1785 to the United States, collecting rhododendrons, hydrangeas and other plants. Perhaps his most significant find was *Rhododendron catawbiense*, which became important in breeding hardier cultivars. Fraser's travels were sponsored by top horticultural establishments such as **Kew**, the **Chelsea Physic Garden** and the Linnean Society (see **Linnaeus**), and he even worked as a collector for Emperor Paul I of **Russia** (who reputedly refused to pay him after his ship was wrecked in the Caribbean). Plants named for Fraser include *Photinia* × *fraseri*, *Rhododendron* 'Fraseri', *Abies fraseri* and *Chamaecyparis* × *lawsoniana* 'Fraseri'.

Frémont, John Charles (1813–1890)

The sun-loving Californian shrub *Fremontodendron* was named in 1842 after this military surveyor and geographer who collected several new species on his travels in the western USA.

Frikart, Carl (1879–1964)

A Swiss plantsman, Frikart raised the successful hybrid *Aster* × *frikartii* in the 1920s and named two of its varieties 'Eiger' and 'Jungfrau' after the mountains of his homeland. Another is named 'Wunder von Stäfa', after the town of Stäfa, where Frikart worked.

Fuchs, Leonhart (1501–1566)

Professor of medicine at the Protestant University of Tübingen in Germany, Fuchs was also a keen field botanist. His book of 1542, *De Historia Stirpium*, described and illustrated some 500 plants and was a key early herbal. In it, he used names for many plant genera that were later confirmed by **Linnaeus**. Fuchs is commemorated by a plant that is now very well known, yet he never saw it. The first fuchsia was collected in 1693 by Father **Charles Plumier** in the West Indies, but fuchsias were not widely grown until the 19th century.

The Garden House, Devon

A number of choice garden plants have a connection with this famous garden just outside the village of Buckland Monachorum on the western flanks of Dartmoor. In a previous incarnation The Garden House was a medieval vicarage, whose ruins are now framed by the luxuriant and hugely varied planting of the walled garden. The first part of the garden to be developed, this was the work of former Eton schoolmaster Lionel Fortescue and his wife, who bought the property in 1945. By then the vicarage had been replaced by a 19th-century house commanding views down a secluded valley. Over the past 30 years this has been filled with creative yet naturalistic contemporary planting. Much of this was carried out by Keith Wiley, who came here as head gardener in 1978, three years before Fortescue's death. The Fortescue Garden Trust continues to maintain the garden, which has been in the care of Matt Bishop since Keith Wiley left in 2003, establishing his own plantsman's nursery and garden, 'Wildside', nearby.

Both the walled garden and the valley gardens abound with beautiful and unusual plants. Most of the mature rhododendrons, camellias and magnolias date from Fortescue's day. Native wild flowers blend with more contemporary planting farther away from the house, with distinct themed areas such as the Cretan cottage garden, the South African garden, the quarry garden and the acer glade offering changes of mood. There is plenty of inspiration to be found at any time of year.

SOME GARDEN HOUSE PLANTS
Anemone nemorosa 'Buckland'
Astrantia 'Buckland'
Campanula latifolia 'Buckland'
Clematis 'Buckland Longshanks'
Epimedium 'Buckland Spider'
Mahonia × *media* 'Buckland'
Mahonia × *media* 'Lionel Fortescue'
Origanum 'Buckland'
Phormium 'Buckland Ruby'
Rodgersia pinnata 'Buckland Beauty'
Vitis vinifera 'Buckland Sweetwater'

Galpin, Ernest (1858–1941)

Tulbaghia galpinii, *Dierama galpinii* and *Kniphofia galpinii* are three of the many plants named after this South African banker and amateur plant collector.

Garden, Alexander (1730–1791)

The genus *Gardenia* and *Fothergilla gardenii* bear the name of this eminent Scottish-born naturalist and doctor who settled in Charleston, South Carolina, in 1752.

Garrya elliptica

Garry, Nicholas (c.1781–1856)

The name of this deputy governor of the Hudson Bay Company is remembered in the shrub *Garrya* and the former trading post of Fort Garry, in what is now Winnipeg.

Gaulthier, Jean-François (1708–1758)

The small evergreen shrubs called *Gaultheria* are named after this botanist and physician to the governor of Quebec.

Gemmell, Alan (1913–1986)

Many British gardeners knew Professor Gemmell as the resident scientific expert on BBC Radio 4's *Gardeners' Question Time* for over 30 years. *Linum* 'Gemmell's Hybrid' is named after him.

Gerard, John (1545–1612)

John Gerard

Gerard was a barber-surgeon and plant collector who had a garden in London's Fetter Lane. His *Herbal* of 1597 is perhaps the most well known of all the early herbals, and was for a long time a key text for students of botany. What perhaps makes Gerard's fame surprising is the fact that his text was largely derived from a herbal of 1554 written by the Dutchman **Rembert Dodoens**. Most of the illustrations had been previously published, too. However, Gerard did include some original material, such as descriptions of plants newly introduced from America, including the potato. Gerard's work was subsequently revised, notably in 1633 by the apothecary Thomas Johnson, who corrected and updated the text to produce a book that was held to be more reputable than the original.

Gerber, Traugott (1710–1743)

Gerbera, the genus of tender daisies mainly from **Africa**, is named after this German doctor who practised in Moscow, where he was also director of the botanic garden. He led plant-hunting expeditions in **Russia** and in 1742 became a doctor in the Russian army, but died the following year.

Giant Snowdrop Company, Gloucestershire

This famous nursery was in business from 1951 to 1968 at Hyde Lodge, Chalford. After Brigadier Leonard Mathias, his wife Winifrede and their gardener Herbert Ransom came here in 1947, they found the neglected garden full of snowdrops of dozens of different kinds, planted before World War II by a previous owner, **Walter Butt**. The finest and most abundant were the excellent variety now known as *Galanthus* 'S. Arnott'. New varieties were raised for sale, too, and the nursery's stylish catalogue found a ready market among the growing numbers of snowdrop connoisseurs.

Gibson, John (1815–1875)

Gibson began his gardening career at **Chatsworth**, working for the Duke of Devonshire who sent him to India on a plant exchange in 1835. The plants that Gibson took with him, destined for the distinguished Dr **Nathaniel Wallich** at Calcutta Botanic Garden, were among the first to travel in the new mini-greenhouses known as Wardian cases (see **Ward**). Gibson stayed on for a time in India and travelled to Assam, where he found many rare orchids and new rhododendrons. After he returned to England, he was in charge of Hyde Park, in London, where he was noted for using subtropical foliage in bedding schemes. *Ricinus communis* 'Gibsonii' is named for him.

Giraldi, Giuseppe (1848–1901)

This Italian Franciscan monk became a missionary and plant collector in **China**. His plants include *Exochorda giraldii*, the yellow-flowered *Daphne giraldii*, early-flowering *Forsythia giraldiana* and, most familiar to gardeners, the distinctive purple-berried *Callicarpa bodinieri* var. *giraldii*, which he discovered in north-west China in 1890. Its cultivar 'Profusion' is becoming an increasingly popular garden shrub. Giraldi was also the first to discover *Kolkwitzia amabilis*, though he did not see it in flower.

Giverny, France

The Normandy garden of the French Impressionist painter Claude Monet (1840–1926) attracts visitors from all over the world. The artist was a keen gardener, and his skill with colour spilled over from his canvases into his planting. Many plants commemorate him, including a canna, a heuchera, a lavender, a rose and a lobelia.

Glasnevin: National Botanic Gardens, Dublin

The Republic of Ireland's principal botanic garden, a mile north of the centre of Dublin on the banks of the Tolka River, was established in 1795. The garden's layout remains largely unchanged from its early days but many of the present trees and shrubs, and the beautiful Victorian glasshouses, date from the years after 1838 when the visionary Dr David Moore and his son Sir Frederick were successive curators of the garden for a period of some 40 years each. In the 1840s

Glasnevin was the first garden to grow orchids from seed, and later in the 19th century another success was developing hardy varieties of agapanthus. Today it is possible to see some 20,000 different plants growing here, including cultivars of Glasnevin origin such as *Solanum crispum* 'Glasnevin', *Buddleja davidii* 'Glasnevin Hybrid' and *Garrya* × *issaquahensis* 'Glasnevin Wine'.

Glebe Cottage Plants see Klein, Carol

Gleditsch, Johann (1714–1786)

The tree genus *Gleditsia* is named after this director of Berlin's botanic garden.

Glendoick, Perthshire

Glendoick is known, first and foremost, for its world-class collection of rhododendrons, built up over some 80 years by three generations of the **Cox** family, who have collected or bred many of the specimens themselves. The estate nursery specializes in ericaceous plants, including many rhododendrons named after the garden. *Calluna vulgaris* 'Glendoick Silver' and *Daphne bholua* 'Glendoick' are among other plants that feature the Glendoick name.

Gmelin, Johann Georg (1709–1755)

This German botanist and doctor from Tübingen became a professor in St Petersburg and later undertook a gruelling ten-year expedition planned by **Russia** to explore the undeveloped wastes of Siberia. He recorded its plant life in his four-volume *Flora Sibirica*, published in 1749–1750. Plants named for him include *Larix* *gmelinii*, *Limonium gmelinii* and *Artemisia gmelinii*.

Goldsworth Nursery, Surrey

One of several important and influential nurseries in the Woking area, Goldsworth Nursery is believed to date back to the 18th century but little is known of its early days. Accounts from the 19th century record an impressive arboretum here, and the nursery appears to have had links with several of the important nursery families in this area, such as the Waterers and the **Jackmans**. In 1877 the nursery was taken over by Walter Slocock, who had trained at Waterer's **Knap Hill Nursery**. Goldsworth remained in the Slocock family until 1976, when the land was sold and the story came full circle with the purchase of Waterer's Knap Hill Nursery by Martin Slocock, Walter's grandson. By then he had become the third generation of the Slocock family to be awarded the RHS Victoria Medal of Honour. The most familiar plant named after the nursery is *Acer platanoides* 'Goldsworth Purple', but there are others including *Calluna vulgaris* 'Goldsworth Crimson', *Fuchsia* 'Goldsworth Beauty' and *Rhododendron* 'Goldsworth Orange', 'Goldsworth Yellow', etc. Many other award-winning rhododendrons were raised here, and there are rhododendrons and other plants named after members of the Slocock family.

Gordon, James (1708–1780)

Gordon was a skilful and progressive London nurseryman who loved to experiment, introducing important foreign plants like camellias, gardenias and *Ginkgo biloba* into the British horticultural trade. He is said to have propagated four original cuttings of gardenia so successfully that he made £500 from the resulting plants in three years. He had a nursery at Mile End and a seed shop in Fenchurch Street.

Gravetye Manor, West Sussex

For 50 years, from 1885, this was the home and garden of the iconoclastic Irish-born gardener **William Robinson**. Already 47 when he bought the estate, he arrived at Gravetye eager to put into practice his vigorous opinions about gardening, gathered through his early horticultural career and on his subsequent travels, and already expressed in his writings such as *The Wild Garden*. Gardeners were set to work, acres of woodland created, pioneering wildflower meadows established, and shrubs and perennials planted informally on the terraces around the house. **Ernest Markham**, later a respected clematis expert, eventually became head gardener, taking charge of the garden as old age and infirmity hampered Robinson himself. Gravetye Manor is now a luxury hotel, and the gardens have been restored, complete with Robinson's meadows and some of the original shrubs and trees. A number of plants are named after the manor, among them *Clematis* 'Gravetye Beauty', *Dianthus* 'Gravetye Gem', *Leucojum aestivum* 'Gravetye Giant' and *Geranium himalayense* 'Gravetye'.

Gray, Asa (1810–1888)

Perhaps the most important American botanist of all time, Asa Gray was professor of botany at Harvard for more than 30 years from 1842. A key figure in the world of plants for much of his life, he was a champion of **Darwin** and a friend and correspondent of **Joseph Hooker**. Gray donated his extensive herbarium and library to Harvard as the basis of what was to become one of the foremost botanical libraries in the world. He wrote many papers and textbooks, and his *Manual of the Botany of the Northern United States* ('Gray's Manual'), published in 1847, remains a respected classic. He collaborated with **John Torrey** on other books, including two volumes of *The Flora of North America*, a hugely ambitious project that was never completed.

Gray, Christopher (*c.*1694–1768)

Gray's influential nursery in the King's Road in Fulham, London, specialized in American shrubs at a time when these were the latest garden novelty. All the great plantsmen of the day – **Catesby**, **Collinson**, **Gordon** and **Miller** – were in Gray's circle, and all the great plants came his way too: for example, his nursery was one of the first places where *Magnolia grandiflora* could be seen. He also published the earliest recorded nursery list, in 1740.

Grayswood Hill, Surrey

This garden in Haslemere is one of Britain's largest private tree collections and has a number of cultivars named after it, including *Betula utilis* var. *jacquemontii* 'Grayswood Ghost', *Betula ermanii* 'Grayswood Hill', *Chamaecyparis lawsoniana* 'Grayswood Pillar', *Pieris japonica* 'Grayswood', *Cistus* 'Grayswood Pink' and *Hydrangea serrata* 'Grayswood'.

Great Dixter, East Sussex

One of the leading gardens of England, loved by British and foreign visitors alike, Great Dixter was the lifelong home of the distinguished gardener, the late **Christopher Lloyd**. He wrote extensively about it in his articles and books, especially *The Year at Great Dixter* (1987) and *Christopher Lloyd's Gardening Year* (1999). The garden was begun in 1910 by his father, the architect Nathaniel Lloyd, and his mother, Daisy, from whom he first acquired his love of plants. Some of the bulb plantings still enjoyed here today were her work. The garden's layout and formal structure, which rely heavily on yew hedging and topiary, were the work of Nathaniel Lloyd and Sir Edwin Lutyens, and have been used very successfully to complement many experimental planting schemes over the years. The arrival of Fergus Garrett as head gardener in 1993 gave the garden new momentum, and it went from strength to strength in the last years of Christopher Lloyd's life. It is famous for bold use of colour, innovative planting of 'exotics', and its meadows, which were developed from the wild garden schemes beloved of Lloyd's mother, who was an admirer of **William Robinson**'s ideas. Plants named after Dixter include *Euphorbia griffithii* 'Dixter', *Crocosmia masoniorum* 'Dixter Flame' and *Campanula lactiflora* 'Dixter Presence'.

Greville, Charles (1749–1809)

Grevillea, from **Australia**, is an appropriately exotic shrub named for the Hon. Charles Greville, whose garden at Paddington, London, was known for its rarities. A vice-president of the Royal Society, he was one of the seven founder members of what later became the **RHS**.

Grey-Wilson, Christopher

This distinguished contemporary botanist, horticulturist, author and photographer has been the Alpine Garden Society's editor since 1990, and has also been the editor of the **RHS**'s learned journal *The Plantsman*. He has written books on alpines, on European wild flowers and on individual plant groups, including cyclamen, poppies, clematis and alpines. *Codonopsis grey-wilsonii* is named after him.

Griffith, William (1810–1845)

Euphorbia griffithii, *Ceratostigma griffithii* and *Arisaema griffithii* are named after this Scottish botanist, plant collector and surgeon, who worked in India and Afghanistan and became director of Calcutta Botanic Garden.

Griselini, Francesco (1717–1783)

Griselinia, a genus of evergreen shrubs from the southern hemisphere that are useful in temperate coastal gardens, are named after this Venetian botanist.

Gronovius, Jan Frederik (1690–1762)

This Dutch botanist and patron of **Linnaeus** described early American plant discoveries in his *Flora Virginica* and introduced Linnaeus to many American species. Much of his information came, together with plant specimens, from the American collector **John Clayton** (whose contribution was not fully acknowledged).

Guincho, County Down

Set on a hillside overlooking Belfast Lough, Guincho is one of Ireland's great private gardens, created by master plantswoman Vera Mackie from 1947 and preserved by subsequent owners. Several plants named after it include *Cardamine heptaphylla* Guincho form and *Erythronium revolutum* 'Guincho Splendour'. Its most famous plant was the first recorded purple-leaved elder, which Vera Mackie found in the wild while on holiday in Scotland. It was later propagated and marketed by **Hillier** and, as *Sambucus nigra* f. *porphyrophylla* 'Guincho Purple', was important in the more recent successful breeding programme at **East Malling** to produce even darker and more durable purple elders.

Gunn, Ronald (1808–1881)

Born in South Africa, Gunn emigrated as a young man to Tasmania, where he spent most of his adult life and became a prolific plant collector, sending hundreds of specimens to the **Hookers** at **Kew**. *Eucalyptus gunnii* is named after him.

Gunnerus, Johan (1718–1773)

Gunnera commemorates this Norwegian botanist who was also a bishop and professor of theology. He collected plants on his travels throughout Norway, ultimately publishing his findings in *Flora Norvegica*.

G

Haast, Johann von (1822–1887)

The daisy bush *Olearia* × *haastii* is probably the most familiar plant named after Haast, a geologist and naturalist who found many new plants in **New Zealand** in the 1860s.

Hahn, Friedrich

Penstemon 'Andenken an Friedrich Hahn' (formerly 'Garnet') is a well-known border perennial, but the derivation of its name is something of a mystery. It was bred in 1918 by Hermann Wartmann

Norman Hadden (1889–1971)

A knowledgeable and creative plantsman who gardened at Porlock in Somerset, Hadden moved there from Aberdeen as a young man, seeking a milder climate that would be less damaging to his delicate constitution. It worked: he lived to be 81, having made a real difference to the world of gardening and plantsmanship during his lifetime. His contribution was acknowledged when he was awarded the RHS Victoria Medal of Honour in 1962.

At his home, Underway, he filled the ever-expanding garden with delicate and lovely plants of many kinds. The mild maritime climate suited tender plants just as well as it suited their owner. His large collection included more than 100 camellias, and he particularly prided himself on the number of winter-flowering plants that he grew. Several plants are named after Hadden and his garden, and one of his most well-known introductions, the award-winning *Rosmarinus officinalis* 'Severn Sea', recalls the alternative name for the nearby Bristol Channel, the estuary of the River Severn.

NORMAN HADDEN AND PORLOCK

Agapanthus 'Norman Hadden'
Cornus 'Norman Hadden'
Cornus 'Porlock'
Genista 'Porlock'
Nerine bowdenii 'Porlock'
Thymus 'Porlock'
Agapanthus 'Underway'
Mahonia × *media* 'Underway'

Hadspen Garden, Somerset

The garden at Hadspen, near Castle Cary, has enjoyed two periods in the care of leading contemporary gardeners. Hadspen House is the family home of **Penelope Hobhouse**'s first husband, and the distinguished garden designer lived here early in her career, taking on an ambitious 1970s restoration of the neglected 9-acre Edwardian garden, documented in her book *The Country Gardener* (1976). From 1987 the garden was redesigned and largely replanted by the Canadian couple Nori and Sandra Pope, known for their particular interest in the use of colour. For some years, until the Popes left in 2005, Hadspen was famed for its creatively planted 'colourist' borders. The nursery at Hadspen sells many plants that are grown there.

SOME HADSPEN PLANTS

Anemone hupehensis 'Hadspen Abundance'
Astrantia 'Hadspen Blood'
Brunnera macrophylla 'Hadspen Cream'
Hosta 'Hadspen Blue'
Lobelia × *speciosa* 'Hadspen Purple'
Rheum × *hybridum* 'Hadspen Crimson'
Salvia involucrata 'Hadspen'

in Switzerland, and may have been named for a German astronomer, Count Friedrich von Hahn (1742–1805).

Hales, Stephen (1677–1761)

The genus *Halesia* is named after this English cleric and botanist whose book describing his research, *Vegetable Staticks* (1727), was the first important work to be published on plant physiology.

An engraving from Hales's Vegetable Staticks

Hall, George R. (1820–1899)

Lonicera japonica 'Halliana' is named after this American doctor who spent several years in Yokohama and introduced a number of important Japanese plants into America, including *Wisteria floribunda*, *Magnolia stellata* and *Hydrangea paniculata* 'Grandiflora'.

Hamilton, Geoff (1936–1996)

A generation of gardeners knew Geoff Hamilton as the well-loved presenter of BBC Television's *Gardeners' World* for 17 years until his sudden death. Plants named after him include *Lathyrus odoratus* 'Geoff Hamilton', Rosa Geoff Hamilton ('Ausham') and *Penstemon* 'Geoff Hamilton'. There is also a *Lychnis coronaria* 'Gardeners' World'.

Hamilton, William (1745–1813)

Hamilton was instrumental in introducing many plants into gardens in the USA. He owned a 300-acre estate near Philadelphia, called The Woodlands, and here he grew practically every plant he could get hold of, including many imported exotics not previously seen in North America. *Ginkgo biloba*, *Acer platanoides* and *Ailanthus altissima* were among them.

Hanbury, Thomas (1832–1907)

A Quaker philanthropist and prosperous tea tycoon with a business in Shanghai, Sir Thomas Hanbury also had considerable horticultural aspirations. In 1867 he bought a huge estate, in a spectacular setting on a hillside above the Mediterranean near Ventimiglia on the Ligurian coast of Italy. With the help of his botanist brother Daniel, he began the extensive planting and landscaping that resulted in one of the classic gardens of Europe, packed with a remarkable range of exotic plants from many countries. It is called La Mortola (not to be confused with another Anglo-Italian garden, **La Mortella**). Sir Thomas settled here after he retired and stayed for the rest of his life. During this time he used his considerable wealth to do something that was to have an even larger impact on the gardening world: he bought the **Wisley** estate in Surrey and presented it to the **RHS**. Sir Thomas's son, Cecil, inherited La Mortola in 1907 but, after his death in 1937, war damage and the difficulty of upkeep took their toll. Cecil's widow, Dorothy, gave La Mortola to the Italian state in 1960, and it is now in the care of Genoa University. *Rosa brunonii* 'La Mortola' is named after the garden, and *Phlox paniculata* 'Dodo Hanbury-Forbes' after Cecil's wife.

Hanmer, Thomas (1612–1678)

A friend of **John Rea** and **John Evelyn**, Sir Thomas Hanmer had a fine garden, at Bettisfield in Shropshire, whose planting included wall-trained fruit and many kinds of bulb – notably tulips, jonquils and fritillaries. He made detailed notes about many plants in his *Garden Book*, a useful and practical early manual written in 1659 but not published until 1932.

Hardy's Cottage Garden Plants, Hampshire

Award-winning displays of cottage perennials from the nursery of Rosy and Rob Hardy near Whitchurch are a familiar sight at horticultural shows all over Britain. Heucheras, penstemons and hardy geraniums are among the many plants listed. Cultivars bred by Hardy's include *Gaillardia* 'Saint Clements' and *Gaura lindheimeri* 'Chiffon'.

Harkness & Co., Hertfordshire

The family-run rose nursery of R. Harkness & Co. at Hitchin dates back to the 1880s, when two young brothers from Yorkshire began exhibiting plants at flower shows. By 1892 the business had established a southern foothold, at Hitchin, and in 1893 the first rose was launched on to the market. Despite the effects of two world wars, by the 1950s some of the most enduring Harkness cultivars, such as the rich red roses 'Ena Harkness' and 'Frensham', were well established. There followed several more roses named after members of the family including Elizabeth, Anne and Rosemary Harkness.

Harlow Carr, RHS Garden, North Yorkshire

Harlow Carr, in Harrogate, was known for many years as the garden of the Northern Horticultural Society. Following the society's merger with the **RHS** in 2001, RHS funding has brought new opportunities for restoration and development schemes. This includes the seven historical gardens from different periods, designed by Dominic Cole and built for the RHS Bicentenary in 2004 as part of *Gardens Through Time*, a garden history project that was the subject of a BBC Television series. The streamside garden, with its wonderful displays of candelabra primulas, blue poppies and astilbes, has long been a magnet for Harlow Carr visitors. Old and new plants named after the garden include *Clematis* Harlow Carr ('Evipo004'), *Primula* Harlow Carr hybrids, *Fuchsia* 'Harlow Carr' and *Rosa* Harlow Carr ('Aushouse').

Hartweg, Theodor (1812–1871)

Hartweg came from a German horticultural family and had worked at the Jardin des Plantes in **Paris**, then at Chiswick for the Horticultural Society. It was on the society's behalf that he went to Mexico and **South America** in 1836 to collect plants. Undaunted by the effects of political turmoil in several countries, and by losing many of the specimens he sent back to England, he made another trip in 1845, this time

Cupressus macrocarpa

to Mexico and California, from where he brought back *Cupressus macrocarpa*, several species of pine, and marvellous orchids. A number of plants bear his name, among them *Pinus hartwegii*, *Penstemon hartwegii*, *Fuchsia hartwegii* and *Asarum hartwegii*.

Hatfield House, Hertfordshire

The historic garden here at the family seat of the Cecils, Earls and Marquesses of Salisbury, dates back to the early 1600s, when the original planting was done by **John Tradescant the Elder**, who was gardener here. The gardening tradition, well established in the Cecil family, was skilfully and enthusiastically upheld in the late 20th century by the 6th Marchioness, a respected plantswoman and committed organic gardener, who has rejuvenated the gardens since 1972. New developments included a parterre, a maze, a herb garden and a woodland garden. *Lamium maculatum* 'Hatfield' and *Hydrangea macrophylla* 'Hatfield Rose' are among the plants named for Hatfield.

Havergal, Beatrix see Waterperry

Hay, Harry

Heuchera americana 'Harry Hay' is dedicated to this gardener and plantsman from Reigate in Surrey, who exchanges plants with fellow enthusiasts all round the world.

Hawera, New Zealand

The charming spring bulb *Narcissus* 'Hawera' is named after this town in the west of **New Zealand**'s North Island, where it was raised in the 1930s.

HDRA see Henry Doubleday Research Association

Heldreich, Theodor von (1822–1902)

This German botanist was director of the botanic garden in Athens. Several plants bear his name, including *Pinus heldreichii*, *Acer heldreichii* and *Jasione heldreichii*.

Dan Heims

Terra Nova Nurseries in Portland, **Oregon**, was established by this well-known American horticulturist and nurseryman in 1991. Heims has travelled widely in the USA and overseas as a plant collector and lecturer, and has introduced hundreds of new perennials to the US nursery trade. At Terra Nova he runs a propagation programme involving many kinds of herbaceous plant, with heucheras and tiarellas a particular speciality. Many of his cultivars are now successful internationally as well as in the USA. He has won numerous awards for new varieties – among them, in 2002, nine RHS Awards of Garden Merit for heuchera cultivars, including 'Can-can', 'Fireworks' and 'Purple Petticoats'.

SOME DAN HEIMS PLANTS

Echinacea purpurea 'Ruby Giant'
Heuchera 'Amber Waves'
Heuchera 'Amethyst Myst'
Heuchera 'Cherries Jubilee'
Heuchera 'Key Lime Pie'
Heuchera 'Plum Pudding'
Hosta 'Jade Cascade'
Hosta 'Pacific Blue Edger'

H

Heligan, Cornwall

This much-celebrated restoration project was masterminded by Tim Smit, who first saw the overgrown, 'lost' garden in 1990 and realized its potential. He put together a team of dedicated enthusiasts to begin the Herculean task of reclaiming the wonderful Victorian kitchen garden, with its glasshouses and pineapple pit, and, later, the surrounding estate, where a fascinating and much older industrial and agricultural landscape was eventually found. Heligan (which has a rhododendron named after it) soon became one of the most visited gardens in Britain, inspiring interest in Victorian gardens and their produce.

Pineapple: a Heligan crop

Hellyer, Arthur (1902–1993)

The Bristol-born nurseryman and horticultural author and editor Arthur Hellyer was a familiar name on the 20th-century gardening scene, chiefly as editor of *Amateur Gardening* and the *RHS Dictionary of Gardening*, and as a founder member of the Hardy Plant Society. He was awarded the RHS Victoria Medal of Honour in 1967, and elected a Fellow of the Linnean Society. A variety of sweet pea is named in his honour.

Hemsley, William (1843–1924)

This botanist from Sussex was apprenticed at **Kew** as a young gardener and eventually became keeper of the herbarium there. He collaborated with F.B. Forbes in cataloguing the flora of **China**, an ambitious but very valuable task that took more than 20 years, at a point when new Chinese plants were arriving all the time. The job was completed in 1905. Hemsley is recalled by several plant names, for example *Styrax hemsleyanus*, a deciduous flowering tree native to China, and the climbing monkshood *Aconitum hemsleyanum*.

Henderson, Louis Forniquet (1853–1942)

One of the grand old men of American botany, Henderson was a remarkable botanist from the Pacific north-west of the USA. During his long and adventurous life he was a teacher, a private plant collector and an expedition botanist. Finally, aged 71, he joined the University of **Oregon** and spent 15 years as an outstanding curator of the herbarium there. Of the 15 species named for him, two are known as garden plants: *Erythronium hendersonii* and *Dodecatheon hendersonii*.

Henri d'Orléans (1867–1901)

Meconopsis henrici and *Rodgersia henrici* are not named after the plant collector **Augustine Henry** (see below), but after a young French prince who had a taste for travel. French law, even a century after the Revolution, prevented Henri from seeking adventure in the military, so instead he travelled independently through much of the 1890s, exploring many remote parts of the Far East that were only later reached by more well-documented plant hunters like

E.H. Wilson, Joseph Rock and Frank Kingdon Ward. Interested in more or less everything, Prince Henri included hundreds of plant specimens in the collections he brought back with him, gathering and pressing all his own material. His specimens of *Incarvillea delavayi*, *Lilium lophophorum*, *Lonicera thibetica*, *Rhododendron primuliflorum* and many other plants, which he submitted to the Muséum d'Histoire Naturelle in Paris on his return, were the first recorded in the West.

Henry, Augustine (1857–1930)

In 1881 this Irish doctor and botanist became a medical officer for the Chinese Imperial Customs Service. He collected large numbers of plants in Hubei, Sichuan and Taiwan on his postings in China, and sent hundreds of herbarium specimens to Kew, including some belonging to genera new to science. Towards the end of his time in China, Henry had the opportunity to advise a newly arrived young plant hunter, E.H.Wilson. The two men met in Yunnan. On his return to Britain in 1900, Henry turned to forestry and was co-author (with H.J. Elwes, of snowdrop fame) of *The Trees of Great Britain and Ireland* (1906–1913). He was professor of forestry at Dublin, and today is commemorated by the Augustine Henry Forestry Herbarium at the National Botanic Gardens, Glasnevin, as well as by his legacy of plants, including *Acer henryi*, *Lilium henryi*, *Lonicera henryi*, *Parthenocissus henryana*, *Sinowilsonia henryi*, *Rubus henryi*, *Tilia henryana* and *Rhododendron augustinii*. He also introduced the well-known garden plants *Rodgersia aesculifolia* and *Rodgersia pinnata*.

Henry Doubleday Research Association (HDRA)

For many years, from its inception in 1954 until recently, the leading organic gardening organization in Europe, now called Garden Organic, was known by this name. The HDRA was founded by the journalist and organic grower Lawrence Hills, who set up the association's first small garden at Bocking, near Braintree, in Essex. Regarded as eccentric at first, the organization gathered momentum through the 1960s and 1970s and, by then under the direction of Alan and Jackie Gear, moved in 1985 to its present main site, Ryton Organic Gardens, near Coventry. The HDRA has pioneered many far-sighted initiatives towards sustainable growing and conservation, such as its Heritage Seed Library, which keeps historic vegetable varieties in circulation, and its other organic gardens at Yalding, in Kent, and Audley End, in Essex.

Henry, Mrs J. Norman (1884–1967)

Phlox divaricata subsp. *laphamii* 'Chattahoochee' is one of the familiar garden plants introduced by this remarkable American plant hunter who lived at Gladwyne, Pennsylvania – now the Henry Foundation for Botanical Research. She found many new plants, mainly in the south-eastern states. She was said to carry with her a little trench spade to defend herself against snakes.

Hergest Croft Gardens, Herefordshire

This very large garden and arboretum in the Welsh border country has a wonderful plantsman's collection of mature trees and shrubs, including many rarities, built up by three generations of the Banks family since 1896. The early plantings included huge rhododendrons and trees that were introduced from the Himalayas by the **Veitch** nurseries – monuments to the last generation of traditional plant hunters such as **Ernest Wilson** and **Frank Kingdon Ward**. There are also National Collections of maples, birches and zelkovas. The garden is commemorated in the plant names *Penstemon heterophyllus* 'Hergest Croft' and *Betula* 'Hergest'.

Hermann, Paul (1646–1695)

Before becoming professor of botany at Leiden in The Netherlands, Hermann spent five years in Sri Lanka (then Ceylon) in the 1670s as medical officer for the Dutch East India Company. He made a significant early collection of plant material, which was useful to **Linnaeus** and many later botanists.

Heronswood see Hinkley, Dan

Herrenhausen, Germany

Origanum laevigatum 'Herrenhausen' and *Polystichum setiferum* (Divisilobum Group) 'Herrenhausen' are two well-established garden plants named after this huge formal garden near Hanover, laid out in the late 1600s by Sophia, Electress of Hanover. *Buxus microphylla* 'Herrenhausen' and *Salvia officinalis* 'Herrenhausen' are other examples.

Herterton House, Northumberland

Geranium sanguineum 'Belle of Herterton' and *Geum* 'Herterton Primrose' are named after this inspired,

Hidcote Manor Garden, Gloucestershire

One of the great showpiece gardens of the 20th century, Hidcote is a unique combination of landscape drama and satisfying structure with a wealth of detailed planting interest. The garden was conceived after World War I by Major Lawrence Johnston, whose mother had bought the estate in 1907. Johnston was a brilliant amateur designer, and his interest in plants grew as he developed his gardens, both at Hidcote and at his other property, Serre de la Madone, near Menton, in southern France. He accompanied **Collingwood Ingram** and **George Forrest** on plant-hunting expeditions, but eventually poor health persuaded him to settle in the south of France and Hidcote was given to the National Trust in 1948.

SOME HIDCOTE PLANTS

Allium cernuum 'Hidcote'
Campanula latiloba 'Hidcote Amethyst'
Dianthus 'Hidcote'
Fuchsia 'Hidcote Beauty'
Helianthemum 'Hidcote Apricot'
Helleborus × *hybridus* 'Hidcote Double'
Hypericum 'Hidcote'
Lavandula angustifolia 'Hidcote'
Penstemon 'Hidcote Pink'
Rosa 'Lawrence Johnston'
Symphytum 'Hidcote Blue'

beautifully planted garden and associated nursery near Cambo. It has been created from scratch, since 1976, by Frank and Marjorie Lawley, who also have plants named after them: *Geranium* × *oxonianum* 'Frank Lawley', *Eucomis* 'Frank Lawley', *Campanula persicifolia* 'Frank Lawley' and *Pulmonaria officinalis* 'Marjorie Lawley'.

Heucher, Johann Heinrich von (1677–1747)
Linneaus named the genus *Heuchera* after this friend and patron, a professor of medicine and botany at Wittenberg University, in Germany.

Highclere Castle, Berkshire
The Highclere holly *Ilex* × *altaclerensis*, a hybrid between the British native *Ilex aquifolium* and a species from **Madeira**, originated in 1835 at this family home of the earls of Caernarvon: *altaclerensis* is a Latinization of 'Highclere'.

Highdown, West Sussex
Sir Frederick Stern (1884–1967) created Britain's most famous chalk garden here on an unpromising downland site west of Worthing. The estate included a large disused chalk pit where he and his wife were assured nothing would grow. Undeterred, they started to make the garden in 1909 and experimented for some 50 years to find plants that were happy in the thin, alkaline soil. This gave them the opportunity to try new plants brought back by the great plant hunters of the day such as **Frank Kingdon Ward**, to whom Sir Frederick dedicated his book *A Chalk Garden* (1960). Sometimes Sir

Frederick brought back plants from his own travels. The result is a surprisingly varied plantsman's garden with many fine lime-tolerant trees and shrubs and a wonderful collection of spring bulbs. Plants named after Highdown and its creator include several cultivars of thyme and sunrose (*Helianthemum*), *Galanthus gracilis* 'Highdown' (Sir Frederick was an expert in snowdrops), *Rosa* 'Highdownensis' and *Helleborus* × *sternii*.

Hill, John (1716–1775)
A prolific writer on plants, John Hill had 76 books to his name, including *Flora Botanica* (1760), which was notable as the first English book to employ **Linnaeus**'s system of classification. His major work was *The Vegetable System*, an enormous project, which took 16 years (from 1759), filled 26 volumes and featured 26,000 plants.

Hillier Nurseries see page 94

Hills, Lawrence see Henry Doubleday Research Association

Hinkley, Dan
One of the élite among contemporary American plant hunters and nurserymen, Dan Hinkley was co-founder of the hugely successful Heronswood Nursery, near Seattle, with architect Robert Jones. From small beginnings in 1987 (and still with only 20 mail-order customers following the launch of its first catalogue in 1992), Heronswood grew exponentially and is now an international plant-lovers' mecca, drawing the world's

The Hillier shop in Winchester

Hillier Nurseries, Hampshire

The Hillier name first entered the gardening world in 1864, when Edwin Hillier and his wife Betsy bought a small nursery and florist shop in Winchester. The enterprise expanded and their sons, Edwin Lawrence and Arthur, joined the business. By the time Edwin Lawrence's son, Harold (1905–1985), became involved in 1921, Hillier was said to be growing a wider range of hardy trees and shrubs than any other nursery in the country. Under Harold's stewardship, the nursery continued to increase in both prestige and size, eventually amounting to some 700 acres.

SOME HILLIER PLANTS

Abutilon × suntense 'Jermyns'
Betula utilis var. jacquemontii
'Jermyns'
Ceanothus 'Blue Mound'
Choisya 'Aztec Pearl'
Cotinus 'Grace'
Daphne 'Valerie Hillier'
Daphne bholua
'Jacqueline Postill'
Eucryphia × hillieri 'Winton'
('Winton' and wintonensis
– from Winchester – usually
indicate Hillier plants)
× Halimiocistus wintonensis
Lonicera × purpusii
'Winter Beauty'
Malus × scheideckeri 'Hillieri'
Phygelius × rectus
'Winchester Fanfare'
Robinia × slavinii 'Hillieri'
Sophora Sun King ('Hilsop')
Thuja plicata 'Hillieri'
Tilia 'Harold Hillier'
Ulmus × hollandica
'Jacqueline Hillier'
Viburnum × hillieri 'Winton'

Harold and his family moved to Jermyns House, Ampfield, in 1953. Here he began the great plant collection that was to become the Sir Harold Hillier Gardens and Arboretum, gifted to Hampshire County Council in 1977. It now boasts many 'champion' trees of record size and 11 National Collections, including one of plants raised by Hillier. After Harold retired, he had more time to indulge his love of plant hunting, and travelled widely overseas. He was knighted in 1983.

Harold's sons, John and Robert, succeeded him, expanding the Hillier garden centre chain. John (now President) retired in 1995. Robert is Chairman and Managing Director. His son, George, and John's sons, Martin and James, from the fifth generation, work for the family business. Three generations of the family have been awarded the RHS Victoria Medal of Honour: Edwin Lawrence in 1941, Harold in 1957 and John Hillier in 1996.

Hillier have exhibited at RHS shows since before World War I. In 2005, they gained their 60th consecutive Chelsea Gold Medal for an exhibit that also won the President's Award and the Lawrence Medal – a unique record. Other outstanding achievements include the indispensable *Hillier Manual of Trees and Shrubs*, regularly updated since 1972 and containing authoritative descriptions of some 10,500 woody plants.

top gardeners and plantsmen. Many come to see and buy Hinkley's own discoveries, usually propagated from small amounts of seed collected in remote parts of the world. The Far East, **New Zealand**, South **Africa**, Mexico, **Turkey** and many other places have hosted his collecting expeditions, and he also lectures widely, both in the USA and abroad. Heronswood was sold to the huge seed company **Burpee** of Philadelphia in 2000, but Hinkley and Jones continue to run it much as before. Plants named after the nursery include *Cercidiphyllum japonicum* 'Heronswood Globe' and *Tiarella wherryi* 'Heronswood Mist'.

Hobhouse, Penelope

Penelope Hobhouse's illustrious career as a gardener, garden designer and author began at **Hadspen** in Somerset. She moved on in 1979 to look after the nearby National Trust property of Tintinhull House. Here she and her second husband, the late Professor John Malins, spent 14 years caring for the classic formal garden, which was designed by its former owner Phyllis Reiss in the years after she moved here in 1933. Alongside her gardening career, Penelope Hobhouse has lectured and designed gardens in several countries and has written many books, including *Plants in Garden History*, *Natural Planting* and the classic *Colour in your Garden*. Since 1993 she has been creating a private garden at her new home at Bettiscombe, in Dorset. *Oenothera* 'Penelope Hobhouse' is named for her. She received the RHS Victoria Medal of Honour in 1996.

Hodgkin, Eliot (1905–1973)

Saxifraga 'Eliot Hodgkin' honours this amateur alpine enthusiast from Twyford, in Berkshire (not to be confused with his contemporary, the artist Eliot Hodgkin). Hodgkin made many plant-collecting trips abroad and became president of the Alpine Garden Society. The charming dwarf *Iris* 'Katharine Hodgkin' was named by the respected plantsman **E.B. Anderson** after Hodgkin's wife.

Hogg, Thomas (1820–1892)

Thomas Hogg and his brother took over their father's New York nursery business after his death in 1855. Thomas spent several years during the 1860s and 1870s in **Japan**, collecting new plants to send back to the nursery, including the first *Cercidiphyllum japonicum* and *Styrax japonicus*. His most renowned introduction was *Hosta* 'Fukurin Fu Giboshi' which, because of its unpronounceable name, very soon became known as *Hosta* 'Thomas Hogg'. Today it is known as *Hosta undulata* var. *albomarginata* (*Hosta* 'Decorata' in the USA).

Hole, Samuel (1819–1904)

One of the most distinguished of many gardening clerics, Hole was vicar of Caunton in Nottinghamshire. In 1887 he became Dean of Rochester, in Kent. His name is familiar to gardeners and nurserymen today through the medal that the Royal National Rose Society still awards in his honour. A lifelong rose enthusiast, he was instrumental in founding the Grand National Rose Show, in 1858, which was taken over

William Jackson Hooker (1785–1865) and Joseph Dalton Hooker(1817–1911)

Sir Joseph Dalton Hooker on his travels

The Hookers, father and son, played key roles in the story of gardening in Britain. Professor of botany at Glasgow University, William Hooker then became the first director of **Kew** in 1841. He fostered a close association between plant science and gardening, opening Kew to the public for the first time and ensuring that its botanists joined expeditions all over the world in order to increase botanical knowledge and collect specimens. Projects under his directorship included Decimus Burton's vast palm house and the tropical waterlily house. Whether for exotic tender plants or hardy herbaceous perennials, shrubs and trees, Hooker realized the importance of making Kew's unrivalled plant collection available to the public and to scientists as living plants, as well as dried herbarium specimens for academic study. By the end of Sir William Hooker's life, the reputation of Kew as an international repository of plant information was second to none.

Hooker's love of plants was inherited by his son Joseph, who spent many years exploring and collecting on his intrepid travels in remote areas, from the Himalayas to the Rocky Mountains and even the Antarctic. He was a well-respected author, detailing his exploits and exciting discoveries in books that remain classics of the botanical world: *The Rhododendrons of Sikkim-Himalaya* (1849–1851), *Flora of New Zealand* (1853), *Himalayan Journals* (1854) and the hugely ambitious *Genera Plantarum* (1862–1883), a 3,000-page work recording all the known plants of the day. Joseph joined his father at Kew in 1855 as assistant director, adding his own herbarium collection and taking responsibility for the day-to-day management of Kew at what was a very busy time for the plant world. Newly discovered plants were arriving all the time, needing to be identified and catalogued – and attracting increasing numbers of visitors. After Sir William's death in 1865, Sir Joseph succeeded him as director, continuing his writing almost until his own death at the age of 94.

SOME HOOKER PLANTS

Bulbinella hookeri
Crinodendron hookerianum
Inula hookeri
Polygonatum hookeri
Raoulia hookeri
Salix hookeriana
Sarcococca hookeriana
Sempervivum ×
barbulatum 'Hookeri'
Silene hookeri

three years later by the **RHS**. One of the founders of the National Rose Society in 1876, he became its first president. He wrote several books, including *A Book about Roses* (1869) and *Our Gardens* (1899), and was awarded the RHS Victoria Medal of Honour in 1897.

Holehird Gardens, Cumbria

Enjoying spectacular views from its setting above Windermere in the Lake District, Holehird is the garden of the Lakeland Horticultural Society and is run entirely by volunteers. It holds national collections of *Astilbe*, *Hydrangea* and *Polystichum*, and has a plant named after it: *Erica australis* 'Holehird'.

Hopleys Plants, Hertfordshire

This nursery and garden at Much Hadham has been responsible for developing and introducing many well-known shrubs and herbaceous plants such as *Lavatera* × *clementii* 'Barnsley', *Potentilla fruticosa* 'Red Ace' and *Osteospermum* 'Whirlygig'. Plants named for the nursery include *Potentilla fruticosa* 'Hopley's Orange' and *Origanum laevigatum* 'Hopleys'.

Hornibrook, Murray (1875–1949)

An expert on dwarf conifers and alpines, Hornibrook lived in Ireland, where he built up a conifer collection which informed his pioneering book *Dwarf and Slow Growing Conifers* (1923). He donated his collection to the botanic garden at **Glasnevin** when he left Ireland, spending his retirement in England and Normandy.

He propagated the award-winning prostrate *Juniperus communis* 'Hornibrookii', which he had found in the wild in County Galway, and is also remembered in *Saxifraga* × *hornibrookii*.

Host, Nicolaus (1761–1834)

Viennese doctor and physician to the Austrian emperor, Host was a keen plantsman and author of *Flora austriaca*, a two-volume book on Austrian plants, written in the 1820s. The genus *Hosta* is named in his honour. Its old name, *Funkia*, commemorates another Austrian doctor, Heinrich Funk (1771–1839), a collector of alpine ferns.

Howard, David

The owner of Howard Nurseries in Wortham, Norfolk, David Howard was formerly a keen dahlia breeder. The robust orange *Dahlia* 'David Howard' was bred by him from the well-known *Dahlia* 'Bishop of Llandaff', sharing its deep bronze foliage.

Hoy, Thomas (1750–1822)

The beautiful but tender plants known as wax flowers (*Hoya*) are named after Hoy, who was head gardener to the Duke of Northumberland at Syon House in west London.

Hugh, Father see Scanlan, Hugh

Humboldt, Alexander von (1769–1859)

An amateur German botanist, Humboldt made an epic five-year expedition to Central and **South**

America with **Aimé Bonpland** at the end of the 18th century. The plant life of the tropics fascinated Humboldt, and when he met the equally enthusiastic Bonpland in Paris in 1798 he saw the opportunity he had been waiting for. Humboldt's family fortune financed the ambitious trip, and the two men braved many dangers in the unexplored rainforests, travelling thousands of miles, from Venezuela to Mexico, and discovering many exotic new plants to send back to France and Spain. These included fuchsias, passion flowers, zinnias, dahlias and orchids. *Rhododendron* 'Humboldt' and *Rosa* 'Alexander von Humboldt' are among the plants named after him.

Huntington Botanical Gardens, California

Railway tycoon Henry Huntington spent much of his considerable family wealth on his estate near Pasadena, in the foothills above Los Angeles. He arrived there in 1903 and spent many years developing the house and land, before eventually dedicating the Huntington estate to the nation as an institution for public research and education. He ensured that it had the best of everything, from a world-class library and art collections to some 200 acres of lavishly planted landscaped gardens. Themed botanical collections include an Australian garden, a Japanese garden and a 12-acre desert garden, which has one of the largest collections of cacti and succulents anywhere. The rose garden alone boasts some 1,500 different rose varieties. Recent additions to the Huntington include a large conservatory for public exhibitions and research, a children's garden and a Chinese garden.

Hyde Hall, RHS Garden, Essex

The smallest of the four gardens of the **RHS**, Hyde Hall came into the ownership of the RHS in 1993. Set on an exposed hill in an especially dry part of East Anglia, the garden has established a reputation for environmental sustainability, and particularly for its award-winning dry garden, opened in 2001. This is designed to inspire visitors to use techniques and plants that do not require irrigation. The garden's ecological credentials have been further advanced by the avoidance of pesticides and by the planting of thousands of trees all around the boundary, helping to make it attractive to wildlife. Hyde Hall is the home of the National Collection of *Viburnum*, and *Clematis* Hyde Hall ('Evipo009') was named to commemorate the bicentenary of the RHS in 2004. *Malus* 'Hyde Hall Spire' and *Verbascum* 'Hyde Hall Sunrise' are other Hyde Hall plants.

Hyrcania

The Hyrcanian Ocean was an ancient name for the Caspian Sea. The botanically rich region once known as Hyrcania lies on its south-eastern shore, in northern Iran, between the Caspian Sea and the Elburz Mountains – around the town now known as Gorgan, an Iranian provincial capital. Several plants, including *Acer hyrcanum* and *Teucrium hircanicum*, preserve the region's old name.

Ikaria

The snowdrop *Galanthus ikariae* is named after this Greek island in the Aegean Sea. It also grows on nearby Andros and Tinos.

Illyria

In ancient times Illyria was a kingdom in the west of the Balkan peninsula, along the Adriatic coast of Croatia and Dalmatia. It is associated with plants bearing the epithet *illyricus*, including *Gladiolus illyricus* and *Ranunculus illyricus*.

Incarville, Pierre d' (1706–1757)

A Jesuit from Rouen, d'Incarville was the first of several French missionaries who collected plants in **China**. He lived in Beijing from 1742, working as a glassmaker and collecting plants in the nearby hills when he could. He had studied under the distinguished French botanist Bernard de **Jussieu**, acquiring an eye for a good plant: several of d'Incarville's finds remain choice species. They include *Sophora japonica*, *Koelreuteria paniculata* and *Albizia julibrissin*. Another of his discoveries, *Ailanthus altissima*, became an invasive pest in **North America** after its arrival there in 1784. The genus *Incarvillea* comprises several species of showy herbaceous plants found mostly in the Himalayas.

Collingwood ('Cherry') Ingram (1880–1981)

One of the most affectionately remembered (and most long-lived) gardening personalities of the 20th century, Ingram began making his garden at The Grange in Benenden, Kent, in 1919. Here he grew some of the many plants he found on his extensive travels – to South **Africa**, **Japan**, **South America**, **New Zealand**, Sikkim and southern Spain. He recounted the links between his travels and his plants in his book *A Garden of Memories*. Another of his books, *Ornamental Cherries*, is a classic on a plant group that was his particular interest, and was the reason why, for much of his life, he was nicknamed Cherry Ingram. (In deference to this, his signature consisted of his initials, 'CI', arranged in such a way that they looked like a cherry.) He became an authority on old Japanese cultivars of cherry, which he studied in Japan, and is said to have reintroduced a lost one, the great white cherry *Prunus* 'Taihaku', to Japan after he found it in a Sussex garden. Other successful garden plants associated with Collingwood Ingram include *Rosmarinus officinalis* var. *angustissimus* 'Benenden Blue' (which he found growing wild in Corsica), the beautiful cultivated bramble *Rubus* 'Benenden' (which he bred in his garden), *Teucrium fruticans* 'Azureum' (from the **Atlas Mountains** in North Africa) and *Omphalodes cappadocica* 'Cherry Ingram'. Plants named for him also include a Japanese maple, a flowering cherry, a primula and a rhododendron. Many of the plants at RHS Garden **Rosemoor** were given by Ingram to the garden's former owner, his friend Lady Anne Berry (formerly Palmer), and Ingram named a variety of cistus that he bred after her: *Cistus* × *fernandesiae* 'Anne Palmer'.

Ingwersen, Walter Edward Theodore (1883–1960)

The name of W.E.Th. Ingwersen has long been synonymous with alpine plants. Born in Hamburg, Ingwersen came to England before World War I, opening his first nursery, and then taking charge of the rock garden at Wisley. He later went into partnership at **Six Hills Nursery** with his contemporary Clarence Elliott, a fellow alpine enthusiast. Here Walter's son Will began to learn the nursery trade. In 1925 **William Robinson** offered Ingwersen the tenancy of Birch Farm, on his Sussex estate at **Gravetye**. Ingwersen founded Birch Farm Nursery in 1927, running it and undertaking plant-hunting expeditions with Will, later a co-founder of the Hardy Plant Society and author of the classic *Manual of Alpine Plants* (1978). Walter's younger son, Paul, eventually joined the business, taking over in 1986. Will died in 1990, since when Paul and his wife Mary have continued to delight customers and visitors to horticultural shows with award-winning displays from Birch Farm's unsurpassed collection of rare and fascinating alpines and other hardy plants. *Geranium macrorrhizum* 'Ingwersen's Variety' is the most widely known plant bearing the name; others include *Liriope muscari* 'Ingwersen', *Halimiocistus* 'Ingwersenii', *Sempervivum ingwersenii* and *Saxifraga* 'Walter Ingwersen'.

Walter Ingwersen

Innes, John (1829–1904)

The John Innes Horticultural Institution was founded in 1909 in Merton, south London, and named after this City businessman, whose bequest of his house and 2 acres of land 'for the promotion of horticultural instruction, experiment and research' had made it possible. The formulae for the famous John Innes composts were developed there in the 1930s. The organization later moved to Norfolk, where it has links with the University of East Anglia. A merger in 1994 established the John Innes Centre, a leading research facility for plant science.

Inverewe Garden, Ross-shire

Primula 'Inverewe' is named after this large, wild garden beside Loch Ewe. It has evolved as a plantsman's garden with a fine collection, including many tender plants from the southern hemisphere. Begun in 1862 by Osgood Mackenzie, who transformed the initially barren, windswept site, Inverewe was left to the National Trust for Scotland by his daughter Mairi when she died in 1953.

Inverleith see Edinburgh

Istanbul, Turkey

Once known as Byzantium and then as Constantinople, Istanbul is represented in plant names by the epithet *byzantinus*, as in *Colchicum byzantinum* and *Gladiolus communis* subsp. *byzantinus*. (See also **Turkey**.)

George Jackman & Son, Woking

The legendary clematis nursery of Jackman in Woking was founded in 1810 by William Jackman. His son George (1801–1869) was the first of three George Jackmans to be involved in the family business, and the one who gave it the name George Jackman & Son. In 1859, he and his son George (1837–1887) raised the beautiful velvety-purple *Clematis* 'Jackmanii'. It won a First Class Certificate in 1863 and has remained one of the most popular of all clematis. Sharing his father's interest in clematis, in 1872 the second George Jackman co-authored the first-ever book on the genus, with Thomas Moore, curator of the **Chelsea Physic Garden**.

The nursery eventually passed to the third generation of the Jackman family: Arthur George Jackman (1866–1926) was involved in the nursery from the age of 16 for some 40 years, until 1923. Many of the Jackman-raised cultivars that are still widely grown today were already well established by this time: 'Duchess of Edinburgh', 'Lady Betty Balfour', 'Mrs George Jackman' and others.

Arthur's son, George Rowland Jackman (1902–1976) trained as a nurseryman elsewhere but returned home to help out when his father fell ill, working in partnership with his uncle Percy for some years after his father's death. Rowland (as he was known) was interested in a wider range of plants than his predecessors, and liked collecting good forms that he found either in gardens or in the wild. *Ruta graveolens* 'Jackman's Blue', *Sorbus aucuparia* 'Sheerwater Seedling' and *Potentilla fruticosa* 'Jackman's Variety' are among his introductions, the last rescued by him when nursery plants had to be dug up to make way for food production during World War II. However, clematis remained a core element of the Jackman catalogue, and Rowland named two that he had raised, *Clematis* 'Barbara Jackman' and *Clematis alpina* 'Pamela Jackman', after his daughters, and another, 'John Huxtable', after a member of his staff. The nursery moved in 1960 when the original site was sold for building, but Rowland Jackman remained in charge until 1967, when it was sold, later to be turned into a garden centre.

Jackson & Perkins, Oregon and California

This leading American rose nursery is most widely known internationally for the ubiquitous rambler 'Dorothy Perkins', named in 1901 after the daughter of George Perkins. (The eponymous British clothing store came later!) Founded in 1872 as a strawberry and grape farm in Newark, New York, the family business soon won a reputation for roses, and for its spectacular rose gardens. The company – which coined the term 'floribunda' – moved west in the 1960s and is now based in Oregon and California.

Jacquemont, Victor (1801–1832)

With a number of fashionable white-barked cultivars, the Himalayan birch *Betula utilis* var. *jacquemontii* is undoubtedly the most well-known garden plant named after this French naturalist who travelled in India and the Himalayas, exploring remote and unexplored regions of Tibet and **Kashmir**. Others are *Androsace villosa* var. *jacquemontii* and *Euphorbia jacquemontii*. Sadly Jacquemont contracted cholera and died in Bombay at the age of only 31.

James, Robert (1873–1960)
Graham Stuart Thomas named the popular fragrant rambler rose 'Bobbie James' after the Hon. Robert James, an eminent gardener who had an outstanding 7-acre garden at St Nicholas, Richmond, in Yorkshire.

Jameson, Vera (1899–1989)
The award-winning *Sedum* 'Vera Jameson' was found by this Gloucestershire plantswoman as a chance seedling in her garden.

Jalapa see Xalapa

Japan see pages 104–105

Jardin des Plantes (Jardin du Roi) see Paris

Jefferson, Thomas (1743–1826)
Jefferson's beautifully preserved estate at Monticello, near Charlottesville, Virginia, is a tribute to his lifelong interest in plants. He inherited the Monticello estate aged 14, later

Gertrude Jekyll (1843–1932)

SOME JEKYLL PLANTS

Helleborus foetidus 'Miss Jekyll's Scented'
Lavandula angustifolia 'Munstead'
Nigella damascena 'Miss Jekyll'
Pulmonaria angustifolia 'Munstead Blue'
Rosa Gertrude Jekyll ('Ausbord')
Sedum telephium 'Munstead Red'
Solenostemon 'Gertrude Jekyll'
Vinca minor f. *alba* 'Gertrude Jekyll'

The genius behind the English garden, Gertrude Jekyll brought together design and planting in a unique and innovative way. Her intuitive grasp of both made her the ideal working partner for the architect Sir Edwin Lutyens, and some of her best gardens were for projects that they developed together. Many of her original gardens have been restored, and countless others around the world owe her an immense debt. Her 13 books, her articles and planting plans, and the survivors among the 200 or so gardens she designed, make up what is probably the most influential body of work in 20th-century gardening.

As a young woman, Gertrude Jekyll studied art, and her skill as a painter undoubtedly influenced her handling of colour and form in gardens. She was an admirer of **William Robinson**'s ideas on naturalistic planting, and of the Arts & Crafts movement, with its emphasis on true craftsmanship (she herself was skilled in many crafts) and the bringing together of the various creative arts. All these ideas found expression in the buildings and garden of her home, Munstead Wood, in Surrey.

building the house and moving there in 1770. He planted many trees, made a huge vegetable garden, and generally took a great interest in the farmland and gardens, teaching himself about botany, farming and horticulture, and keeping detailed records. His many horticultural experiments included the planting of olive cuttings here in 1774. As third president of the United States, he favoured the introduction of many foreign plants as well as encouraging botanists and naturalists to discover the North American flora, and was instrumental in setting up the expedition of **Lewis** and **Clark** in 1803.

Jeffrey, John (1826–1854)

A plant collector from the Royal Botanic Garden **Edinburgh**, Jeffrey was sent to **North America** in 1850 to find plants for a syndicate of Scottish landowners, but came to a mysterious and sad end. He reported his progress from Hudson Bay through Canada and down to the Sierra Nevada, and it is known that on the way he discovered some 20 new conifers including the Jeffrey pine, *Pinus jeffreyi*, which he found in the Shasta Valley of northern California in 1852, sending back seed and identification samples. However, by 1854 contact with Jeffrey had been lost and he was never heard of again.

Jermyn, Jim see Edrom Nurseries

Jermyns see Hillier

Jessopp, Euphemia (1861–1935)

One of the most useful cultivars of common rosemary, *Rosmarinus*

officinalis 'Miss Jessopp's Upright', is named after this amateur gardener who lived in Enfield, north London, and was a friend and frequent garden visitor of **E.A. Bowles** at nearby Myddelton House.

Johnson, A.T. (1873–1956)

Arthur Tysilio Johnson was a Welsh amateur plantsman and gardener whose 4-acre garden was at Ty'n-y-Groes, in the Conwy Valley in north Wales. Here he and his wife, Nora, grew shrubs, old roses and semi-naturalized hardy herbaceous plants. A number of plants are associated with Johnson, including the award-winning *Daphne cneorum* 'Eximia', which he raised in his garden, and, more obviously, *Geranium* × *oxonianum* 'A.T. Johnson', the excellent winter-flowering heather *Erica* × *darleyensis* 'Arthur Johnson' and the indispensable *Geranium* 'Johnson's Blue'. *Ceanothus* 'A.T. Johnson' was named in his honour by the **Burkwood** brothers, who raised it at their nursery. Johnson is also remembered as the co-author of *Plant Names Simplified*, first published in 1931 and still in print. He had several other books published, and wrote on gardening in the national press.

Johnson, Helen

The highly popular *Verbascum* 'Helen Johnson' occurred as a chance seedling at the Royal Botanic Gardens, **Kew**, and was named after the horticulturist who found it there. She later named *Verbascum* 'June Johnson' after her mother.

Japan

Lilium auratum

Japan has an extraordinarily rich flora, with something approaching 6,000 native species, as well as a very long tradition of breeding and cultivating ornamental plants. However, it was one of the very last places to share its plants, wild or cultivated, with the rest of the world.

Today it is hard to comprehend how isolated Japan was until the middle of the 19th century. In the early 1600s, Christian missionaries had been seen increasingly as unwelcome troublemakers, and to prevent further incursions Japanese ports were eventually closed to all but the Chinese – a ban that lasted more than 200 years. The Dutch East India Company, however, had historic links with Japan and managed to establish an exclusive trading agreement. Japanese people were forbidden any contact with the outside world, so the Dutch traders who came here were confined to Deshima, a tiny man-made island in Nagasaki harbour. The island had about a dozen permanent Dutch residents, a population that was temporarily swelled from time to time by the arrival of a Dutch ship bearing goods from Europe and silk from China. In return, the ships took away Japanese porcelain, which was so fashionable in The Netherlands that it was later extensively copied there.

GARDEN CLASSICS FROM JAPAN

Acer japonicum
Aucuba japonica
Carex hachijoensis
Chaenomeles japonica
Cryptomeria japonica
Fatsia japonica
Hamamelis japonica
Hosta sieboldiana
Kirengeshoma palmata
Ligularia japonica
Lilium auratum
Lonicera japonica
Magnolia stellata
Parthenocissus tricuspidata
Primula japonica
Pseudosasa japonica
Rodgersia podophylla
Rosa rugosa
Skimmia japonica
Vitis coignetiae
Wisteria floribunda

Three important botanists worked on Deshima at different times in this long period: **Engelbert Kaempfer** in the 1690s, **Carl Thunberg** in the 1770s and **Philipp von Siebold** in the 1820s, all of them there as physician to the Dutch governor of the day. They had few opportunities to see anything of Japan, except on the expected annual ambassadorial gift-bearing pilgrimage to the Japanese imperial court in Tokyo. There was little freedom, and the Europeans were always heavily guarded: only Siebold was able to see more of Japanese life. In spite of the restrictions, all three somehow managed to satisfy their passion for plants by collecting specimens, which they sometimes cared for in a garden on Deshima until a ship arrived to carry them, carefully packed, back to The Netherlands.

It seems that Siebold claimed some of the credit for the eventual opening-up of Japan, for in 1853 he persuaded William II to make representations to the Shogun recommending trading with Europe. Also in that year America had the same idea but a different technique, sending a fleet of warships to

Plants for America

Japan's climate and geology make it a particularly good source of garden plants for temperate **North America**, and it was the origin of the first consignment of live plants sent from Asia to the USA, in 1862. The plants had been prepared in the Yokohama garden of **Dr George Hall**. Packed in 'Wardian cases' (see **Ward**), they were sent to Parsons of Flushing, Long Island and some were then sent on to Britain. These included the first *Zelkova serrata* (keaki), an ornamental tree native to northern **China**, Japan and Korea.

Tokyo under Admiral Perry. One or both methods succeeded, for in 1854 two ports were opened and an American consul was put in place. Restrictions gradually lifted. Word spread to the world's nurseries. Within a few years there was a rush of collectors to Japan, and many plant introductions were duplicated. The year 1860 saw the arrival of the young English nurseryman John Gould **Veitch**, the Scot **Robert Fortune**, the German **Max Wichura** and the Russian **Carl Maximowicz**, as well as Siebold himself. Veitch had the good fortune to be invited to join the first European party to climb the sacred Fujiyama (Mount Fuji), successfully collecting conifer seeds along the way including those of *Chamaecyparis obtusa* and *Cryptomeria japonica* Elegans Group. The consignment he later sent to England included 15 other new conifers, several primulas, *Magnolia stellata*, *Lilium auratum* and *Parthenocissus tricuspidata*.

Chaenomeles japonica

Later collectors in Japan included **Charles Maries**, **Charles Sprague Sargent**, **E.H. Wilson** and **Collingwood Ingram**. Making up for lost time, they sent back seeds and specimens of rhododendrons, maples, camellias, hydrangeas, peonies, bamboos, hostas, cornus, cherries and countless other choice Japanese plants that have become well established favourites in Western gardens.

Skimmia japonica

SOME JAPANESE EPITHETS

japonicus from Japan
niponicus, nipponicus from Japan
hachijoensis from Hachijo-jima, an island south of Tokyo
hakusanensis from Haku-san, a mountain on Honshu
oshimensis from O-shima, an island near Tokyo
yakushimanus from Yaku-shima, an island in the south
yedoensis, yesoensis, yezoensis from Tokyo (formerly Yedo)

FUJIYAMA

Some of the many cultivars named after the sacred Japanese mountain

Argyranthemum 'Fuji Sundance'
Clematis 'Fuji-musume'
Cornus kousa 'Mount Fuji'
Dracocephalum argunense 'Fuji White'
Fuchsia 'Fuji-San'
Hosta 'Mount Fuji'
Hydrangea serrata 'Fuji Waterfall'
Hydrangea serrata 'Shirofuji'
Penstemon Fujiyama ('Yayama')
Phlox paniculata 'Mount Fuji'
Prunus 'Shirotae'

Johnson, Hugh

An eminent writer on wine, trees and gardening, Hugh Johnson (under the nom-de-plume of Tradescant) is a long-standing columnist in the RHS journal *The Garden*, for which he is also a consultant. His garden is at Saling Hall, near Braintree, in Essex. There is a daylily, *Hemerocallis* 'Mrs Hugh Johnson', named after his wife.

Johnson, Thomas see Gerard, John

Johnston, Lawrence see Hidcote

Joly, Charles (1818–1902)

Acer platanoides 'Charles Joly' and the lovely double, deep purple lilac *Syringa vulgaris* 'Charles Joly' (introduced by Victor **Lemoine**) are named after this vice-president of the Société Nationale d'Horticulture Française and president of the editorial board of the horticultural periodical *Le Jardin*.

Joséphine, Empress see Malmaison

Jouin, Emile see Simon-Louis Frères

Judd, William (1888–1946)

Viburnum × *juddii* is named for this propagator at the **Arnold Arboretum** who had worked at **Kew**, from 1910 to 1913.

Jury family

Camellia × *williamsii* 'Jury's Yellow', whose lovely double, creamy flowers were first seen in 1971, is the most widely known of several award-winning plants raised by, and named for, the Jury family at their nursery in Tikorangi, **New Zealand**. Others are *Camellia* × *williamsii* 'Les Jury' and 'Elsie Jury'. Les's brother Felix, who died in 1996, was known for his magnolia hybrids: 'Iolanthe', 'Vulcan' and 'Apollo' are prized all over the world. Felix's son Mark, also a distinguished magnolia and camellia breeder, now runs the nursery.

Jussieu family

A Métro station near the Jardin des Plantes in **Paris** is named for this French family, several of whom were significant figures in the botanical world of their day. The two eldest Jussieu brothers, sons of a pharmacist, were Antoine (1686–1758) and Bernard (1699–1777), both eminent professors of botany at the Jardin du Roi (later Jardin des Plantes). Bernard's pupils there included **d'Incarville**, **Dombey** and other plant hunters. A networker and general facilitator in the plant-hunting world, Bernard de Jussieu also devised a method of plant classification. A younger brother, Joseph (1704–1779), found new plants, including the heliotrope, on an expedition to **South America** with the explorer Charles-Marie de la Condamine. He stayed on in Peru as a doctor, but his last years there were dogged by mental illness. Bernard's nephew Antoine-Laurent de Jussieu (1748–1836) wrote *Genera Plantarum*, an important book on plant classification based on the work of **Linnaeus** and **Adanson** and published in 1789. His son, Adrien Henri Laurent de Jussieu (1797–1853), became professor of botany at the Muséum d'Histoire Naturelle in Paris in 1826, and later its director.

Heliotropium arborescens

Kaempfer, Engelbert (1651–1716)

The first Western descriptions of *Ginkgo biloba* and *Camellia* were in the notebooks of this German doctor who worked in **Japan** for the Dutch East India Company. He is commemorated by the tropical genus *Kaempferia*, by *Larix kaempferi* and its many cultivars, and by *Rhododendron kaempferi*.

Kalm, Pehr (1716–1779)

Lobelia kalmii and the genus of American evergreen shrubs called *Kalmia* are named after this Finnish student of **Linnaeus** who visited **North America** in 1742 and spent three years there, collecting plants to take back to Sweden. He later became professor of botany at Abo University.

Kamchatka

This volcanic region in the remote far east of **Russia** includes the 700-mile-long Kamchatka peninsula. The area, explored in the 1740s by the intrepid **Georg Steller**, is represented in plant names by the epithet *camtschatcensis* or *camtschaticus*, as in *Lysichiton camtschatcensis*, *Filipendula camtschatica* and *Aruncus dioicus* var. *kamtschaticus*.

Kamel, Georg (1661–1706)

A Czech missionary working in the Philippines, Kamel was one of the first people to collect plants in the Far East and bring them safely to Europe. Despite the misleading differences in spelling and (usually) pronunciation, his name – Latinized as Camellus – is the derivation of *Camellia*.

Karatau

This mountain range in Kazakhstan is noted for its flora. It is recalled in the names of *Thymus karatavicus* and *Allium karataviense*.

K

Arboretum Kalmthout, Belgium

Arboretum Kalmthout, near Antwerp, began life in 1856 as a nursery, later specializing in rhododendrons, conifers and *Hamamelis* under the ownership of Antoine Kort. Like many nurseries, the business fell into ruin during World War I and was forced to close. However, the second half of the 20th century saw Kalmthout transformed into a world-class arboretum, with rare trees and shrubs of many kinds including some of the original plants from Kort's nursery beds. The masterminds behind its rebirth were the late Robert and Jelena de Belder. Robert and his brother Georges had bought the land in 1952; Jelena came here two years later from Slovenia as a new graduate in horticulture, and subsequently became Robert's wife. Two very successful cultivars of the hybrid witch hazel *Hamamelis* × *intermedia* rescued from the old nursery were named 'Jelena' and 'Diane' after Jelena and her daughter. The de Belders also raised several excellent cultivars of *Hydrangea paniculata*, including 'Unique', 'Brussels Lace' and Pink Diamond ('Interhydia'). An agapanthus is named after the arboretum, while the unusual oak cultivar *Quercus ellipsoidalis* 'Hemelrijk' takes its cultivar name from a second, even larger arboretum created by Robert and Jelena.

Kashmir

The beautiful and botanically rich, but politically troubled, region of Kashmir, at the western end of the Himalayas, was visited by a number of plant hunters in the 19th and 20th centuries. Many plant names refer to Kashmir (with several different spellings): some examples are *Aralia cachemirica*, *Iris kashmiriana* and *Lavatera cachemiriana*.

Keay, Alister

Keay is a **New Zealand** breeder of some newer clematis varieties that quickly became popular, such as *Clematis* 'Snow Queen', 'Allanah' and 'Prince Charles'.

Kelmscott, Gloucestershire

The award-winning monkshood *Aconitum carmichaelii* Wilsonii Group 'Kelmscott' is named after Kelmscott Manor near Lechlade, the summer home of craftsman and writer William Morris (1834–1896).

Kelways, Somerset

This important hardy plant nursery at Langport, established by James Kelway in 1851, is known especially

GOLD MEDAL, ST. LOUIS, 1904.

HARDY PERENNIALS.

The most satisfactory plants for the Garden and amongst THE MOST BEAUTIFUL are the following:—

Kelway's Pæonies

Kelway's Delphiniums
Collection C, 42/- per dozen.

Kelway's Gaillardias Kelway's Pyrethrums

Carriage and Package Free for Cheque with Order, this Paper being mentioned. OTHER COLLECTIONS AT DIFFERENT PRICES.

KELWAY & SON, LANGPORT, SOMERSET.

for its long history of breeding and introducing perennials, particularly bearded irises and peonies. The company is still one of the leading suppliers of both. Many peonies are named after the nursery and members of the Kelway family, but more widely known is a cultivar of the attractive but invasive plume poppy, *Macleaya microcarpa* 'Kelway's Coral Plume'.

Kennedy, Lewis see Vineyard Nursery

Kerr, William (d.1814)

Hawick-born Kerr travelled to **China** in 1803, sent by **Sir Joseph Banks** as a representative of the Royal Botanic Gardens, **Kew**, where Kerr had been a gardener. He was the first in a long line of Scottish botanists and plant hunters working in China and the Himalayas. *Euonymus japonicus*, *Lilium lancifolium*, the white-flowered *Rosa banksiae* var. *banksiae* (named for Sir Joseph Banks's wife) and *Begonia grandis* were among the plants that Kerr sent back to Kew, and a specimen of *Cunninghamia lanceolata* grown from his original batch of seed still grows at Esher, in Surrey. The charming spring-flowering shrub *Kerria japonica* 'Simplex' was one of his first introductions – though its more familiar double-flowered form, *Kerria japonica* 'Pleniflora', is believed to have been in cultivation in Europe since about 1700.

Kiftsgate Court, Gloucestershire

Old roses are the classic attraction in this lovely garden, and a giant among them, the rambler *Rosa filipes* 'Kiftsgate', makes a magnificent specimen here, where it has the run of a huge beech tree. Kiftsgate Court has been nurtured since 1920 by three generations of the same family. The garden's creator was Heather Muir, who planned the areas close to the house as informal planting in a formal layout, in a similar vein to nearby **Hidcote**. (*Continued on page 110*)

Kew: Royal Botanic Gardens, London

The gardens of Kew House were already well known in the 17th century, when the property was owned by Lord Capel. Its royal connections began in 1730 when the house was let to the king's son, Frederick, Prince of Wales, whose circle included members of the botanical fraternity of the day, notably **John Stuart**, 3rd Earl of Bute. Frederick died in 1751, but his widow, Princess Augusta, continued to invest her energies in the garden, with Bute as her adviser and **William Aiton** as gardener. They devoted themselves to improving both the landscaping and the planting, and by the time her son came to the throne as George III, the scene was set for Kew to become a significant botanic garden. After Augusta's death, George III bought the freehold of Kew House and, as the personal property of the monarch, the Royal Botanic Gardens came into being. Kew flourished

The Chinese pagoda, built in 1761

under the direction of **Sir Joseph Banks**, and by 1789 William Aiton was able to publish *Hortus Kewensis*, a formidable and immensely valuable list of the plants grown there, which numbered 5,535 species. In 1803, with the despatch of **William Kerr** to **China**, Kew's tradition of sending out professional plant hunters got under way.

After the death of both Sir Joseph Banks and King George III in 1820, Kew suffered a period of decline, though its collections were maintained by the diligent head gardener, **William Townsend Aiton**. The arrival of a new director, **Sir William Jackson Hooker**, in 1841, heralded a new era, which continued under the subsequent directorship of his son, **Sir Joseph Hooker**, who took Kew into the 20th century. The Hookers restored the status of Kew as a scientific centre of excellence, and their incumbency saw many improvements, from specialist gardens and splendid buildings that remain flagship features today – notably Decimus Burton's Palm House (1840s) and the Temperate House (1890s) – to the founding of the formal programme of botanical and horticultural training that has gained Kew worldwide prestige.

SOME KEW PLANTS

Buddleja colvilei 'Kewensis'
Caryopteris × *clandonensis* 'Kew Blue'
Cytisus × *kewensis*
Euonymus fortunei 'Kewensis'
Iris chrysographes 'Kew Black'
Lavatera × *clementii* 'Kew Rose'
Skimmia × *confusa* 'Kew Green'
Sorbus × *kewensis*

Conservation of the world's threatened plant life, and related educational initiatives, have become an increasingly important part of Kew's work. Today more than 1 million visitors a year come here, and Kew's unique position at the centre of integrated environmental issues in the 21st century is reflected in its designation as a UNESCO World Heritage Site.

Frank Kingdon Ward (1885–1958)

A long career as a prolific and courageous plant hunter in the Far East links Kingdon Ward firmly with the tradition of the great 19th-century plant hunters, although his travels did not begin until 1907 when, aged 22, he left for **China** to become a schoolteacher in Shanghai. As a child, Kingdon Ward's interest in wildlife and outdoor pursuits had been nurtured by his father, who was professor of botany at **Cambridge**. Tales of the Far East provided further inspiration, and by 1911 he was on his first fully fledged plant-hunting trip, for **Arthur Bulley**. This was the start of more than four decades of professional plant hunting in difficult but spectacular Himalayan terrain. Documented in Kingdon Ward's 12 books, his travels involved every kind of crisis and hardship, from malaria and many injuries, to a major earthquake on the Assam-Tibet border. He made several trips to Burma, where he spent much of World War II in the British Army, attached to the Special Operations Executive. His growing reputation as a successful and knowledgeable plant collector won him sponsorship from wealthy garden owners and, later, from the **Arnold Arboretum**, the **New York Botanical Garden** and the **RHS**, whose Victoria Medal of Honour was one of many accolades including, in 1952, the OBE. Among the plants he collected are *Meconopsis betonicifolia*, *Cotoneaster conspicuus*, *Cotoneaster sternianus*, *Primula alpicola*, *Primula burmanica*, *Rhododendron wardii* and dozens more rhododendron species. The giant *Primula florindae* is named for his first wife, Florinda, and *Lilium mackliniae* for his second wife, Jean Macklin, whom he met in India. She accompanied him on six plant-hunting trips.

Mrs Muir's daughter, Diany Binny, took over the garden next, and now it is in the care of her granddaughter Anne Chambers and her husband. They have turned a former tennis court into a stylish, minimalist contemporary garden, which complements the profusion of planting elsewhere.

Killerton, Devon

This historic estate a few miles east of Exeter was the seat of the Acland family. Sir Thomas Acland began to create the garden in the 18th century with John **Veitch**, who became his land steward and later went on, with Sir Thomas's encouragement, to found a business that was to become an international nursery legend. The Veitch nurseries began in a small way at nearby Budlake. Many special trees and shrubs on the Killerton estate are a testament to the connection between the two families, for they were propagated from seed gathered abroad by collectors working for Veitch in the 19th century. Another famous name linked to Killerton is **William Robinson**, who designed the part of the garden that included the mixed borders still to be seen near the house. Two varieties of cider apple are named after Killerton, as is *Osteospermum jucundum* 'Killerton Pink'.

Kirstenbosch see Africa

Kitaibel, Paul (1757–1817)

An eastern European genus of herbaceous plants, *Kitaibelia*, is named after this Hungarian doctor and botanist who became director of the botanic garden in Budapest.

Kivistik, Uno (1932–1998)

A useful new group of compact and hardy late-flowering clematis hybrids, including the popular 'Romantika', were bred between 1979 and 1996 by this pioneering Estonian nurseryman and his wife, Aili, on their farm in Harjumaa, near the Baltic coast.

Klein, Carol

Warkleigh, in the heart of rural north Devon, is the home of Glebe Cottage Plants, the nursery and garden owned by this well-known plantswoman and television gardener. It offers a wide selection of garden-worthy perennials including many rarities. *Pulmonaria saccharata* 'Glebe Cottage Blue' is one of the plants named for it.

Knap Hill Nursery, Surrey

The oldest nursery of the Waterer family of Woking is believed to date back to the 1760s and still features in plant names. It was the second and third generation of Waterers at the nursery, a father and son both called Michael, who set the business on the road to success by their expert breeding of rhododendrons. By 1829, after the death of the elder Michael Waterer, his son bought a second nursery, at Bagshot. In the same year the famous gardener **J.C. Loudon**, visiting the nursery, was impressed by its fine collection of American plants (though he also found the place too weedy for his liking). For the rest of the 19th century Knap Hill went from strength to strength, opening a retail outlet in London's King's Road and developing a brisk export business to supply discerning gardeners in Europe and even America. By this time the nursery was in the care of another father-and-son team, both called Anthony Waterer, who continued to command the respect of the gardening world for their hardy rhododendrons and azaleas. The younger Anthony took over the business after his father's death in 1896 but, like many nurseries, Knap Hill suffered a decline in World War I and its era as an exclusively family-run business ended in the mid-1920s. However, subsequent generations of Waterers retained an interest and Donald Waterer, another rhododendron specialist, was instrumental in building up the nursery after World War II, remaining involved until he retired in 1976.

SOME KNAP HILL PLANTS

Chaenomeles × *superba* 'Knap Hill Scarlet'
Cotoneaster × *watereri* 'John Waterer'
Erica cinerea 'Knap Hill Pink'
Lonicera etrusca 'Donald Waterer'
Potentilla fruticosa 'Knap Hill Buttercup'
Rhododendron 'Knap Hill Apricot' and 'Knap Hill Red'
Rhododendron 'Michael Waterer'
Rhododendron 'Mrs Anthony Waterer'
Rhododendron 'Souvenir of Anthony Waterer'
Rhododendron campanulatum 'Knap Hill'
Rosa 'Mrs Anthony Waterer'
Spiraea japonica 'Anthony Waterer'

K

Knaut, Christoph (1638–1694)

This German botanist and doctor and his brother Christian (1654–1715) are remembered in the genus *Knautia*.

Knightshayes Court, Devon

Built from 1867 for the Heathcoat Amory family, who gave it to the National Trust in 1972, Knightshayes, near Tiverton, has long been famous for its fine ornamental garden, a blend of formal and wild, planted with a remarkable collection of trees, shrubs, perennials and naturalized spring bulbs. Plants named after the estate include *Carex elata* 'Knightshayes', *Gentiana asclepiadea* 'Knightshayes', *Erythronium revolutum* 'Knightshayes Pink' and *Anemone nemorosa* 'Knightshayes Vestal'. The huge walled Victorian kitchen garden has recently been restored.

Kniphof, Johann Hieronymus (1704–1763)

Kniphofia, the southern African genus commonly known as red-hot pokers, was named after this German professor of medicine at Erfurt.

Koehne, Bernhard (1848–1918)

A German botanist and author, Koehne was an expert on trees and shrubs. He helped to name some of the woody plants **E.H. Wilson** found in **China**. *Sorbus koehniana* is named for him.

Kolkwitz, Richard (1873–1956)

The shrub *Kolkwitzia amabilis* (beauty bush), first discovered by **Giuseppe Giraldi** and introduced to Britain in 1901 by **E.H. Wilson**, is named after this professor of botany in Berlin.

Kölreuter, Joseph (1733–1806)

The genus *Koelreuteria* is named for this German doctor and pioneering botanist, who was among the first scientists to experiment with hybridization and to understand the importance of insects in pollination.

Komarov, Vladimir (1869–1945)

Syringa komarovii commemorates this Russian botanist and explorer, whose journeys took him to Siberia, Manchuria and Korea in the 1890s. A native of St Petersburg, he collected many herbarium specimens for the botanic garden there.

Kos

Cyclamen coum is named for the Greek island of Kos, but is no longer believed to grow there. 'Cos' lettuce was found on the island and named after it.

Cyclamen coum

Kurume

A nursery in this town on the island of Kyushu in southern **Japan** was the origin of a successful group of compact, free-flowering evergreen azaleas first seen by **E.H. Wilson** in another nursery near Tokyo in 1914. Wilson recognized the plants as something special, and came back for more on his last trip to the Far East, in 1917–1918. He selected 50 plants to send to the **Arnold Arboretum**, prompting a breeding programme that resulted in numerous named hybrids. Many of the Kurume azaleas retain their star quality today.

K

La Mortola see Hanbury, Thomas

La Mortella, Italy
Laid out in an old stone quarry by the legendary garden designer Russell Page, La Mortella is on the island of Ischia, in the Bay of Naples. It is the garden of Lady Walton, widow of the English composer Sir William Walton, and was conceived as a memorial to him.

Ladakh
The name of *Clematis ladakhiana* comes from this remote, high plateau district in the far western Himalayas, part of Jammu and **Kashmir**. It was once an independent Buddhist kingdom.

Lamarck, Jean-Baptiste (1744–1829)
Amelanchier lamarckii is named after this neglected but visionary French botanist and zoologist. He coined the term invertebrate, and invented the idea of using a key as a process of elimination when identifying unknown species. His inspired early support for evolutionary theory was widely regarded as mere eccentricity.

Lambert, Aylmer (1761–1842)
The Australian genus *Lambertia* is named after this English botanist.

Lanarth, Cornwall
A number of well-established plants have connections with this early 20th-century garden and the nearby village of St Keverne. The garden was made by P.D. Williams (1865–1935), a cousin of **J.C. Williams** of **Caerhays Castle**. The cousins were both keen plantsmen and kept in close touch, sharing a fondness for the exotic new plants of the day, particularly flowering shrubs: rhododendrons, magnolias and camellias from the Far East were still novelties, and enthusiastic breeding programmes were producing ever more cultivars. The mild Cornish climate suited these plants, and they flourished in many favoured gardens, of which Lanarth was one. Its rhododendron collection, boosted by plants of Williams' own breeding, was one of the best in the country. Williams also hybridized daffodils, and there are still cultivars named after both Lanarth and St Keverne. The most familiar Lanarth plants are *Viburnum plicatum* f. *tomentosum* 'Lanarth', the award-winning *Hydrangea macrophylla* 'Lanarth White', and the choice *Magnolia campbellii* subsp. *mollicomata* 'Lanarth'. Plants selected by Williams and named for St Keverne include a heather, an escallonia and a viburnum.

Lancaster, Roy
The well-known contemporary plantsman, author and broadcaster Roy Lancaster began his career at Moss Bank Park, Bolton, moving on after five years to **Cambridge University Botanic Garden**. He joined **Hillier Nurseries** in 1962 and within two years was working at the Sir Harold Hillier Gardens and Arboretum, of which he became the first curator, in 1970. His numerous plant-hunting trips to **China** and Nepal are documented in some of his many books. He became known in the 1970s for his regional television broadcasts, then appeared for several years on the

BBC's *Gardeners' World*; he has also been a regular panellist on BBC Radio 4's *Gardeners' Question Time*. Awarded the RHS Victoria Medal of Honour in 1988, he features in the plant names *Hypericum lancasteri* and *Cotoneaster lancasteri*.

Lapham, Allen (1811–1875)

Dr Increase Allen Lapham was the full name of this self-taught American scholar who settled in Wisconsin and became an outstanding naturalist, cartographer and historian. Travelling west from New York with early colonizers, he made maps and recorded the plant life, geology and archaeology of the Midwest as it was before the arrival of white settlers. *Phlox divaricata* subsp. *laphamii* is named for him.

Lavallée, Pierre (1836–1884)

The ornamental hawthorn *Crataegus × lavalleei* 'Carrierei' is the most widely grown of several plants named after this French botanist.

Lawley, Frank and Marjorie see Herterton House

Lawson, Charles (1794–1873)

The Lawson cypress, *Chamaecyparis lawsoniana*, is named after this Scottish nurseryman and botanical author.

Laxton, Thomas (1830–1890)

A nurseryman with a keen interest in science, Laxton experimented with plant breeding and produced improved varieties of fruit and vegetables. His sons, who took over the business, concentrated on fruit, producing a number of now well-established apple varieties, including 'Laxton's Superb' and 'Lord Lambourne', and the strawberry 'Royal Sovereign', at their nurseries and trial grounds at Bedford and Sandy.

Lazistan

Iris lazica comes from this region on the south-eastern shore of the Black Sea, now partly in **Turkey** and partly in Georgia.

Le Vasterival see Sturdza

Lee, James (1715–1795)

A leading London nurseryman, Lee was a partner, with Lewis Kennedy, in the **Vineyard Nursery** at Hammersmith. He was a gifted scholar and botanist, corresponding with some of the great names of his day, including **Linnaeus** (whose work Lee translated), and exchanging seed with plantsmen in other countries. He also published *An Introduction to Botany*, in 1760.

Leichtlin, Max (1831–1910)

Leichtlin was the owner of a private botanic garden at Baden-Baden in Germany. Among the plants that especially interested him was *Clematis texensis*, which had been introduced into Europe in 1868. He improved it through selective breeding to achieve larger flowers, and crossed it with large-flowered hybrids.

Chamaecyparis lawsoniana

This eventually gave rise to a new type of clematis, with large, bright, bell-shaped flowers: 'Duchess of Albany' is such a cultivar still seen today, as is 'Sir Trevor Lawrence' (named after a president of the RHS). *Camassia leichtlinii* and *Lilium leichtlinii* are two of several plants that bear Leichtlin's name.

Philadelphus coronarius

Leiden University Botanical Garden, The Netherlands

This is one of the world's historic botanic gardens, notable among other things as the place where tulips were planted, by **Carolus Clusius**, in 1593. The hugely successful Dutch bulb industry later grew from small beginnings here, and it is fitting that the 16th-century garden has been restored and includes some of the bulbs that gave rise to 'tulipomania'.

Leigh, Norah (1884–1970)

The variegated *Phlox* 'Norah Leigh' has long been popular as a connoisseurs' plant. It is named after a keen gardener from the Cotswolds whose daughter married the nurseryman Joe Elliott, son of Clarence Elliott of **Six Hills Nursery** in Stevenage. It was Joe who propagated it and named it after her, and the same is true of the less well-known *Viola* 'Norah Leigh'.

Lemoine et fils, France

Victor Lemoine (1823–1911) and his son Emile (1862–1942) ran this important French nursery based in Nancy. Plants brought back from Japan by the German collector **Philipp von Siebold** were propagated here, and this was the first nursery to propagate hydrangeas from seed. Lemoine also developed many cultivars of other flowering shrubs, notably lilacs and philadelphus. Their herbaceous specialities included bearded irises, of which they produced more than 100 cultivars in the first half of the 19th century. Plants that still carry their name include *Malus* × *purpurea* 'Lemoinei', *Philadelphus* × *lemoinei* and *Syringa vulgaris* 'Madame Lemoine'.

Lenné, Peter Josef (1789–1866)

Magnolia × *soulangeana* 'Lennei' is named for this leading German landscape architect and botanist who designed a neoclassical garden at Sanssouci, near Potsdam, and Pfaueninsel, a magical landscaped island in the Havel Lakes near Berlin.

Leonardslee, West Sussex

Several rhododendrons are named after Leonardslee and the Loder family, who have built up an outstanding collection of rhododendrons and other choice woodland plants here. The 240-acre garden has several lakes, a rock garden, an alpine house and a resident colony of wallabies. It was Sir Edmund Loder (1849–1920) who introduced them; he began the woodland garden, in 1889, and was also the breeder of the Loderi group of rhododendron hybrids, known for their large, scented flowers, which were first seen here in 1907. From the 1940s to 1981 the garden was in the care of Sir Edmund's grandson, Sir Giles (1914–1999), and his wife, Lady Marie Loder (1914–2005). Both dedicated gardeners, and much involved in the **RHS**, they were the first couple each to be awarded the RHS Victoria Medal of Honour. The estate is now in the care of their younger son, Robin.

Leschenault de la Tour, Jean-Baptiste (1773–1826)

This well-travelled French botanist sailed with Captain Baudin in 1800 to **Australia**, where he found evergreen shrubs of the genus that was subsequently named *Leschenaultia*. He had to leave the ship through illness on the return journey but, having recovered, used the opportunity to make a prolonged exploration of Java. He later spent several years in India.

Lewis, Meriwether (1774–1809)

In 1803, President Thomas Jefferson of the United States launched an ambitious expedition with Captain Meriwether Lewis as one of its two leaders, and **William Clark** as the other. The aim was to travel across the vast tract of land newly acquired in the Louisiana Purchase, which had more than doubled the size of the United States. It was hoped that Lewis and Clark would find the 'missing link' in a possible route from coast to coast across **North America** by travelling up the Missouri River and then down the Columbia River. Their all-embracing brief was to make maps, describe flora and fauna, and study the native peoples

they encountered. Lewis and Clark eventually reached the Pacific coast, on a monumental adventure that lasted more than two years. Lewis, who died less than four years after their return, is commemorated in the North American alpine genus *Lewisia*. Bitterroot (*Lewisia rediviva*) was one of the plants discovered on the historic journey. Cooked, it was an important winter food crop for the native Americans, but the travellers found it most unpalatable. Other plants named for Lewis include *Mimulus lewisii* and *Philadelphus lewisii*. These and other plants found by Lewis and Clark were new to science: some, such as gaillardia, snowberry and the Oregon grape (*Mahonia aquifolium*), later became very familiar and widespread as garden plants.

Leyland, Christopher (d.1931)

The first specimens of the popular – and now notorious – Leyland cypress, × *Cupressocyparis leylandii*, were grown from a cone collected from a Nootka cypress (*Chamaecyparis nootkatensis*) by this Victorian botanist at his brother-in-law's home, Leighton Hall near Welshpool, in 1888. The trees were grown on in his own garden at Haggerston Castle in Northumberland. The other parent is thought to have been a Monterey cypress (*Cupressus macrocarpa*).

L'Haÿ-les-Roses, France

This town near Paris was renamed in 1910, in honour of its famous rose garden, La Roseraie du Val-de-Marne. The landscape architect **Edouard André** was commissioned in 1892 to design a garden for a collection of roses, to include some rescued from **Malmaison**, the legendary garden of the Empress Joséphine. The garden is the source of the name of the robust and popular rugosa rose, *Rosa* 'Roseraie de l'Haÿ'.

Libert, Marie (1782–1863)

The genus *Libertia* was named for this Belgian botanist who was an expert in liverworts.

Libertia formosa

Lindsay, Norah (1876–1948) and Nancy (d.1973)

The eccentric but reputedly brilliant Irish-born gardener and socialite Norah Lindsay moved in fashionable circles. Through her much-admired and influential garden, at the Manor House, Sutton Courtenay, she became an unofficial garden adviser to society figures of her day, such as the Astors at Cliveden. Her commissioned design projects included a parterre and shrub border for the Astors' friend Lord Lothian, at Blickling Hall, in Norfolk, and a parterre at Mottisfont. Her most lasting influence was probably at **Hidcote**, where, as a close friend of Lawrence Johnston, she had considerable input into the garden. Her sudden death upset Johnston's plans for her to move to Hidcote after his proposed move to France, but her daughter Nancy, a knowledgeable plantswoman, briefly took charge until the National Trust took over. Nancy kept in touch with Johnston after his move, and eventually inherited Serre de la Madone, his French Riviera garden and house, on his death in 1958. Plants named for Nancy

John Lindley (1799–1865)

Lindley's name is most often heard in connection with the **RHS** Lindley Library, which is named after him and began with his book collection, bought by the RHS after his death. Lindley's career is an exhausting roll-call of the most prestigious jobs in horticulture. He joined the RHS aged 23, having already worked in **Sir Joseph Banks**'s library. By the time he was 30 he was combining the job of assistant secretary to the RHS with the Chair of Botany at London University and the editorship of the *Botanical Register*. He was later also editor of the RHS *Journal* and of the *Pomological Magazine*, founder of the *Gardener's Chronicle*, director of the **Chelsea Physic Garden** and author of a dozen or so learned books. He instigated the first flower shows, and identified and named plants sent to the RHS by its collectors overseas, tackling the notoriously complex area of the classification of orchids, which became something of a speciality for him and resulted in two books. Plants named after him include *Aeonium lindleyi* and *Rhododendron lindleyi*, and many garden plants are still familiar to us under names that Lindley gave to them.

SOME PLANTS NAMED BY LINDLEY

Garrya elliptica
Jasminum nudiflorum
Lonicera fragrantissima
Rhododendron fortunei
Rosa xanthina

Carl Linnaeus (1707–1778)

Now universally known as the origin of modern botanical nomenclature, Linnaeus's book *Species Plantarum* was first published in 1753. His system of classification had gained wide acceptance by 1768, when it was used in the eighth edition of **Philip Miller**'s *Gardener's Dictionary*, but it was not officially adopted internationally until 1905. His revolutionary taxonomy gave every plant two names – genus and species. Plants were classified according to the structure and number of the flower's stamens and pistils.

> 'I am tempted to ask whether men are in their right minds who so desperately risk life and everything else through their love of collecting plants.'
> Carl Linnaeus, *Glory of the Scientist* (1737)

Linnaeus became professor of medicine at Uppsala, in Sweden, where he had been a student, in 1741. The post carried with it responsibility for the botanic garden, which had been damaged by a fire in 1702 and fallen into disrepair. He restored it, and it became both laboratory and classroom for him. It has been reconstructed, with the help of Linnaeus's own plans and plant lists, and visitors can see the garden as it was in his day.

Linnaeus named many plants after colleagues, friends and patrons and it seems strange that the only ones named after him are the obscure *Lobelia linnaeoides* and *Linnaea borealis* (twinflower). Linnaeus's self-deprecating comment on the renaming of the latter (which he found in Lapland in 1732) was: '*Linnaea* was named by the celebrated **Gronovius** and is a plant of Lapland, lowly, insignificant and disregarded, flowering but for a brief space – from Linnaeus, who resembles it.'

THE LINNEAN SOCIETY

The stated aim of this historic organization is 'the cultivation of the Science of Natural History in all its branches', and this has remained unchanged since its inception, in London, in 1788. It was founded by Sir James Edward Smith, who had bought Linnaeus's collections and library from his widow. With many distinguished scientists among its membership through the ages, the Linnean Society is a forum for research and discussion, as well as a repository of a large body of information on the biological sciences.

Lindsay include cultivars of colchicum, hosta, arum and iris.

Little Court, Hampshire
Ribes sanguineum 'Elkington's White' was found in Patricia and Andrew Elkington's garden here at Crawley, also named in *Ajuga reptans* 'Little Court Pink'.

Liss Forest Nursery see Catt, Peter

Lizé Frères, France
This nursery in Nantes was where the evergreen bigeneric hybrid × *Fatshedera lizei*, a cross between *Fatsia japonica* and the common ivy *Hedera helix*, was discovered by chance in 1910.

William Lobb (1809–1864) and Thomas Lobb (1817–1894)

The Lobb brothers, from Cornwall, marked the beginning of a new era in plant hunting in the mid-19th century. Most previous expeditions had been funded either by scientific establishments such as **Kew**, or by syndicates of wealthy garden owners. The Lobbs were the first collectors to be sent out by the **Veitch** nursery business, with the primarily commercial aim of obtaining large quantities of seed of desirable species. This was needed in order to grow plants cheaply in sufficient numbers to satisfy the burgeoning nursery market, which was now finding ready customers on a larger scale than ever before, with increasing industrialization, urbanization, and the rise of the middle classes.

South America was the chosen destination for the first Veitch expedition, in 1840–1844. William Lobb's prize on this trip was some 3,000 seeds of the monkey puzzle tree, *Araucaria araucana*, which he sent back from Chile. Veitch were soon able to sell seedlings of what became the most sought-after novelty of the day. William Lobb's trip was heralded a success, and more expeditions followed. His introductions from a subsequent trip to South America included *Berberis darwinii*, *Crinodendron hookerianum*, *Luma apiculata* and *Tropaeolum speciosum*. Later he had two extended stays in California, where he collected commercial quantities of seed of some of the conifers that had been discovered by **David Douglas**. On the first trip he was also involved in one of the most momentous plant discoveries ever: that of the giant sequoia or Wellingtonia, *Sequoiadendron giganteum*, in 1853. He lost no time in bringing seeds back to Veitch. They offered seedlings of the immense tree for sale the following year, and another Victorian fad was born.

Meanwhile the Veitch nursery had identified another gap in the market – exotic plants to fill the glasshouses that were springing up in the gardens of their wealthier clients. Thomas Lobb, inspired by his brother's early exploits, was keen to be a plant hunter too, and Veitch sent him east to Singapore and Java to explore the rainforests and bring back orchids, pitcher plants and ferns. By the early 20th century the growing market for these was already causing early conservation worries, but for Lobb, with unimaginable swathes of virgin habitat as his collecting ground, this was hardly an issue. He continued to collect until the 1860s, adding to his itinerary the Philippines, Borneo, India (where he was offered assistance by **Joseph Hooker,** but refused) and Burma. He came back with many conservatory, house and garden plants – the last including a good form of *Cryptomeria japonica* and the impressive giant lily *Cardiocrinum giganteum*. Unlike his brother, who died in California in middle age, Thomas returned from his travels to enjoy a long retirement in Cornwall.

Plants named after the Lobb brothers include *Rosa* 'William Lobb', *Ribes lobbii* and *Hydrangea lobbii*.

Lloyd, Christopher (1921–2006)

Widely respected as one of the most influential contemporary gardeners and gardening writers, Christopher Lloyd combined a lifetime's knowledge and experience of traditional horticulture with a creative and innovative approach to gardening. This rare blend of talents resulted in his world-renowned garden at **Great Dixter** and in over 20 authoritative and witty books and hundreds of articles. His magazine work, which began in 1953 with a piece in *Gardening Illustrated*, included a column in the *Guardian* every Saturday, occasional features for *Horticulture* magazine in the USA, and the weekly articles that he wrote for *Country Life* for 42 years until October 2005. His books span a period almost as long, from the late 1950s. *The Well-Tempered Garden* (1970) is often quoted as his classic work, but more recent, and offering an equally compelling mix of fresh ideas and expert opinion, are *Meadows* (2004) and *Succession Planting for Adventurous Gardeners* (2005) – both written in his 80s. *Gazania* 'Christopher Lloyd' seems to be the only plant named after him, though others are named after Dixter, and he introduced the bronze-leaved celandine *Ranunculus ficaria* 'Brazen Hussy', which he found locally in the wild. He was awarded the RHS Victoria Medal of Honour in 1978, and the OBE in 2000.

L'Obel, Mathias de (1538–1616)

The genus *Lobelia* was named after this Belgian botanist and physician. Born in Lille, he became William I of

Lobelia

Orange's physician for a time, later travelling to England, where he was botanist to King James I. His book, *Stirpium Adversaria Nova*, a study of some 1,300 plants he had found in France and England, was written with Petro Pena in 1570 and is an important early botanical work. It emphasized the importance of careful observation and discussed the identification and classification of plants by their leaves. Other plants named after him include *Ulmus × hollandica* 'Lobel' and *Acer lobelii*.

Löbner, Max (1900s)

Magnolia × loebneri – a cross between *Magnolia kobus* and *Magnolia stellata* – is named after its breeder, Max Löbner, who worked at the botanic gardens of Dresden and Bonn for many years.

Lochinch Castle, Wigtownshire

One of the best garden buddleias, *Buddleja* 'Lochinch' is named after Lochinch Castle near Stranraer, in the far south-west of Scotland.

Loddiges of Hackney, London

One of the most famous and prolific of the early London nurseries, Loddiges was founded by a German, John Busch, around 1760. It was taken over in 1771 by the Dutchman Conrad Loddiges (1743–1826), who went on to acquire additional land and build up the business, eventually handing it on to his sons. The nursery went from strength to strength. It was able to plant its own arboretum in 1816, and regularly published a beautifully illustrated catalogue and magazine, *The Botanical Cabinet*, which ran from 1817 to 1833, to advertise the huge range of plants on offer. The nursery became one of the first commercial growers of orchids, as well as a leading supplier of hardy garden shrubs, trees and herbaceous plants: by 1818 Loddiges' rose list alone numbered more than 1,500 varieties. New treasures were continually arriving from plant-collecting expeditions around this time, and Loddiges had many eager customers waiting to be the first to plant these novelties in their gardens. The nursery had particular connections with new plants from **North America** discovered by William Bartram

and later **David Douglas**. Loddiges eventually closed after auctioning off its entire stock of orchids in 1856.

Loder, Giles and Marie see **Leonardslee**

Loder, Gerald see **Wakehurst Place**

Logan Botanic Garden, Wigtownshire
The Royal Botanic Garden **Edinburgh** is responsible for this remarkable exotic garden set on a peninsula in south-west Scotland. Many of the plants are from the southern hemisphere: tree ferns, cordylines, eucalyptus, salvias and fuchsias all thrive, with the help of the Gulf Stream to temper the climate. The woodland garden has areas devoted to the plants of Australia and Chile, while other features include a gunnera bog and a historic garden with peat walls. Constructed in 1927 to grow some of

L

Loddon Nursery, Berkshire

Named after a river that runs into the Thames near Twyford, Loddon Nursery's name has survived in an amazing number of plants that have remained popular for more than 50 years. The 7-acre nursery at Twyford was started in 1920, as his first solo venture, by Thomas Carlile, who had previously worked at other well-known nurseries, including Waterer's (see

SOME LODDON PLANTS
Anchusa azurea 'Loddon Royalist'
Campanula lactiflora 'Loddon Anna'
Helianthus 'Loddon Gold'
Heliopsis helianthoides var. *scabra* 'Light of Loddon'
Lavandula angustifolia 'Loddon Blue' and 'Loddon Pink'
Monarda 'Loddon Crown'
Veronica prostrata 'Loddon Blue'

Knap Hill) and **Perry**'s. His success was such that he could soon claim to be offering more plants that held the RHS Award of Merit than any other nursery. Carlile brought up his family there, and one of his daughters joined him in the business. It was she who selected the pink campanula that has proved one of the most enduring Loddon plants: *Campanula lactiflora* 'Loddon Anna', which Carlile eventually named after his granddaughter. *Delphinium* 'Mrs T. Carlile' is named for his wife.

the newly arrived Chinese plants of the time, this was completely restored in 2002–2003. Plants named after the garden include a fuchsia, a form of phygelius and a rhododendron.

London, George see Brompton Park Nursery

Longstock Park Gardens and Nursery, Hampshire

Part of the John Lewis Partnership's Leckford Estate, the water garden here on the River Test near Stockbridge was created by John Spedan Lewis after World War II. An oasis of beautiful planting surrounds a chain of lakes and streams: candelabra primulas, blue poppies, gunneras and ferns all thrive here. The nearby nursery, a treasure trove of unusual plants, has a walled garden and holds National Collections of *Buddleja* and *Clematis viticella*.

Longwood Gardens, Pennsylvania

One of the major gardens of **North America**, Longwood began as an arboretum in 1798 and was bought in 1906 by the industrialist Pierre S. du Pont. Extending to more than 1,000 acres, it attracts nearly 1 million visitors each year to see its outdoor and indoor gardens and attend the many horticultural events that take place here. Longwood also has a long tradition of plant hunting all over the world, celebrating its 50th expedition in 2006.

Lonitzer, Adam (1528–1586)

The honeysuckle genus *Lonicera* is named after this Frankfurt physician and naturalist.

Lord, Tony

A leading authority in the world of plants and gardening, Tony Lord is a horticultural author, editor and photographer, and was gardens adviser for the National Trust until 1989. An expert on plant nomenclature, he edited the first ten editions of the *Plant Finder*, and is now consultant editor. His books include *The Encyclopedia of Planting Combinations*, *Designing with Roses* and *Best Borders,* and he was the photographer for *Gardening at Sissinghurst* and *Rosemary Verey's Making of a Garden*. He was awarded the RHS Victoria Medal of Honour in 2005.

Loudon, Jane (1807–1858)

A pioneering gardening writer, Jane Loudon was author of the bestselling *Gardening for Ladies*, published in 1840, and a number of other books on gardening, several of which were intended for a female readership. Although her marriage to **John Claudius Loudon** (see below) was a famous horticultural partnership, it lasted only 13 years, from their meeting and marriage in 1830 until John Claudius Loudon's death.

Loudon, John Claudius (1783–1843)

Loudon's unique contribution to the plant world was as a hugely prolific author of gardening books and as the publisher of *The Gardener's Magazine*, the first regular gardening periodical, established in 1826. His books were a mine of information for those who suddenly found themselves dragged into the 19th-century boom in gardening.

He explained how to do everything from managing glasshouses to laying out public squares. His most famous book, the *Encyclopaedia of Gardening* (1822), ran to nine editions in 21 years. Like his more ambitious, eight-volume tree book, *Arboretum et Fruticetum Britannicum* (1838), it contains much information that is still relevant today.

Lucombe & Pince, Devon

William Lucombe founded his Exeter nursery in 1720 and it became Lucombe & Pince about 100 years later, remaining in the same family for most of the 19th century. Introductions from the nursery include the Lucombe oak, *Quercus × hispanica* 'Lucombeana', the white passion-flower *Passiflora caerulea* 'Constance Elliott', and many fuchsias and glasshouse plants.

Ludlow, Frank (1885–1972)

This British traveller and collector is nearly always mentioned with **George Sherriff**, with whom he shared many Himalayan expeditions. The two first met in 1929 in Turkestan, where Sherriff was Vice-Consul. Their first trip, to Tibet, came four years later and was followed by further expeditions as they combed inaccessible regions of the Himalayas in search of choice plants, returning with dozens of rhododendrons, primulas and other new introductions. *Paeonia delavayi* var. *ludlowii* was one. After their last trip, in 1949, Ludlow worked at **Kew**.

Lyall, David (1817–1895)

Like many plant collectors, Lyall travelled for much of his life as a surgeon in the navy, having gained experience as a newly qualified young doctor on a voyage to Greenland aboard a whaling ship. His first naval voyage was a scientific expedition to Antarctica in 1839, under Sir James Ross. His brief included plant collecting, and he succeeded in finding some 1,500 herbarium specimens on the trip. He later found himself in **New Zealand**, attached to a coastal survey expedition. Here he continued to collect plants: notable discoveries were *Parahebe lyallii* and *Ranunculus lyallii* (which, sadly, Lyall never saw in flower). Subsequent surveying trips took him to the Arctic again, and to Canada, where he worked with the team surveying the boundary of British Columbia, a task that enabled him to record vegetation zones and to return with another impressive herbarium collection. Plants named for him include *Hoheria lyallii*, *Anemone lyallii* and *Penstemon lyallii*.

Lyon, John (1765–1814)

Born in Scotland, Lyon went to America and worked in the Philadelphia garden of **William Hamilton** before becoming a plant collector, mainly in the southern States, in the early 1800s.

Lyte, Henry (1529–1607)

Lyte was a scholar and antiquarian whose *Niewe Herball or Historie of Plantes* (1578) was a translation of **Rembert Dodoens**. Lyte's home, Lytes Cary in Somerset, still stands but unfortunately the botanic garden he made there has been lost.

Maack, Richard (1825–1886)

A Russian professor in the remote eastern Siberian city of Irkutsk, Maack undertook plant-hunting expeditions in eastern Asia. Plants commemorating him include *Euonymus maackii*, *Lonicera maackii* and *Prunus maackii*.

McBeath, Ron

Ron McBeath is a contemporary gardener, nurseryman and plant hunter with a specialist nursery at Lamberton in Berwickshire, Scotland. He spent more than 20 years at the Royal Botanic Garden **Edinburgh**, and has undertaken many plant-hunting expeditions in **China** and the Himalayas. Plants named after him include *Persicaria affinis* 'Ron McBeath' and *Potentilla nepalensis* 'Ron McBeath'.

McGredy, Sam

Before he moved his business to **New Zealand** in 1972, this world-famous rosarian from Portadown, in Northern Ireland, was the fourth Sam McGredy to run the family rose nursery established there in the 1890s by his great-grandfather, who died in 1926. More than 100 rose cultivars were bred by Sam McGredy IV, who took over the business in 1952, when he was only 20. There are roses named for many members of the McGredy family.

MacKenzie, Bill (1904–1995)

The yellow-flowered *Clematis* 'Bill MacKenzie' is named after this former curator of the **Chelsea Physic Garden** who had also worked at the Royal Botanic Garden **Edinburgh**.

Macleaya

MacLeay, Alexander (1767–1848)

This Scottish entomologist was secretary of the Linnean Society (see **Linnaeus**) from 1798 until he emigrated to **Australia** in 1825 to become Colonial Secretary of New South Wales, a post that carried responsibility for Sydney's botanic garden. The herbaceous perennial *Macleaya* bears his name.

M'Mahon, Bernard (1775–1816)

In 1796 M'Mahon emigrated from Ireland to America, where he founded a nursery in Philadelphia in 1802 and published the first American practical gardening book, the *American Gardener's Calendar*, in 1806. It includes a list of plants that he sold – a useful record of what was being grown in America at the time. M'Mahon was clearly a well-respected plantsman, for he was a major supplier of plants to **Thomas Jefferson** for his estate at Monticello, and it was to M'Mahon that Jefferson entrusted seeds of new plants found on **Lewis** and **Clark**'s pioneering expedition to the west coast. One of them became the first species in a newly named genus: *Mahonia aquifolium*.

Madagascar

This 1,600-mile-long island off the east coast of **Africa** is top of the list of the many islands that have extensive

M

endemic floras: its plant life numbers some 10,000 species, of which 8,000 occur nowhere else. Gardeners in temperate climates are most likely to encounter the tender patio plant *Plectranthus madagascariensis* and

Catharanthus roseus

perhaps the glasshouse shrub *Buddleja madagascariensis*. Another Madagascar native, the rosy periwinkle *Catharanthus roseus*, is grown as a bedding plant or houseplant, and is also used in the pharmaceutical industry as an anti-cancer agent.

Madeira

Situated on ancient trading routes, the island of Madeira has been on the itineraries of long-haul ships since earliest times. Plants from **Africa**, **North** and **South America**, Asia and Europe have often reached temperate gardens via these ships and the sailors, scientists, plant collectors and missionaries who travelled on them. Plant names connected with the island include *Argyranthemum maderense* (actually native to Lanzarote and Fuerteventura rather than Madeira), *Genista maderensis*, *Hedera maderensis* and *Ilex × altaclerensis* 'Maderensis'. *Geranium maderense*, now endangered in the island's laurel forests, has become a popular, though tender, garden plant.

Magellan, Ferdinand (1480–1521)

A famous Portuguese navigator, Magellan was not in fact the first person to circumnavigate the world, but he did lead the first expedition to attain this historic goal, in 1522. Magellan himself travelled only as far as the Philippines, where he was killed in a fight. A number of South American plants are named after him (or after the straits that bear his name): they include *Fuchsia magellanica*, the diminutive and little-known *Gunnera magellanica*, *Elymus magellanicus*, *Oxalis magellanica* and *Primula magellanica*.

Magnol, Pierre (1638–1715)

Linnaeus named *Magnolia* after this distinguished Frenchman, who was physician to Louis XIV and professor of botany in his native city, **Montpellier**, where he was also in charge of the botanic garden.

Makino, Tomitaro (1862–1957)

This pioneering Japanese botanist and taxonomist named and described many Japanese plants and produced an illustrated flora of **Japan**. *Gentiana makinoi*, *Polystichum makinoi*, *Sedum makinoi* and *Rhododendron makinoi* are among the plants that are named for him.

Malmaison, France

The country retreat of Napoleon's wife, the Empress Joséphine (1763–1814), Malmaison has many resonances for gardeners, particularly for rose and carnation enthusiasts. Joséphine had a passion for plants, and treasured extravagant collections of roses, begonias and dahlias at Malmaison, near Paris, where the garden was as much a focus of attention as the house.

M

She was the first major collector of roses anywhere, and by the end of her life, her collection of over 1,000 plants included all the known varieties. *Rosa* 'Souvenir de la Malmaison' and *Dianthus* 'Souvenir de la Malmaison' are among the plants named after the garden. Joséphine's maiden name was de la Pagerie, and the lovely but rather tender Chilean bellflower, *Lapageria rosea*, was named in her honour.

Margaret, Crown Princess of Sweden (1882–1920)

The **David Austin** rose Crown Princess Margareta ('Auswinter') is named for this granddaughter of Queen Victoria who wrote gardening articles and books.

Maries, Charles (1850–1902)

Maries, a foreman at the **Veitch** nursery, spent three years in the late 1870s collecting plants in **Japan** and **China**, later settling in India. Important finds include *Hamamelis mollis* and *Viburnum plicatum* f. *tomentosum* 'Mariesii'. Among other plants that bear his name are *Hydrangea macrophylla* 'Mariesii' and *Platycodon grandiflorus* 'Mariesii'. He was one of the first recipients of the RHS Victoria Medal of Honour, in 1897.

Markham, Ernest (1881–1937)

Markham joined **William Robinson**'s team of gardeners at **Gravetye Manor** in 1910, later becoming head gardener there. He had a special interest in clematis, and his book on them was published in 1935, the year Robinson died. Subsequently, Markham became increasingly interested in breeding and

showing clematis. After his death, the Gravetye clematis collection, which had originated with the French nursery of **Morel et fils**, passed to Rowland Jackman. He gave the name 'Ernest Markham' to a clematis that Markham had raised and called simply 'Red Seedling'. There is also a macropetala type of clematis called 'Markham's Pink'.

Marwood Hill Gardens, Devon

Magnolia sprengeri 'Marwood Spring' and *Tulbaghia* Marwood seedling originated in this garden near Barnstaple, which has National Collections of *Iris ensata* cultivars, *Astilbe* and *Tulbaghia*.

Mason, Maurice (1912–1993)

Begonia masoniana and *Rodgersia pinnata* 'Maurice Mason' are named after this East Anglian farmer, an amateur plantsman and collector with a particular interest in begonias, cacti, pineapples and other glasshouse plants. He was known for his varied and impressive entries at the Chelsea Flower Show and other **RHS** shows for more than 35 years. He received the RHS Victoria Medal of Honour in 1960.

Mathew, Brian

A leading contemporary botanist and taxonomist, Brian Mathew has special expertise in bulbs and hellebores, and has written books on both. He has worked at **Wisley** and **Kew**, and has been editor of *Curtis's Botanical Magazine*. He was awarded the RHS Victoria Medal of Honour in 1991, and the MBE, for services to horticulture and botanical science, in 2005. *Crocus*

Francis Masson (1741–1805)

The first in a long line of **Kew** plant hunters, Masson is chiefly noted for his intrepid expeditions in southern **Africa**, which resulted in the introduction of many prized exotic plants not previously seen in northern gardens. Born in Aberdeen, Scotland, he was apprenticed at Kew and distinguished himself sufficiently to be chosen, in 1772, as the first government-sponsored plant collector to be sent on a major expedition. The Cape was to be his destination, and his captain, on the *Endeavour*, James Cook. In South Africa Masson met **Carl Thunberg**, and the two travelled through the veldt and into the Blue Mountains. Despite hardships and setbacks ranging from heat exhaustion and shortage of water to icy storms and wild animals, Masson sent many seeds, bulbs and herbarium specimens back to **Kew**, and returned safely to England in 1775. He wrote delightedly to **Linnaeus** that he had 'added upwards of 400 new species to his Majesties collection of living plants'. They included *Protea repens* (the first protea in Europe, which took six years to flower), many different Cape heaths, pelargoniums, gladioli, irises, lobelias and kniphofias, as well as tender succulents and the extraordinary bird of paradise flower, *Strelitzia reginae*. A cycad that Masson brought back from this trip still grows in the palm house at Kew.

His next adventure, in 1778, took him to **North America** via **Madeira**, the Canary Islands and the Azores to the West Indies. Echiums and *Senecio cineraria* were among the plants he sent back to Kew on the early part of the voyage, but in Grenada he was taken prisoner during the French revolutionary war. Eventually released, he moved on to St Lucia, only to lose his new plant collection and his journal in a hurricane. He returned home in 1781, but within two years he was off to Portugal and North Africa, then, in 1785, to South Africa again, where he spent ten years exploring the interior and nurturing his finds in his Cape Town garden. This trip yielded the arum lily, *Zantedeschia aethiopica*.

Masson's last voyage took him across the Atlantic again. After surviving awful weather and two attacks by pirates, the passengers arrived in New York. From here Masson went to Canada, where he died – but not before he had sent more new plants, including *Trillium grandiflorum*, as his last offering to Kew.

M

mathewii is a new autumn-flowering species he found in **Turkey** in 1992.

Matteuci, Carlo (1811–1868)

Matteuccia struthiopteris, the stately woodland plant known as the ostrich fern or shuttlecock fern, is the most widely grown member of the genus named after this Italian physician.

Mattioli, Pierandrea (1501–1577)

The genus *Matthiola* (stocks) takes its name from this Italian botanist and writer from Siena. His book on medicinal herbs, based on the work of **Dioscorides**, was in circulation for many years, and was translated into several languages.

Carl Maximowicz (1827–1891)

One of **Russia**'s most important botanists and plant collectors, Maximowicz combined an adventurous plant-hunting career with lifelong work at St Petersburg's important botanic garden, where he became principal botanist and, eventually, director. He corresponded regularly with the **Hookers** at **Kew**, and was the leading authority of his day on the flora of eastern Asia. His first trip there was by accident: a Russian ship on which he had travelled to South America, in 1853, as botanist and collector on a world voyage, was recalled from Honolulu the following year at the start of the Crimean War. The ship, now with priorities other than exploring, was sent straight to the Gulf of Tartary, and Maximowicz found himself unceremoniously dumped on the coast of Manchuria. By 1857 he had travelled back, along the Amur River and through Siberia, to St Petersburg, having amassed an impressive collection of largely unknown plants on the way. Two years later he began another long trip, to Manchuria and **Japan**, returning via the Cape of Good Hope in 1864 and settling down at the botanic garden to a life of sorting, classifying and writing about his collections and those of other travellers.

SOME MAXIMOWICZ PLANTS
Acer maximowiczii
Allium maximowiczii
Ampelopsis brevipedunculata var. maximowiczii
Betula maximowicziana
Euonymus maximowiczianus
Geranium maximowiczii
Primula maximowiczii
Prunus maximowiczii
Tulipa linifolia Maximowiczii Group
Weigela maximowiczii

M

Menzies, Archibald (1754–1842)

Menzies travelled thousands of miles as a naval surgeon, to the Americas and beyond, including one trip round the world. He had been apprenticed as a young man at the Royal Botanic Garden **Edinburgh** and had collected plants in the Scottish Highlands, but was not primarily a plant hunter. However, he is known for one of the most famous (though unsubstantiated) plant-collecting stories, involving the introduction of the monkey-puzzle tree, *Araucaria araucana*. The story goes that edible nuts from this distinctive tree were served as dessert at a diplomatic banquet that Menzies was attending in Chile in 1795, and he pocketed some of them and raised plants from their seeds on the voyage home. It is mainly for his discoveries of American plants that Menzies is remembered by botanists and gardeners, but many of these plants were actually introduced later by others, notably **David Douglas**. However, his records of plant discoveries were extensive, and he was the first to find the coast redwood, *Sequoia sempervirens*, in 1794, as well as various maples, rhododendrons, pines and other conifers. The plants he

Araucaria araucana

André Michaux (1746–1803)

Had he lived in a less turbulent age, Michaux may well have become a household name on both sides of the Atlantic, for he travelled many thousands of miles and collected hundreds of new plants. However, many never reached the gardens for which they were intended, but instead were lost or destroyed in the turmoil of the Middle East, or of France at the time of the Revolution. Michaux nevertheless played an important role in the spread of garden plants around the world, especially in **North America**.

Ginkgo biloba

The son of a French farmer, Michaux became a botanist at the Jardin du Roi in **Paris**. He cut his plant-collecting teeth in the botanically rich but often dangerous Middle East, enduring hardships and disasters such as robbery and freak weather, but returning with many plants, including those that were to become known as *Michauxia campanuloides* and *Dionysia michauxii*. His next trip, in 1785, with his 15-year-old son François, was across the Atlantic. He was sent in search of new American trees, particularly species that could be grown in France for much-needed timber for shipbuilding. Michaux spent 11 years in North America, undertaking ambitious plant-collecting trips over a huge area, from the Bahamas and Florida to Quebec and Hudson's Bay, and west to the Mississippi and Illinois rivers. He is said to have sent 60,000 live plants back to France, many of them raised in nurseries he set up for the purpose: one near New York and the other in Carolina. He also successfully introduced into American gardens some of the native plants he had discovered, as well as European and Asian plants not yet seen in America: sweet bay (*Laurus nobilis*), pomegranate (*Punica granatum*), *Ginkgo biloba*, *Rhamnus alaternus* and *Camellia japonica* to name a few. On his eventual return to France, he was distraught to find that many of his treasured plants had suffered neglect, damage or destruction in the aftermath of the Revolution. He had no money to return to America, so joined a sponsored voyage bound for Australia instead. He left the ship at **Madagascar**, where he eventually died, probably of malaria. His memorial consists of numerous plants in American gardens, as well as a book on American oaks and a more comprehensive account of American trees, *Flora Boreali Americana*.

did introduce were significant, including as they did not only the monkey-puzzle tree but also *Ribes speciosum* and the tree lupin, *Lupinus arboreus*. The shrub genus *Menziesia*, from North America and Asia, is named in his honour, and other Menzies plants include *Arbutus menziesii*, *Nothofagus menziesii*, *Sanguisorba menziesii*, *Nemophila menziesii*, *Delphinium menziesii* and the Douglas fir, *Pseudotsuga menziesii*.

Meserve, Kathleen (1906–1999)
The hardy 'blue holly' hybrids *Ilex* ×
meserveae were bred by this Long Island
gardener on the windowsill of her
home in the 1950s.

Mesny, William (1842–1919)
Resembling winter jasmine but
flowering in summer, the Chinese
shrubby climber *Jasminum mesnyi*
was introduced into cultivation by
E.H. Wilson but was originally found
in 1880 by Mesny, a remarkable
adventurer from the Channel Islands.
He ran away to sea at the age of 12
and went to **China**, where he began a
new life. He was made a general in the
Chinese Imperial Army, and spent his
retirement editing a weekly magazine,
Mesny's Chinese Miscellany.

M

Messel, Leonard see Nymans

Meyer, Frank (1875–1918)
Syringa meyeri was discovered in **China**
by this Dutch-born American gardener
and botanist whose pioneering work for
the US government entailed travelling
the world collecting mainly new varieties
of economic plants – such as timber trees,
fruits and cereals – to use in breeding
programmes. He is believed to have
been the first Westerner to see *Ginkgo
biloba* in the wild, and the popular shrub
Kolkwitzia amabilis is among the plants
he introduced into the USA.

Michaux, André see page 129

Miller, Philip (1691–1771)
When the society doctor and
benefactor **Sir Hans Sloane** appointed

the former Pimlico florist Philip
Miller as curator of the **Chelsea Physic
Garden**, he placed him firmly at the
centre of a world full of exciting new
plant discoveries. Miller received seeds
and plants from collectors in many
countries, corresponding with them
and gathering information as well as
invaluable first-hand experience of the
new plants and how to grow them.
He turned this great opportunity to
the advantage of plantsmen present
and future by producing one of the
most important gardening books
ever: *The Gardener's Dictionary*
(1731). It appeared in a number of
updated editions during his lifetime,
was translated into several European
languages, and remains useful today.

Misczenko, P.I. (1869–1938)
The spring bulb *Scilla mischtschenkoana*
is named after this Russian botanist.

**Missouri Botanical Garden,
St Louis**
As the meeting place of three great
North American rivers, St Louis was
the gateway to the unexplored West
and the hub of an area of strategic
importance to early travellers and plant
hunters. **Michaux** explored the area
in 1795 and **Nuttall** in 1810, with
the expedition of **Lewis** and **Clark**
in between. It was therefore a fitting
home for America's first botanic garden,
established in 1859 by Henry Shaw, a
wealthy English settler who had built
a profitable cutlery business. **Asa Gray**
and **William Hooker** advised on the
garden, as did local doctor and botanist
George Engelmann. Today there are

more than 30 different gardens here, celebrating both native and exotic plants. The garden's research and educational programmes are among the world leaders in their field.

Mitchell, Alan (1922–1995)

Mitchell's work in various arboreta complemented his travels around the British Isles to make him the leading authority on temperate trees. His *Trees of Britain and Northern Europe* (1974), a Collins Field Guide, was the standard work on its subject for many years. This distinguished dendrologist's detailed records of the history of particular tree species, incorporating his notes on individual specimens, were published posthumously in the companion volume *Trees of Britain* (1996). He founded the Tree Register as a charity in 1988, and recorded details of over 100,000 trees during his lifetime.

Mlokosiewicz, Ludwik (1831–1909)

Paeonia mlokosewitschii – the peony with the most notoriously unpronounceable of all plant names (and therefore usually known as Molly the Witch) – was discovered by, and named for, this Polish aristocrat whose interest in plant collecting began in his 20s when he was stationed in the **Caucasus** with the Russian army. He spent much of his later life in that botanically rich region where, as the official inspector of forests, he made frequent trips into the mountain wilderness, collecting plants and other specimens, which he sent back to the museums of **Russia**. He also travelled in Persia. *Primula juliae* is named after

Julia, his daughter, who discovered it in the south-eastern Caucasus in 1900, and sent plants to **Oxford University Botanic Garden**.

Moerheim Nursery, The Netherlands

This influential nursery, founded in 1888 by the distinguished plant breeder Bonne Ruys, was the home of *Helenium* 'Moerheim Beauty', *Hosta* 'Moerheim', *Scabiosa caucasica* 'Moerheim Blue' and numerous other classic perennials. The respected garden designer Mien Ruys, daughter of Bonne, used many of her father's plants in her naturalistic contemporary design schemes. *Impatiens glandulifera* 'Mien Ruys' is named after her, and *Phlox paniculata* 'Mia Ruys' after her sister.

Monardes, Nicolas (1493–1588)

The genus *Monarda* is named after this early Spanish botanist and doctor who was physician to Philip II of Spain. He became one of the first Europeans to describe American plants after his son Dionisio emigrated to Peru. The English translation of his book, published in 1577, was *Joyfull Newes out of the Newe Founde Worlde*. It described sunflowers, tobacco and many medicinal plants.

Monet, Claude see Giverny

Monksilver Nursery, Cambridgeshire

Narcissus 'Monksilver' and *Pulmonaria* 'Monksilver' are named after this plantsman's nursery at Cottenham, near Cambridge. Run by Joe Sharman and Alan Leslie, it specializes in pulmonarias, variegated plants, sedges and bulbs, including snowdrops.

Monticello see Jefferson, Thomas

Montpellier, France
The medical faculty at Montpellier was the focus of much early study of plants, and botany was first recognized as an academic subject here, under the direction of Guillaume Rondelet. Many well-known botanists studied at Montpellier, including **Clusius**. The specific epithet *monspeliensis* refers to Montpellier and its botanic garden, as in *Cistus monspeliensis*.

Morel et fils, France
Francisque Morel (1849–1925) was a nurseryman and clematis breeder in Lyon. His introductions around the turn of the 20th century included some of the most popular clematis cultivars such as 'Ville de Lyon', 'Comtesse de Bouchaud' and 'Perle d'Azur'.

Morin, René (d.1657) and Pierre (d.1658)
The genus *Morina* commemorates these notable French nurseryman brothers, who specialized in breeding bigger and better spring bulbs, such as hyacinths and anemones, for use in the fashionable parterres of the time. They exchanged letters with the **John Tradescants**.

Morris, Cedric (1889–1982)
This legendary artist and plantsman lived and gardened at Benton

End, at Hadleigh in Suffolk. The garden he created there from 1940 was inspired by Monet's garden at **Giverny**, in France. Sir Cedric was especially known as a breeder of irises, raising several hundred seedlings every year. These are the subject of some of his most famous paintings, such as *Iris Seedlings* (1943), in the Tate collection. Sir Cedric's garden and plants, and his propagation work, were an important influence on **Beth Chatto**, whose nursery still offers a number of plants raised by him, including *Narcissus* 'Cedric Morris' and *Papaver orientale* 'Cedric Morris'. A rose and a pink are also named after him, as well as several irises with 'Benton' in their name.

Moser et fils, France
Jean-Jacques Moser (1846–1934) founded this nursery in Versailles, which introduced one of the most famous of all clematis in 1897 and named it 'Nelly Moser'. *Clematis* 'Marcel Moser', a similar cultivar raised there, is also still available.

Mottisfont Abbey, Hampshire
This National Trust property on the River Test, near Romsey, is known to gardeners mainly for its lovely walled garden, where **Graham Stuart Thomas** assembled a National Collection of old shrub roses in the 1970s. More than 300 labelled varieties are set among herbaceous planting and formal evergreens, filling the air with summer perfume. All date from the 19th century or earlier, and

Morina longifolia

some were acquired from a famous earlier rose garden, that of the Empress Joséphine at **Malmaison** in France.

Mount Hope Nurseries, New York

This influential nursery business was founded in Rochester, New York State, in 1840, by **Patrick Barry** and **George Ellwanger**. The business began with fruit trees, which always remained a speciality, and eventually grew to be one of the USA's largest and most notable nurseries. By 1851 there were several regional branches, including one in Toronto. Mount Hope was known for introducing many new ornamental plants into cultivation, and in 1900 won a gold medal at the Paris Exhibition for its display of 118 varieties of pear. It eventually closed down in 1918, when the plant collection and the site were given to the city of Rochester. Perhaps surprisingly, there seems today to be only one commercially available plant named after the nursery: *Hosta* 'Mount Hope'.

Mount Stewart, County Down

The mild climate of this important and large garden near Belfast, in Northern Ireland, encouraged the planting of a huge range of the exotic new plants of the day: trees and shrubs in the 19th-century outer landscape garden, with flamboyant herbaceous colour in the 1920s formal gardens near the house. Created by the 7th Marchioness of Londonderry, they are beautifully maintained today by the National Trust. Plants associated with the garden include *Agapanthus* 'Mount Stewart', *Geranium clarkei* 'Mount Stewart' and *Iris* 'Mount Stewart Black'.

Mount Stuart, Isle of Bute

An impressive Victorian pinetum and an arboretum of internationally endangered coniferous trees, established in recent years in association with the Royal Botanic Garden **Edinburgh**, are among the attractions of this great landscape garden. It has been in the family of the Stuarts, Marquesses of Bute and influential gardeners, since the 1700s.

Mount Usher, County Wicklow

The large *Eucryphia* × *nymansensis* 'Mount Usher', in its summer flowering season, is a star attraction of this wonderful woodland garden whose favourable microclimate allows tender and unfamiliar plants to thrive, including many from the southern hemisphere, such as eucalyptus. *Crocosmia* × *crocosmiiflora* 'Mount Usher' is also named after the garden.

Moyes, Revd E.J. (1800s–1900s)

Rosa moyesii is named after this missionary in western **China** who met **E.H. Wilson** on his travels there. Wilson introduced the rose into Europe in 1903.

Mueller, Ferdinand von (1825–1896)

An Austrian who emigrated to **Australia** at the age of 17, von Mueller trained as a chemist and later became a leading botanist and plant hunter there. He covered huge distances overland on expeditions into the remote mountain ranges and river valleys of Victoria

M

and later travelled extensively in the north of the country. He discovered thousands of new plants, embarking on a huge project, *Flora Australiensis*, which aimed to catalogue them all in its seven volumes.

Muncaster Castle, Cumbria

This historic garden is home to an extensive collection of species rhododendrons, mainly introduced in the 1920s and 1930s by **Frank Kingdon Ward**, **Frank Ludlow** and **George Sherriff**. Magnolias, maples, camellias and hydrangeas complete the transformation of the Lakeland fells into a Himalayan paradise. Plants named for the garden include *Acer palmatum* 'Muncaster' and several old rhododendron cultivars, including 'Muncaster Mist'.

Munstead Wood see Jekyll, Gertrude

Mupin see Baoxing

Museum of Garden History, London

The two **John Tradescants** are buried in the graveyard of the Lambeth church that became the museum in 1979. They are commemorated by a knot garden, designed by the Dowager Marchioness of Salisbury (of **Hatfield House**, where the Tradescants worked), behind the museum. This is a good place to study plant introductions: the knot garden features 17th-century plants, some introduced by the

Tradescants, and the labels on many of the other plants include the date they were introduced into Britain.

Mussin-Puschkin, Apollon (1760–1805)

The small spring bulb *Puschkinia scilloides* is named after this Russian diplomat and mineralogist. He had lived in England for a time before making an expedition into the **Caucasus** between 1800 and 1805. From here he sent seeds and specimens to **Sir Joseph Banks** at **Kew**.

Myddelton House Gardens, Enfield, London

Named afer its 17th-century owner, Sir Hugh Myddelton, this was the 4-acre garden of the great plantsman **E.A. Bowles**, familiar to many through the three books he wrote about it. A prolific plant collector, Bowles lived and gardened here from childhood throughout his life. Thanks to recent restoration work, many of his plants can now be seen much as he knew them: favourites such as hellebores, cyclamens, crocuses and other bulbs; his famously eccentric 'lunatic asylum' of quirky plants like corkscrew hazel; and 'Tom Tiddler's ground' – plants with golden, variegated or coloured leaves. He also made an exquisite rock garden. There is a National Collection of irises, with some 300 varieties, and a conservatory with exotic plants and an exhibition on Bowles. *Penstemon* 'Myddelton Gem' is named after the garden.

Iris germanica

National Botanic Garden of Wales, Carmarthenshire

A fascinating blend of traditional and contemporary, this new botanic garden was established in 2000 on the 400-year-old estate of the Middleton family. They sold up in 1776, and the estate flourished under a later owner, wealthy Scotsman William Paxton, who bought it in 1789 after making his fortune in India. No expense was spared: he built a new mansion (which was destroyed by fire in 1931) and had the grounds lavishly landscaped into a complex water park with ponds, cascades, bridges and streams. There was also a double walled garden, and a bathhouse to take advantage of the mineral springs that were found on the land.

All fell into disrepair after Paxton's death, and most of the land was farmed until the initiatives of the late 20th century. The new developments focus on a huge, stylish hilltop glasshouse by Foster & Partners. The landscaped interior shelters plants of more than 1,000 species from the world's five main Mediterranean climate zones, in an elliptical area measuring 100yds by 60yds. These botanically rich zones – in South **Africa**, **Australia**, Chile, California and the Mediterranean itself – occupy less than 2 per cent of the earth's surface, but contain 20 per cent of known species of flowering plants, many of them now threatened. Conservation and education are at the heart of the garden's work, and native species form a key part of the outdoor planting.

National Arboretum see Washington

Neckham, Alexander of (1157–1217)

This English scholar became a teacher and Abbot of Cirencester. His manuscript *De Naturis Rerum*, written before 1200, was among the first works to discuss garden plants, recommending the cultivation of violets, marigolds, poppies, daffodils, lilies, roses and acanthus, and also of many herbs.

Ness Botanic Gardens, Cheshire

Now the botanic garden of the University of Liverpool, Ness began life as the private garden of **Arthur Bulley**, who bought the land in 1897 and built a house and garden here on Mickwell Brow, above the River Dee. Bulley's ambitious ideas for the realization of his garden involved sponsoring several plant hunters, over a period of years, to collect plants for him. They included **George Forrest**, **Reginald Farrer** and **Frank Kingdon Ward**. The garden eventually fell into neglect during World War II and after Bulley's death in 1942 his daughter gave it to the University of Liverpool. It has subsequently built on its historical significance and varied planting to become a valuable facility for research and propagation with a new visitor centre in 2006.

Newby Hall, North Yorkshire

Newby Hall, near Ripon, already had a fine formal garden by the late 17th century but the present garden has mainly been created and cared for by

Newry, County Down: Daisy Hill Nursery

The few plants listed today that originated at this great Irish nursery represent only a tiny fraction of a roll-call of more than 250 introductions, most of which no longer exist. Daisy Hill Nursery operated for more than a century. It was founded in 1887 by Thomas Smith, who advertised it confidently as 'the only Nursery in Ireland worth a button, and the most interesting nursery probably in the World'. Smith attracted customers from far and near with the huge range of plants that he grew, especially Michaelmas daisies, lupins, bergenias and delphiniums. **E.A. Bowles** wrote that 'Mr Smith's magic wand makes everything grow', and his legendary 'green fingers' were acknowledged when he was awarded the RHS Victoria Medal of Honour in 1911. After his death in 1919, his son George Norman Smith (nicknamed 'Great Northern Smith') took over. The nursery kept going for two more generations, through a long series of ups and downs, finally closing in 1996 on the retirement of Thomas Smith's great-grandson.

> **SOME DAISY HILL PLANTS**
>
> Aconitum 'Newry Blue'
> Cotoneaster newryensis
> Cytisus 'Daisy Hill'
> Erica cinerea 'Atrorubens, Daisy Hill'
> Escallonia 'Newry',
> Hebe 'Autumn Glory'
> Phlox subulata 'Daisy Hill'
> Primula 'Our Pat'
> Prunus subhirtella 'Autumnalis'
> Rosa 'Daisy Hill'
> Rosa × odorata 'Mutabilis'

three generations of the Compton family. *Salvia microphylla* var. *microphylla* 'Newby Hall' is one of a prized collection of salvias grown here, and there is a National Collection of *Cornus*.

New York Botanical Garden

A spectacular 250-acre site in the Bronx is the home of this world-class garden, which was founded in 1891 at the suggestion of a botanist from Columbia University. Inspired by **Kew**, and financed by some of the big business names of the day – Vanderbilt, Carnegie and Morgan – the garden now boasts 50 distinct collections and gardens, including a conifer arboretum, the USA's largest Victorian glasshouse (with a near-comprehensive collection of palms), and the International Plant Science Center. The research programme, founded with the garden, runs a large herbarium and library as well as a busy publishing operation.

Noisette, Philippe (d.1835)

This nursery owner in Charleston, South Carolina, bred and selected the first Noisette rose in the early 19th century, introducing it into Europe in 1814 through his Parisian brother Louis, also a nurseryman. *Rosa* 'Noisette Carnée' (formerly 'Blush Noisette') is still a favourite today.

Noll, Wladyslaw

The popular rich red *Clematis* 'Niobe' is one of the significant new varieties raised by this contemporary Polish clematis breeder.

New Zealand

New Zealand's climate ranges from subtropical to cool temperate, with a rich mixture of different habitats, and the flora is correspondingly varied. As with many islands, a large proportion of the native flora – around three-quarters – is endemic, with many strange and wonderful plants, from the gaunt and newly fashionable *Pseudopanax ferox* to the exotic *Clianthus puniceus*, the lobster claw or parrot's bill, which was first discovered, growing in Maori gardens, by the young **Joseph Banks** when he came here in 1770 with Captain Cook. The islands have always appealed to plant hunters and botanists: **Joseph Hooker** visited in 1841, Johann von Haast in 1858, and Captain Dorrien-Smith of **Tresco Abbey Gardens** in 1910. **Allan Cunningham** and his brother Richard were here at different times in the 1820s and 1830s, **David Lyall**, **Johann von Haast** and **John Buchanan** in the second half of the 19th century. Through them, New Zealand plants gradually began to take their place in herbaria, in botanic gardens, and then in nurseries such as **Loddiges** in London.

Phormium cookianum

SOME GARDEN PLANTS FROM NEW ZEALAND

Brachyglottis species
Carex buchananii
Carex comans
Cordyline australis
Griselinia littoralis
Hebe species
Hoheria lyallii
Leptospermum scoparium
Olearia × *haastii*
Phormium cookianum
Phormium tenax
Pittosporum tenuifolium
Podocarpus nivalis
Sophora tetraptera

A surprising number of today's garden plants are New Zealand natives. Many, such as sedges, hebes and phormiums, have found their niche in the contemporary design idiom, helped by their architectural qualities and by the warming climate of temperate gardens. However, phormiums are nothing new. Among the earliest recorded New Zealand plants, they were used by early Maoris for ornament and for their durable fibres, which were used to make ropes, nets and fabrics.

Plant names with New Zealand links include *Hebe canterburiensis* (from the Canterbury Plains around Christchurch), the grass *Festuca novae-zelandiae*, *Geranium sessiliflorum* subsp. *novae-zelandiae* and the so-called pirri-pirri bur, *Acaena novae-zelandiae*.

New Zealand gardens in Britain

The **Savill Garden**'s New Zealand collection was a gift to the Queen from the people of New Zealand, in 1986. It includes varieties of *Carex*, *Hebe*, *Podocarpus*, *Phormium*, *Acaena* and *Pittosporum*. **Ventnor Botanic Garden** also has a New Zealand garden, developed since 1989, where New Zealand plants familiar to gardeners grow alongside lesser-known plants, sometimes in experimental plantings to test their suitability for the British climate.

North America

With a climatic range as great as any subcontinent on earth,
North America is home to an extraordinarily varied flora. Its
native plants range from perennial prairie species, such as
daisies and grasses, to the world's largest conifers, and from
exquisite woodland perennials to some of the most drought-
tolerant plants known. Over the past 400 years this cornucopia of
plants has made a dramatic impact on gardens and landscapes in many countries.

Magnolia grandiflora

The earliest settlers grew mostly familiar plants they had imported from
Europe, though the crops of the native Americans – squashes, maize and beans
– were soon in gardens and kitchens. Making homes
and finding food were the main preoccupations, and it
was the mid-17th century before ornamental American
plants began to make much impact. **John Tradescant
the Younger** brought many American trees and shrubs to
Europe, as well as species of aster and rudbeckia, *Yucca
filamentosa* and *Aquilegia canadensis*. By 1688, assisted by
John Banister, the English botanist **John Ray** was able to
publish the first record of the flora of America. Within
50 years the developing colony had its first home-grown
botanist and plant hunter, the self-taught **John Bartram**.
His influence spread far and wide: about one in four
of all the American plants that were new to science in
his lifetime were found by him. These discoveries were
welcomed into the gardens of America as well as Europe.

SOME BORDER PLANTS FROM NORTH AMERICA

Aquilegia canadensis
Aster lateriflorus
Aster divaricatus
Echinacea purpurea
Liatris spicata
Lupinus arboreus
Monarda species
Penstemon species
Phlox species
Rudbeckia species
Solidago species
Trillium erectum
Trillium grandiflorum

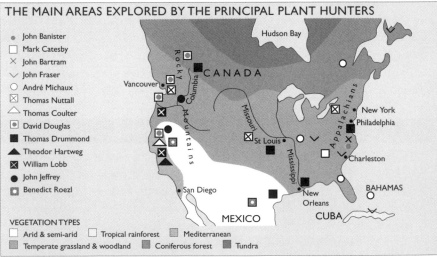

THE MAIN AREAS EXPLORED BY THE PRINCIPAL PLANT HUNTERS

- John Banister
- Mark Catesby
- John Bartram
- John Fraser
- André Michaux
- Thomas Nuttall
- Thomas Coulter
- David Douglas
- Thomas Drummond
- Theodor Hartweg
- William Lobb
- John Jeffrey
- Benedict Roezl

Hudson Bay
CANADA
Vancouver
New York
Philadelphia
St Louis
Charleston
San Diego
New Orleans
BAHAMAS
MEXICO
CUBA

VEGETATION TYPES
- Arid & semi-arid
- Tropical rainforest
- Mediterranean
- Temperate grassland & woodland
- Coniferous forest
- Tundra

N

albertianus from Alberta

alleghaniensis from the Allegheny
Mountains

canadensis from Canada or the
eastern USA

catawbiensis from the Catawba River
area (North and South Carolina)

columbianum from the Columbia
River or British Columbia

marilandicus from Maryland

nootkatensis from the Nootka Sound
(British Columbia)

novae-angliae from New England

novi-belgii from New York

oreganus, oregonensis, oregonus from
the north-western USA including
(but not restricted to) Oregon

Ironically, many of the native plants that arrived in American gardens in the 18th century got there through naturalists and collectors from Europe: **Clayton**, **Garden**, **Catesby** and **Michaux**. They also took new plants home with them: *Magnolia grandiflora*, *Kalmia latifolia* and *Rhododendron maximum* were important introductions of the period.

These and other early plant hunters had largely confined themselves to the east. Michaux had travelled as far as the Mississippi in 1795, but by the early 1800s the territories farther to the west were claiming attention, and the race was on to find a route to the west coast. In the Louisiana Purchase of 1803, President Jefferson paid the French emperor Napoleon $16 million for a huge area of land west of the Mississippi, which became 12 new states. The momentous journey of **Lewis** and **Clark** to investigate this new territory in 1804–1806 literally put the West on the map. Plant collecting was not the main purpose of their trip, but a number of plants grown from seed that Lewis and Clark collected reached Europe later in the 19th century: the snowberry *Symphoricarpos albus* var. *laevigatus* in 1817 and the Oregon grape *Mahonia aquifolium* in 1893. They had been grown in the Philadelphia nursery of **Bernard M'Mahon**, a key figure in early American gardening, who not only set up a brisk transatlantic plant trade but also supplied plants – native and imported – to the developing gardens of east coast landowners, and even to the president himself at Monticello. A gardening tradition was already well established in the eastern states: garden plots at Williamsburg, Virginia, had been sold and developed from the early 1700s while, farther south, exotic and native plants flourished side by side in the balmy plantation gardens around Savannah and Charleston.

In parallel, a mix of indigenous plants and introductions – in this case mainly from **South America** – was also the formula for the feted mission gardens of California. Here ceanothus, eschscholtzia, fremontodendron and other lovely plants thrived, awaiting discovery by 19th-century explorers. The 1820s and 1830s saw **David Douglas** and **Thomas Nuttall** plant hunting in the west coast states and western Canada, followed by **William Lobb** and **John Jeffrey**. Among their finds were seeds of many large new conifers that were later to settle happily in much of western Europe, transforming the tree flora, providing valuable new timber resources, and satisfying the Victorian hunger for novel garden plants.

Aquilegia canadensis

North, Marianne (1830–1890)

The richness and colour of the plant world is memorably expressed in the collection of more than 800 paintings by this remarkable Victorian. Marianne North painted the pictures on a phenomenal series of travels over five continents; she had a gallery built at **Kew** for the express purpose of displaying them all. From early expeditions around the Mediterranean with her father, she graduated to increasingly intrepid solo journeys. Ambitious even by today's standards, they were almost beyond belief for a single woman during the 19th century. Japan, California, New Zealand, Chile, the Seychelles and Borneo were just a few of her chosen destinations. *Kniphofia northiae*, one of hundreds of plants she depicted, is named after her.

Notcutts, Suffolk and Surrey

This well-known British nursery business was founded in the 1880s when Roger Crompton Notcutt (1869–1938), then still in his teens, bought a nursery in Ipswich, specializing at first in chrysanthemums.

Thomas Nuttall (1786–1859)

Nuttall travelled in 1808 from his native Liverpool to Philadelphia, where he became the protégé of **Benjamin Smith Barton**, a distinguished scientist who inspired Nuttall's career as an enthusiastic and prolific plant collector. Barton even financed some of his expeditions, including one in 1810 to the Great Lakes, from where Nuttall joined the first leg of a big fur-trapping expedition heading towards the Rockies and the west coast. Collecting plants was his only aim, to the extent that others in his team nicknamed him *le fou* (the madman) because his obsession made him oblivious to other people and his own safety alike. Nuttall left the party at St Louis, continuing down the Mississippi to New Orleans, from where he left for England, first despatching some of his plants to Barton, and giving others to Liverpool Botanic Garden on his return.

Within a few years Nuttall was back in Philadelphia. He compiled a remarkably comprehensive flora of America – only the third ever published – and made another trip to the Midwest before settling for a while in Massachusetts, where he was curator of Harvard University's botanic garden. Finally, in 1834, the chance of a third trip, even farther west, proved irresistible and this time he reached the west coast at last, spending several months in 1835 collecting new plants – including *Cornus nuttallii* – in the Columbia River area, where **David Douglas** had previously been. Finally he travelled down the coast to California and sailed from San Diego round Cape Horn and back to Boston. In 1841, the terms of a legacy compelled him to return reluctantly to England, where he spent his last years gardening. His plant names include *Rhododendron nuttallii* and the bulb *Zigadenus nuttallii*, and he also introduced species of evening primrose, penstemon, artemisia, camassia and rudbeckia.

By 1897, when the expanding business moved to Woodbridge, the list had grown to around 1,000 plants, and by 1936 to nearly 3,000. Still in the same family today, Notcutts acquired the Surrey nursery business of Waterer's (see **Knap Hill**) in 1982 and, three years later, Mattocks Roses. Like several successful traditional nurseries, Notcutts have also developed a chain of retail garden centres. The current chairman, Charles Notcutt, grandson of the founder, is active in the **RHS** and received the OBE for services to horticulture in 1993. His son William is managing director of the firm.

Notcutts have raised many well-known plants over the years, among them *Hibiscus syriacus* 'Woodbridge', *Viburnum opulus* 'Notcutt's Variety', *Cotinus coggygria* 'Notcutt's Variety' and *Syringa vulgaris* 'Maud Notcutt'.

Nymans, West Sussex

One of the great plantsman's gardens of southern England was started here at Handcross near Hayward's Heath in 1890 by Ludwig Messel (1847–1915). The garden remained in the care of the Messel family for three generations, and is most often associated with Ludwig's son, Leonard (1873–1953), who played a key role in its development, assisted by his head gardener, James Comber (1866–1953). Leonard Messel introduced many new plants, especially in the 1930s, an exciting time for new arrivals from the Himalayas. His interest in hybridizing and the selection of new cultivars gave rise to a number of successful new garden plants here. His wife, Maud, created the rose garden, which was later restored by their daughter, Anne, Countess of Rosse, who lived here until her death in 1992.

Nymans was given to the National Trust after Leonard Messel's death in 1953: the house had been almost completely gutted by fire in 1947 but survives as a romantic ruin. The garden, with its fine collection of trees and shrubs, remained intact. However, the great storm of 1987 brought devastating damage to Nymans: most of the trees and the famous pergola were flattened and the pinetum destroyed. Since then, energetic restoration and replanting by the National Trust have set the garden back on its feet. It derives part of its special character from its judicious blend of formal and informal: immaculate topiary contrasts with the romantic dovecote, and spring bulbs and wildflowers give way to the herbaceous borders with their blazing summer colours. Plant enthusiasts will find much of interest everywhere, with many choice mature shrubs and trees such as magnolias, camellias, rhododendrons, styrax and cornus.

> ## SOME NYMANS PLANTS
> *Camellia* 'Leonard Messel'
> *Camellia* 'Maud Messel'
> *Cyclamen coum* subsp. *coum* f. *coum* Nymans group
> *Eucryphia* × *nymansensis* 'Nymansay'.
> *Forsythia suspensa* 'Nymans'
> *Magnolia* × *loebneri* 'Leonard Messel'
> *Nyssa sinensis* Nymans form
> *Polygonatum* 'Nymans Variety'
> *Skimmia japonica* 'Nymans'
> *Sorbus* 'Leonard Messel'

N

Oakington, Cambridgeshire

Dianthus 'Oakington', *Campanula cochlearifolia* 'Oakington Blue' and *Heuchera* 'Oakington Jewel' are some of the plants raised, in his early career, by the late Alan Bloom. Oakington, near Cambridge, was where he had his first nursery, building his reputation as a successful plantsman through the late 1920s and 1930s. He sold the premises after World War II and founded **Blooms of Bressingham**.

Oehme, Wolfgang

Since 1977, this influential landscape architect has been a partner, with James van Sweden, in Oehme, van Sweden & Associates, a landscape design practice in Washington DC. Oehme trained in his native Germany and moved to the USA in 1957. Oehme and van Sweden became known for the 'New American Garden' style of planting, using robust perennials and grasses. The golden-edged palm sedge *Carex muskingumensis* 'Oehme' was found in his garden.

Ogisu, Mikinori

This contemporary Japanese botanist and plant collector has brought many new plants into cultivation from his travels in **China**, **Japan**, **South America** and elsewhere. They include hostas, witch hazels, irises, epimediums and the beautiful *Bergenia emeiensis*. Plants named for him include *Epimedium ogisui* and the shrubby, double-flowered white cherry *Prunus incisa* 'Mikinori', while *Epimedium leptorrhizum* 'Mariko' was named by him for his wife.

Omei, Mount see Emei Shan

Oregon

The specific epithets *oreganus*, *oregonus* or *oregonensis* appear in many plant names, for example *Erythronium oregonum*, *Geranium oreganum* or *Sedum oregonense*. Usually the terms cover not only the present-day state of Oregon, but the north-western USA generally – the area once covered by the Oregon division of the Hudson's Bay Company, which also embraced Washington State. This region, especially the Columbia River, is particularly associated with the plant hunter **David Douglas**, who first came here in April 1825.

Oudolf, Piet

An influential contemporary Dutch garden designer and nurseryman, Piet Oudolf has a string of internationally renowned planting schemes to his credit. His style has become distinctive and recognizable: dense, naturalistic drifts of grasses and structural perennials, best in late summer and autumn but chosen for winter interest too, usually in the form of long-lasting architectural seedheads. Echinaceas, achilleas, stachys, rudbeckias, alliums and grasses are typical examples of his choice of plants. Perennials Oudolf has bred include *Achillea* 'Martina' and *Heuchera* 'Pewter Moon'. Several cultivars of Bergamot (*Monarda*), including 'Fishes', 'Mohawk' and 'Squaw', are Oudolf's selections, and *Stachys officinalis* 'Hummelo' is named after the Netherlands town where he lives and works. Places to see Oudulf's work in the UK include RHS Garden **Wisley** and Trentham Gardens, Staffordshire.

Overbeck's, Devon

One of mainland Britain's best exotic gardens, this National Trust property enjoys a favoured setting on a terraced slope above the Salcombe estuary. The garden is a mass of lush subtropical planting, best in late summer but offering other seasonal delights such as mimosa in spring and a huge *Magnolia campbellii* in late winter. Summer highlights include palms and towering blue echiums, astelias, aeoniums, eucomis and banana plants. Overbeck's changed its name when its previous owner, the eccentric scientist and inventor Otto Overbeck, bequeathed it to the National Trust in 1937 and wanted the garden to carry his name. Its previous name, Sharpitor, lives on in a well-known fuchsia cultivar, *Fuchsia magellanica* var. *molinae* 'Sharpitor'.

Oxford University Botanic Garden

Britain's oldest botanic garden was founded in 1621. The university needed a place to grow plants used in the teaching of medicine: a gift from Sir Henry Danvers made it possible to set aside a space and build the walls and archways that still enclose the older part of the garden. One venerable plant survives from the garden's infancy: the yew tree planted in 1645, when **Jacob Bobart** worked there. Other early plantings include an Austrian black pine, whose seed was brought here in 1795 by **John Sibthorp**. Helped by bequests and endowments, the garden developed as an aid to the teaching of botany

The main gateway in 1713

– increasingly valuable as its new glasshouses enabled plants from other climates to thrive. Today there is much to interest gardeners and botanists alike.

Careful labelling identifies everything from the spring shrubs and perennials along the riverside walk to the dahlias, tulips and purple foliage of the exciting contemporary borders. Part of the walled garden is organized in a series of 'family beds' of related plants, and there is also a National Collection of euphorbias, a border of variegated plants, and the fascinating 'economic beds', with plants used for practical purposes such as medicines, fuels and fabrics. The old stone walls shelter many slightly tender garden shrubs and a fern collection, while exotic treasures such as tropical waterlilies, desert plants and sparkling alpines benefit from the controlled conditions of the various glasshouses.

The terms *oxonianus* and *oxoniensis* denote a link with Oxford. *Geranium ×
oxonianum* is a successful but invasive hybrid between *Geranium endressii* and *Geranium versicolor* which is available in many named forms. Cultivars with Oxford associations include several (agapanthus, eryngium etc.) called 'Oxford Blue', *Salvia microphylla* 'Oxford', *Dahlia* 'Bishop of Oxford', *Iris* 'Oxford Tweeds' and even *Geum rivale* 'Oxford Marmalade'!

Padua: Orto Botanico

Padua and Pisa had the first botanic gardens in the world, founded within a few months of each other in 1545. Unlike Pisa, the garden in Padua is still on its original site. Like most early botanic gardens, it was established by the university in order to teach medical students about medicinal plants. Botanic gardens soon became centres for the study of plants generally, with herbaria, libraries, collections of botanical drawings, and later laboratories. The plants were systematically laid out in formal beds so as to be easily found and identified. Today Padua's botanic garden – one of some 500 in Europe alone – plays an important role in plant conservation and is a designated UNESCO World Heritage Site. The oldest plant here is a palm planted in 1585.

Pagels, Ernst

This German nurseryman and garden designer was a pupil and one-time employee of the famous plant breeder **Karl Foerster**, from whom he learned rigorous selection techniques, choosing naturally robust and hardy perennials that require little maintenance and provide a long season of interest. The plants Pagels raised suit contemporary schemes, and have proved understandably popular with nurserymen from many countries, and with landscape and garden designers. Many of his award-winning plants are now seen everywhere, and are featured in a garden dedicated to him in Bad Zwischenahn, Germany. Pagels' most significant introductions include cultivars of *Miscanthus*, *Achillea* and *Salvia*, such as *Miscanthus sinensis* 'Kleine Fontäne' and *Salvia nemorosa* 'Ostfriesland'. His hybridization work with *Miscanthus* gained him the RHS **Reginald Cory** Memorial Cup in 2006.

Pakenham, Thomas

Thomas Pakenham captured the public imagination with his unusual 1996 book *Meetings with Remarkable Trees*, a series of portraits of individual trees of special interest in the UK. It was made into a successful television series and was followed by two sequels.

Palmer, Lady Anne see Rosemoor

Palmer, Lewis (1894–1971)

A knowledgeable and widely respected plantsman, the Hon. Lewis Palmer was the second son of the Earl of Selborne and a friend of the great plantsman E.A. Bowles. Palmer's home was at Headbourne Worthy, near Winchester, in Hampshire, and here he bred the well-known hardy *Agapanthus* Headbourne hybrids. He had spent part of his childhood in South **Africa**, and on a later business trip there he brought back from Kirstenbosch seed of the hardiest agapanthus he could find. With this he began his breeding programme, which ultimately led to RHS **Wisley** trials of some 60 agapanthus. He often gave away unnamed offspring of his plants, which people came to know as Headbourne hybrids – a name that stuck. Another agapanthus, 'Penelope Palmer', is named after his daughter. Palmer's garden was full of choice plants; he had particular expertise in cyclamens, hellebores and snowdrops, and he also bred the highly successful *Philadelphus* 'Beauclerk'. He is remembered in the lovely blue *Pulmonaria* 'Lewis Palmer'.

Paris, France: Jardin des Plantes

The botanic garden in Paris traces its origins to 1626, when Louis XIII began to plan a first-class French educational and research establishment for the teaching of anatomy, chemistry and botany. A good collection of medicinal herbs was a prerequisite, and this grew into the royal garden later officially named the Jardin du Roy (Roi). In 1793, after the French Revolution, the institution was reorganized as the Muséum d'Histoire Naturelle, while the garden shook off its royal label and became the Jardin des Plantes. It remained very much at the centre of botanical discoveries and international scientific networking, later receiving some of the first plants to be introduced from America and many from the Far East. Great names of science such as **Tournefourt** and the **Jussieu** family worked and taught here, and some of their pupils in turn became important botanists and plant hunters.

Parkinson, John (1567–1650)

Parkinson, a royal apothecary and botanist, was working at an exciting time in the history of gardening, when many of the hardy garden plants we know today were introduced as a

The title page of John Parkinson's Theatrum Botanicum

result of the international trade that had blossomed during the reign of Elizabeth I. Parkinson's horticultural treatise *Paradisi in Sole Paradisus Terrestris*, published in 1629, is a key work in plant history because it broke the tradition of the medieval herbal and portrayed the ornamental qualities of plants. The rather strange title is partly a pun on the author's name: *Paradisi in Sole* = 'park in sun'! Parkinson's later work *Theatrum Botanicum* (1640) classified plants into 17 categories (two of which were 'strange and outlandish plants' and 'venomous sleepy and hurtful plants'). A subtropical genus, *Parkinsonia*, is named after him, as is *Crocus biflorus* subsp. *biflorus* 'Parkinsonii'.

Parks, John Damper (*c.*1792–1866)

Parks, a gardener for the **RHS**, travelled to Canton (now Guangzhou) and Macao in 1823 on behalf of the society. He stayed for two years in **China**, collecting chrysanthemums, camellias and roses, most of which came from local nurseries and gardens.

P
Q

Parrot, F.W. (1792–1841)

The Persian ironwood, *Parrotia persica*, is named after this German explorer and naturalist. The first specimen was found in the **Caucasus** by the German botanist Carl Meyer, who worked at the botanic garden in St Petersburg. It was introduced to **Kew** around 1840, but took nearly 30 years to flower.

Paul, William (1822–1905)

Several classic roses – 'Paul's Lemon Pillar', 'Paul's Scarlet Climber' and 'Paul's Himalayan Musk' – as well as the popular ornamental hawthorn *Crataegus laevigata* 'Paul's Scarlet' originated at the Royal Nurseries at Waltham Cross, founded by William Paul in 1860. He also wrote several books, including *The Rose Garden* (1848) and *The Villa Garden* (1855), and contributed articles to the *Gardeners' Chronicle*. Along with his nephew George Paul (1841–1921), also a nurseryman, he was one of the 60 original recipients of the RHS Victoria Medal of Honour in 1897.

Paulowna, Princess Anna (1795–1865)

The Chinese tree genus *Paulownia* is named for the daughter of Tsar Paul I of Russia. She became the wife of King William II of The Netherlands.

Paulownia

Pemberton, Joseph (1852–1926)

The beautiful, and still popular, Hybrid Musk roses 'Penelope', 'Cornelia' and 'Felicia' were bred in the 1920s by this Essex clergyman who wrote a book on roses and was president of the National Rose Society.

Pennells Nurseries, Lincolnshire

Seven generations of Pennells have been growing plants since 1780 in this Lincoln nursery business, long known chiefly for its climbers, especially clematis. Several cultivars – *Clematis* 'Pennell's Purity', 'Vyvyan Pennell',

'Walter Pennell' and 'Richard Pennell' – are named after family members, and *Clematis* 'Lincoln Star' is also a Pennell cultivar. The nursery has always grown a wide range of other plants, and among its lastingly popular introductions over the years have been *Hedera colchica* 'Dentata Variegata' and the apple 'Ellison's Orange'.

Perkins, Dorothy see Jackson & Perkins

Perny, Paul (1818–1907)

The Chinese holly species *Ilex pernyi* and the unusual woodland perennial *Disporopsis pernyi* are named after Abbé Paul Perny, a French missionary who collected many plants in the Chinese provinces of Guizhou and Sichuan.

Perovski, Vasili (1794–1857)

Perovskia (Russian sage) is named after this general from Turkestan who settled in St Petersburg.

Perraudière, Henri de la (1831–1861)

Epimedium perralderianum is named after this French botanist and entomologist.

Perry, Frances see Perry, Amos

Phillips, Roger

An influential photographer and author, Roger Phillips is known mainly for the pioneering series of photographic guides to wild and garden plants that he co-produced with **Martyn Rix** from the 1970s to the 1990s.

Amos Perry (1871–1953)

SOME PERRY PLANTS

Achillea ptarmica 'Perry's White'
Erysimum 'Perry's Peculiar'
Geranium himalayense 'Frances Perry'
Iris sibirica 'Perry's Blue'
Meconopsis cambrica 'Frances Perry'
Papaver orientale 'Perry's White'
Papaver orientale 'Mrs Perry'
Viola 'Frances Perry'

This remarkable nurseryman was one of the most prolific breeders of hardy perennials the horticultural world has ever seen. Nurseries still list many plants named after him and members of his family, but many more, sadly, are no longer available. Perry's Hardy Plant Farm was in business for 50 years until its land was compulsorily purchased for house building after World War II. During that time it launched more than 400 new cultivars.

Amos Perry's father was a nurseryman, and the young Amos joined him in Thomas Ware's nursery in Tottenham, where he was a partner. A few years later Amos began his own nursery in north London, moving after three years to settle on a larger site at Enfield, where his father came to join him in the business. Here plants were grown in their thousands, typified by one legendary show exhibit in 1910 which incorporated 25,000 separate delphinium spikes. As well as border perennials, such as irises, daylilies and Michaelmas daisies, Perry grew and bred waterlilies and other aquatics, staging Britain's first-ever water garden at a show in 1902. Several waterlily cultivars bearing his name are still available, and many more have only recently disappeared from the *RHS Plant Finder*. Hardy ferns and bulbs were other specialities, the latter a legacy of Perry's days as bulb foreman for Thomas Ware.

The wife of Perry's son Gerald was Frances Perry (1907–1993), who became well known in her own right for her classic book on water gardens and for her gardening articles. She took over from **Vita Sackville-West** as gardening correspondent for *The Observer*. Her son, who was killed in a car accident, is commemorated by an oriental poppy, *Papaver orientale* 'Marcus Perry'.

P
Q

Picton, Percy (1904–1985)

Picton was a great plantsman and a skilled propagator. Early in his gardening career he had spent 15 years working for **William Robinson** at **Gravetye Manor**, where he met and was influenced by great gardeners of the day, including **Ernest Markham** and **Walter Ingwersen**. He later became head gardener at **Hagley Court**, near Hereford. By 1948 he was nursery

Percy Picton judging

manager for **Ernest Ballard**, at Old Court Nurseries, Colwall, near Malvern. After Ballard's death, Picton bought the business and he later became well known through his lectures and television appearances, and as a horticultural judge. He is remembered as a breeder of Michaelmas daisies (*Aster*) and as the raiser of successful clematis

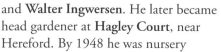

cultivars including the still popular 'Hagley Hybrid', 'Picton's Variety' and 'Joan Picton'. Other Picton plants include *Ranunculus ficaria* 'Picton's Double'. A ceanothus and a euphorbia named after him are unfortunately no longer in commerce, but there are a number of *Aster* cultivars, a Shasta daisy, a crocosmia and a hebe named for Colwall, and a kniphofia called 'Old Court Seedling'. Picton's son and daughter-in-law, Paul and Meriel Picton, continue to run the nursery, which celebrated its centenary in 2006. They hold a National Collection of autumn-flowering asters.

Pissard, René (1800s)
The well-known purple-leaved plum *Prunus cerasifera* 'Pissardii' was found in Persia in 1878 by this Frenchman who was gardener to the Shah.

Pitlochry, Perthshire: Scottish Plant Hunters' Garden
The 18 Scots commemorated in this series of gardens adjacent to Pitlochry's Festival Theatre include all the famous names: **James Drummond**, **George Forrest**, **Archibald Menzies** and others. The garden is also an excellent introduction to less well-known botanical travellers, such as **Thomas Thomson**.

Platt, Jane Kerr (d.1989)
Magnolia stellata 'Jane Platt' and *Leptinella squalida* 'Platt's Black' are named after this prominent Oregon plantswoman whose Portland garden, created mainly from the 1950s to the 1970s, remains well known in the

USA and abroad for its extraordinary collection of rarities. A trained artist, Jane Platt combined a great knowledge of plants with design skills learned from her Scottish father, who came to Portland as a young man and made a wonderful garden nearby at Elk Rock.

Platt, Karen
Phormium 'Platt's Black' is named after this plantswoman and author who has a special interest in coloured foliage plants.

Pliny the Elder
This 1st-century AD Roman scholar and naturalist was renowned for his prodigious energy and wide-ranging intellectual curiosity. His 37-volume work *Naturalis Historia* is a valuable record of early plants, plant names and gardens, containing not only the views of Pliny himself but also borrowings from his contemporaries and predecessors: he described its content as '20,000 important matters, taken from 100 selected authors'. Beautiful illustrated copies of Pliny's work were made in medieval times.

Plumier, Charles (1646–1706)
The first fuchsia known to Europeans – probably either *Fuchsia triphylla* or *Fuchsia coccinea* – was described by this French Roman Catholic priest in his book *Nova Plantarum Americanum Genera* (1703). He found the plant on one of his expeditions to the tropics of Central America. *Fuchsia* was one of about 50 genera named by Father Plumier after distinguished botanists or patrons, including **Mathias de l'Obel** (*Lobelia*) and **Michel Bégon** (*Begonia*).

P
Q

Polunin, Oleg (1914–1985)

Polunin taught botany at Charterhouse School, in Surrey, and was an authority on European flora. He is known mainly for his books on the subject, including *Flowers of the Mediterranean* (1965), co-authored with Anthony Huxley, and *Flowers of Europe* (1969). He explored and collected in many areas of botanical interest including Nepal, **Kashmir**, **Turkey**, the Lebanon and Iraq. *Saxifraga poluniniana* is named after him.

Pontus

Pontus was the ancient name of a botanically rich area of Asia Minor, to the south of the Black Sea. A number of plants associated with the

Rhododendron ponticum

region have the specific epithet *ponticus*, for example *Rhododendron ponticum*, *Daphne pontica* and *Fritillaria pontica*.

Popple, Mrs see Six Hills Nursery

Porlock see Hadden, Norman, and Butt, Walter

Potanin, Grigori (1835–1920)

Indigofera potaninii and *Rhus potaninii* are named after this Russian explorer and prolific plant collector who made four ambitious expeditions in **China** and eastern Asia. Unusually among plant hunters, he was accompanied on his trips by his wife, Alexandra, until she fell ill and died in China. *Rheum alexandrae* is named after her.

Potts, John (d.1822)

Potts, a gardener for the **RHS**, was sent to **China** by the society in 1821 in search of potentially valuable plants. He returned with a successful collection including *Paeonia lactiflora* 'Pottsii', *Primula sinensis* and *Camellia euryoides*.

Powis Castle, Powys

Artemisia 'Powis Castle' is named after this imposing Welsh border fortress, now owned by the National Trust. The steeply terraced gardens are famous for their huge, billowing clipped yews, rare plants and stylishly planted containers.

Prichard, Maurice & Sons, Dorset

'Riverslea' plants, such as *Geranium* × *riversleaianum* 'Russell Prichard', *Saxifraga* 'Riverslea' and *Erica australis* 'Riverslea', are named after the nursery of Maurice Prichard at Purewell, near Christchurch. Established in 1890, the Riverslea nursery was famed for its border perennials and alpines, particularly geraniums, irises, saxifrages and crocosmias. The business prospered for many years, but closed after Maurice Prichard's death in the 1950s. Plants named after the Prichard family include *Campanula lactiflora* 'Prichard's Variety', *Trollius* × *cultorum* 'Prichard's Giant' and *Primula marginata* 'Prichard's Variety'.

Przewalski, Nikolai (1839–1888)

Ligularia przewalskii is the most well known of the many tongue-twisting plant names honouring this Russian soldier, explorer and collector (whose name is pronounced 'Shur-val-ski'). The epithet is shared by a salvia, a

P
Q

rhododendron and a cotoneaster, among others, and Przewalski's horse also commemorates this remarkable man. He made several epic expeditions to the remotest wilds of Tibet, **China** and central Asia and his collections of both plants and zoological specimens were prodigious. However, he never realized his life's ambition: to reach the forbidden city of Lhasa, in Tibet.

Purdom, William (1880–1921)

Although he is not usually mentioned with the same awe as other plant hunters, Purdom achieved much in his short life and was perhaps eclipsed by illustrious and more communicative contemporaries in **China** at the same time, such as **Farrer**, **Wilson** and **Forrest**. As a young man, Purdom moved from his native Westmorland to London where he worked for the **Veitch** nursery and then at **Kew**. His first plant-hunting expedition to China was sponsored by Veitch and the **Arnold Arboretum**. Leaving England in 1909, he spent three years travelling widely in China and sent back more than 300 packages of seed including *Malus transitoria*. He gained valuable knowledge of China on this expedition, and his next trip, to Gansu province in 1914–1915, was at the invitation of Reginald Farrer. *Viburnum farreri*, named for Farrer and often thought to have been introduced by him, was in fact first found by Purdom, whose other introductions included *Clematis macropetala*, *Gentiana gracilipes*,

Allium cyaneum and *Syringa pubescens* subsp. *microphylla*. Plants bearing his name include *Rodgersia purdomii*, *Rhododendron purdomii* and the cultivars *Potentilla fruticosa* 'William Purdom' and *Betula albosinensis* var. *septentrionalis* 'Purdom'.

Purpus, Carl Albert (1853–1941) and Joseph Anton (1860–1932)

The fragrant winter-flowering honeysuckle *Lonicera* × *purpusii*, the herbaceous perennial *Penstemon purpusii* and the houseplant *Tradescantia zebrina* 'Purpusii' are named after these German brothers who were well-known plant collectors.

Puschkin, Count Apollon Mussin- (d.1805)

Puschkinia scilloides is named after this Russian botanist and plant collector.

Puschkinia scilloides

Quinta Arboretum, Cheshire

The man behind this remarkable tree collection near Congleton was the astronomer and founder of the pioneering radio telescope at Jodrell Bank, Sir Bernard Lovell. He and his wife bought a house called The Quinta, in the village of Swettenham, in 1948, and today its grounds have become a 40-acre arboretum with 25,000 trees, many collected on his travels by Sir Bernard himself, and most of them planted by him. In 2003 the arboretum passed to the Tatton Garden Society, ensuring its survival for the future.

Radde, Gustav (1831–1903)

Campanula raddeana and *Betula raddeana* are named for this German naturalist.

Raiche, Roger

A leading contemporary American botanist and garden designer working in Berkeley, California, Raiche has a particular interest in Californian native plants and has introduced a number of new species into cultivation. *Erigeron glaucus* 'Roger Raiche' is named for him, and a new grey-leaved zauschneria that he found in the wild has also been named in his honour and is available in the USA.

Raulston, J.C. (1940–1996)

The J.C. Raulston Arboretum at North Carolina State University was named, after his death, in honour of its founder, a respected plantsman and collector. Raulston had a special interest in garden-worthy plants, and ran an extensive programme of trials with the aim of bringing new plants into the nursery trade.

Rauwolff, Leonhardt (*c*.1540–1596)

This German doctor and traveller journeyed through **Turkey** and the Middle East in the 1570s. Rauwolff's memoirs record not only a curious new drink – coffee – but also many plant discoveries, then unknown in Europe, which have become garden favourites: *Cotinus coggygria*, *Canna indica*, *Acanthus spinosus*, hyacinths and many kinds of tulip, fritillary and lily. Like many early travellers, he collected and pressed some of the plant specimens he found, and his herbarium is preserved at the University of Leiden in The Netherlands.

Raven, John (1914–1980) and Faith Raven

John Raven, the eminent field botanist and classicist, and his wife Faith (after whom *Artemisia arborescens* 'Faith Raven' is named) were a keen and knowledgeable gardening partnership. Their two very different gardens, at **Docwra's Manor** and **Ardtornish**, are described in John Raven's book *A Botanist's Garden*. Their daughter is the Sussex gardener, lecturer and author Sarah Raven, the wife of **Vita Sackville-West**'s grandson Adam Nicolson.

Ray, John (1627–1705)

This landmark English botanist (he even coined the term botany) and early taxonomist was the son of the village blacksmith at Black Notley, near Braintree, in Essex. He compiled a local flora at Cambridge, where he was a student and then a professional academic until he resigned as a conscientious objector to the 1662 Act of Uniformity, which excluded nonconformists from Cambridge degrees. He later travelled widely in Europe, gathering information that was eventually to contribute to his multi-volume life's work, *Historia Plantarum*, which was published between 1686 and 1704 and covered something approaching 20,000 species. Though it was considered rather unmanageable, Ray's classification system laid the foundations for much later work, such as that of Antoine-Laurent de **Jussieu**.

R

Rea, John (d.1681)

A Shropshire gardener and nurseryman at Kinlet, Rea was one of the earliest recorded professional florists (see panel). His collection of tulips was reputedly the largest in the country. He wrote an early gardening book, *Flora, Ceres & Pomona* (1665), giving advice on making gardens and on growing flowers from seed, cultivating bulbs, and fruit-growing. The book was dedicated to Rea's neighbour and gardening friend Sir **Thomas Hanmer**.

Ranunculus asiaticus

FLORISTS AND THEIR FLOWERS

In the 17th and 18th centuries, 'florists', like John Rea, were not people who worked with cut flowers, but committed plantsmen who bred a very specific range of 'florists flowers'. The breeders applied themselves to hybridizing these choice plants, aiming to produce ever more refined and exquisite forms for connoisseurs and collectors to appreciate in close-up detail. Shows were held and societies of florists formed. At different times the most fashionable florists' flowers included auriculas, anemones, ranunculus, tulips, hyacinths and pinks.

Redouté, Pierre-Joseph (1759–1840)

One of the most familiar names in botanical art, this prolific Belgian illustrator came from an artistic family, and spent his early years training in his father's studio and studying art on later travels abroad. By the age of 23 he was in France, soon discovering the Jardin du Roi (see **Paris**) and the world of botanical painting. Redouté's most famous role, as botanical artist to the Empress Joséphine at **Malmaison**, came later. He recorded many plants from her prodigious collections there in his eight-volume *Les Liliacées* (1802–1816) and *Les Roses* (1817–1824), and illustrated two other books on Malmaison and its plants. He also left hundreds of original watercolour paintings on vellum, but it was through newly developed printing techniques involving 'stipple engraving' that Redouté's work became so widely known and appreciated.

Reeves, John (1774–1856)

An enthusiastic naturalist, Reeves lived in **China** for some 20 years as an inspector of tea for the East India Company in Canton (now Guangzhou). He corresponded with **Sir Joseph Banks** and with the Horticultural Society of London (see **Royal Horticultural Society**), sending plants and botanical drawings. His gifts included camellias, azaleas, peonies, roses and cherries, all carefully established in pots in his garden on the island of Macao, where foreigners in Canton on business had to live. He also introduced *Wisteria sinensis* to Europe, sending two plants back from Canton nurseries. He later became Chairman of the RHS's China Committee. His son, John Russel Reeves, later helped the plant collector

Robert Fortune, who named a skimmia (now known as *Skimmia japonica* subsp. *reevesiana*) after him.

Rehder, Alfred (1863–1949)

Rehder was a dendrologist at the **Arnold Arboretum** in Massachusetts. The sweetly scented, autumn-flowering *Clematis rehderiana* is named after him.

Renard, Charles Claude (Karl Ivanovich) (1809–1886)

Geranium renardii, introduced from the **Caucasus** in 1935, is named for this respected naturalist based in Moscow.

Requien, Esprit (1788–1851)

Delphinium requienii and the diminutive yet pungent Corsican mint, *Mentha requienii*, are named after this French naturalist who founded the natural history museum in Avignon.

Réunion (Ile Bourbon)

This strategically placed island in the Indian Ocean played a significant role in early exploration and hence in the story of plants. In 1817 the first Bourbon rose flowered here – a chance hybrid. The specific epithet *borbonicus* is associated with the island.

Rhodope Mountains

This mountain range in south-western Bulgaria is indicated by the term *rhodopensis*, as in *Haberlea rhodopensis*.

RHS see Royal Horticultural Society

Riccarton, Edinburgh

Fuchsia 'Riccartonii' was raised by John Young, a gardener in the 1830s at Riccarton, an estate on the edge of Edinburgh and now part of Heriot-Watt University.

Thomas Rivers & Son, Hertfordshire

The renowned nursery firm Rivers of Sawbridgeworth dates back to 1725, when John Rivers founded a business that was to become one of the best rose nurseries in the country. A catalogue of 1836 lists nearly 700 varieties. This was largely due to his descendant, Thomas Rivers (1798–1877), a devoted and knowledgeable rose expert who, later in life, also began to study fruit, pioneering fruit-growing in glasshouses – the fashionable 'orchard houses' of the mid-19th century. His son, also Thomas (1831–1899) continued the fruit-growing interest of his father, and many of the numerous varieties developed by the nursery in the 19th century remain popular, for example the 'Conference' pear, and the plum named 'Czar' to commemorate the visit of the Russian emperor in 1874, the year in which the plum first fruited. The nursery closed in 1985 but an orchard has been preserved in memory of the nursery and the Rivers family. The name lives on in a number of fruit varieties.

Plum

SOME RIVERS FRUIT VARIETIES
Cherry: 'Early Rivers'
Apple: 'Thomas Rivers'
Plum: 'Rivers's Early Prolific'
Nectarines: 'Early Rivers', 'John Rivers'

Rice, Graham

The author of a range of books and articles on plants and gardening, as well as a lecturer and photographer, Graham Rice regularly gardens on both sides of the Atlantic. He trained at **Kew**, and is an **RHS** committee member.

Rickard, Martin

A leading fern expert and former nurseryman of Rickard's Hardy Ferns, Martin Rickard is author of several books on the subject.

Rivers, Thomas see page 153

Riverslea Nursery see Prichard

Rivis, Frances (1900s)

One of the loveliest spring-flowering alpina-type clematis is named after this lady from Saxmundham, Suffolk. She is thought to have collected clematis seed in Tibet, from which **Sir Cedric Morris** raised the plant in the 1960s.

Rix, Martyn

Former botanist to the **RHS** at **Wisley**, and now editor of *Curtis's Botanical Magazine*, Martyn Rix has studied and collected plants in many countries. He has written numerous scientific papers and books, including a series of photographic guides to plants in collaboration with **Roger Phillips**. An iris cultivar is named after him.

Robb, Mary Anne (1829–1912)

Euphorbia amygdaloides var. *robbiae*, 'Mrs Robb's bonnet', is named after

this Victorian traveller who brought this indispensable though invasive plant back from **Turkey** in her hat box.

Robin, Jean (1550–1629) and Vespasian (1579–1662)

This father-and-son team were both French royal gardeners and avid plantsmen. Jean Robin had been responsible for the gardens at the Louvre in Paris, and was known for his fine collection of plants on the Ile de la Cité, where, in 1601, the first recorded *Robinia pseudoacacia* was planted. The younger Robin travelled in Europe and North **Africa**, returning with new plants. Contemporaries and friends of the two **John Tradescants**, they exchanged letters, as well as gifts of many important rare plants, with their counterparts across the English Channel.

Robinia hispida

Robinson, Thomas Romney (1792–1882)

Romneya coulteri commemorates both this Irish physicist and astronomer at the observatory at Armagh, and his friend **Thomas Coulter**.

Rock, Joseph (1884–1962)

Though usually thought of as American, Joseph Rock was born in Vienna, and emigrated to the USA in 1905. He worked for some years in Hawaii as a botanist, but his first love was the East, and he seized an opportunity to travel to India as a plant collector for the US Department of Agriculture. This led to a job collecting herbarium specimens

William Robinson (1838–1935)

William Robinson c. 1925

The opinionated and fiercely intelligent Robinson was one of the most influential and colourful figures in recent gardening history. He left his respectable but impoverished Irish family at a young age to pursue a career in horticulture, beginning at **Glasnevin**, in Dublin, and then moving to London. There he worked with native plants at the Royal Botanic Society's garden in Regent's Park, eventually becoming head gardener. He later travelled in Europe and America, wrote for the *Gardeners' Chronicle* and *The Times*, published three books and founded a magazine, *The Garden*, which he edited until 1899. (Its title later fell out of use until it was adopted by the **RHS** for its journal in 1975.) Robinson's travels and experiences served only to strengthen his contempt for many of the fashionable gardening practices of the day, such as topiary and the labour-intensive and artificial system of seasonal 'bedding out'. Instead, he championed hardy perennials, wild plants and informality – and, above all, the importance of plants, rather than contrived formal architecture, as the essence of gardening. Having put his opinions into words in his books and articles, he proceeded to put them into practice in the garden he made at **Gravetye Manor**, the house in Sussex where he spent the last 50 years of his life. It is appropriate that a spring woodland flower is the most familiar plant named after Robinson: the charming pale blue *Anemone nemorosa* 'Robinsoniana'.

---

in **China** on behalf of the Smithsonian Institution and the National Geographic Society. China became Rock's first love, and he was soon an authority on the Naxi people of Yunnan, learning their language and translating Naxi manuscripts. A number of plants he collected in China were successfully introduced into cultivation. The golden-berried rowan *Sorbus* 'Joseph Rock' is the most familiar tribute to him, and he is also remembered in *Erica cinerea* 'Joseph Rock' and the exquisite *Paeonia rockii*, which he found in a Gansu monastery garden, sending seed to the **Arnold Arboretum** and to Sir Frederick Stern, who grew it at **Highdown.**

Rodgers, John (1812–1882)

A commodore in the US Navy, Rodgers discovered *Rodgersia podophylla* in **Japan** in 1855. Other collectors later found five related species from the Far East, all making up the genus of valuable foliage plants that bears his name.

Roezl, Benedict (1824–1885)

The son of a Czech gardener, Roezl trained in some prominent European gardens and nurseries, including **Van Houtte**'s nursery in Ghent, before emigrating to Mexico, where he set up in business. Only after he lost an arm in an industrial accident did

R

this energetic and colourful character become a plant collector. He followed exhausting itineraries around Central, **South** and **North America** and collected huge quantities of seeds and plants, especially orchids, bromeliads and other exotics, but also conifers and hardy plants, including *Darmera peltata*, which he introduced from California. Despite suffering countless dangers and disappointments on his travels, and being robbed rather frequently, he managed to supply plants to many European nurseries, botanic gardens and private subscribers.

Rohde, Eleanour Sinclair (1881–1950)

A prolific writer and researcher who specialized in medieval gardens and herbs, Eleanour Sinclair Rohde wrote many books including *A Garden of Herbs*, *Oxford College Gardens* and *The Story of the Garden*.

Roper, Lanning (1912–1983)

A Harvard graduate who became a teacher in New York City, Roper spent time in England in the US Navy during World War II and settled there after the war. Inspired by British and European gardens he visited, he studied at **Kew** and the Royal Botanic Garden **Edinburgh** and by 1951 had a job with the **RHS**. He subsequently became a freelance gardening journalist and garden designer, and wrote seven books, including *Successful Town Gardening* and *Hardy Herbaceous Plants*. In his later career Roper became involved in increasingly prestigious garden design projects in the UK

and Europe, including RHS Garden **Wisley** and the Prince of Wales's home, Highgrove, in Gloucestershire. He remains an important name in 20th-century garden history.

Rosemoor, RHS Garden, Devon

The **RHS** acquired this garden in 1987 as the gift of its owner Lady Anne Berry (formerly Palmer), whose family had bought the estate in 1923. A skilful gardener and plantswoman, she made the garden, with her first husband, Colonel Palmer, from 1959. She was a friend of **Collingwood Ingram**, and many plants at Rosemoor, including ornamental cherries, peonies, rhododendrons, acers and cistus, were gifts to Lady Anne from his legendary garden at Benenden, in Kent. Plants associated with Rosemoor include *Geranium* × *magnificum* 'Rosemoor' and *Clematis* Rosemoor ('Evipo002').

Roseraie de l'Haÿ see L'Haÿ

Rothschild, Miriam (1908–2005)

A key influence on the trend towards wildlife gardens in the second half of the 20th century, Dame Miriam was an eminent scientist, perhaps inheriting her keen interest in natural history from her father, Charles Rothschild, who founded what was to become the Royal Society for Nature Conservation. Dame Miriam's estate, Ashton Wold in Northamptonshire, was celebrated for its wild flowers and she was among the first writers and broadcasters to introduce gardeners to the idea of meadows. She was awarded the RHS Victoria Medal of Honour in 1990.

Royal Horticultural Society

The RHS celebrated its bicentenary in 2004 but its story began in 1801, when John Wedgwood, son of the famous Josiah of pottery fame, suggested the idea to **William Forsyth**, Royal Gardener at Kensington, and **Joseph Banks**. On 7 March 1804, the inaugural meeting was held, at Hatchard's bookshop in London's Piccadilly. Also there were the Hon. **Charles Greville** and Richard Salisbury (both gentleman gardeners and amateur botanists), **William Townsend Aiton**, royal gardener at **Kew**, and nurseryman **James Dickson**. The stated purpose of the society was 'to collect every information respecting the culture and treatment of all plants and trees, as well culinary as ornamental'.

The Chelsea Flower Show in the 1950s.

Within a year the Horticultural Society (not yet 'Royal') had 28 members and, by 1818, its own garden, at Kensington – necessary for the growing numbers of plants that were arriving. In 1821 this was replaced by 33 acres at Chiswick – the society's first experimental garden. Here the society eventually began two of its key activities: administering a system of qualifications for gardeners and organizing flower shows. It also began to sponsor plant-hunting expeditions overseas, identifying and distributing the resulting plants.

All this took its toll on the society's finances. The herbarium, the library and many plants were sold but the society continued to struggle until Prince Albert came to the rescue, becoming president in 1858. In 1861 the society gained its Royal Charter and opened a new garden in Kensington, on a site now occupied by the Science Museum, Imperial College and the Royal College of Music.

The 1860s saw financial recovery, and the establishment of many activities and traditions that continue today. The Society replaced the lost library by purchasing that of its former secretary **John Lindley**, in 1866, and the same year saw the first edition of the RHS *Journal*, later renamed *The Garden*. Regional shows were established, and national conferences held for apples (1883) and pears (1885). The focus of many RHS activities was the London gardens: Kensington was maintained until 1888, while the Chiswick garden was abandoned only in 1903–1904 on the acquisition of **Wisley** and the royal opening of the fine new headquarters in Vincent Square. The most famous of all RHS institutions, the Chelsea Flower Show, began in 1913, and ever since then the society has maintained and expanded its programme of specialist committees, various awards (for plants and for people), horticultural education, and the promotion of gardening to the general public through its shows and gardens, which numbered four by 2001 when the RHS amalgamated with the Northern Horticultural Society and **Harlow Carr** joined **Wisley**, **Rosemoor** and **Hyde Hall**.

R

Rovelli Nurseries, Italy

Plants collected in **Japan** by **Philipp von Siebold** were propagated and sold by Ratello Rovelli at this nursery near Lake Maggiore. The first *Abelia* × *grandiflora* was also raised there, in 1886.

Rowallane Garden, County Down

Rowallane, south of Belfast, is a world-famous garden of some 50 acres, now in the care of the National Trust. It was created in the first half of the 20th century by master plantsman Hugh Armytage Moore, who inherited the garden in 1903 from his uncle and cared for it for some 50 years until his death. He subscribed to plant-hunting expeditions and nurtured the resulting plants, as well as selecting and encouraging many good forms that appeared as seedlings in the garden. The result is a paradise of rare and exotic mature shrubs and trees, from rhododendrons, magnolias and tree peonies to Rowallane's own award-winning plants: *Hypericum* 'Rowallane', *Chaenomeles* × *superba* 'Rowallane' and *Crocosmia masoniorum* 'Rowallane Yellow'. Other plants named after the garden, which give an idea of its variety, include the candelabra primula called 'Rowallane Rose', *Tanacetum parthenium* 'Rowallane' and *Viburnum plicatum* subsp. *tomentosum* 'Rowallane'. The 2-acre walled garden is especially densely planted, with unusual and interesting primulas, hostas, astilbes and meconopsis carpeting the ground beneath shrubs and trees.

Royal Botanic Garden Edinburgh see Edinburgh

Royal Botanic Gardens, Kew see Kew

Royal Horticultural Society see page 157

Rudbeck, Olaus (1630–1702)

Linnaeus named *Rudbeckia* after this professor of botany at Uppsala, and his son of the same name, who was a friend of Linnaeus and succeeded his father to the Chair. Rudbeck senior founded Uppsala's botanic garden, successfully cultivating many plants from warmer climates. He was also the author of a huge but unfinished botanical treatise, *Campi Elysii*, for which thousands of illustrations had been made with the intention of representing all known plants, but the woodcuts, and almost all the extant copies of the first two volumes, were destroyed in a fire shortly before Rudbeck's death.

Russell, George (1857–1951)

Russell lupins – one of the great flower-breeding successes of the 20th century and stars of many a show bench – were raised by this Yorkshire gardener, who spent over 20 years hybridizing and selecting bigger and better lupin spikes on his allotment. He finally agreed to sell his seeds to Bakers Nursery, who exhibited the lupins for the first time in 1937 to great acclaim. Russell was awarded the MBE for services to horticulture.

Russell, James see Sunningdale Nursery

Ryton Organic Gardens see Henry Doubleday Research Association (Garden Organic)

Russia

Scilla siberica

Hardy plants are the mainstay of temperate gardens, but in the early days of plant hunting, before the colonization of **North America** and the opening up of **China** and **Japan**, opportunities for finding suitable new species were limited. For centuries, the vast lands of Russia and its former empire offered variety and potential to the intrepid, from the Arctic flora of Siberia and **Kamchatka**, in the far north-east, to the botanical riches of the **Caucasus** region in the south-west.

John Tradescant the Elder was probably the first plant hunter to visit Russia, in 1618, travelling as part of a fruitless diplomatic mission to the Tsar. It is thought that he returned with the first cones of the common larch, *Larix decidua*, as well as a number of unfamiliar berrying shrubs from the region around the Bay of St Nicholas in the far north-west, where his ship moored.

A century later, Russia was recruiting scientists and men of learning from overseas. In the newly founded city of St Petersburg, Peter the Great planned a prestigious academy of sciences. It began with a garden of medicinal herbs, which was soon famous for its trees and shrubs, and in the 1820s it became the Imperial St Petersburg Botanical Garden. It was later the source of significant expeditions and was associated with respected botanists and plant collectors such as **Maximowicz**. As the Komarov Botanical Institute, it remains important in plant research and conservation today.

Most of Russia's 18th-century influx of scientists were from Germany, and this was how the contemporaries **Gmelin** and **Steller** came to make up the second generation of plant hunters in Russia, in the 1730s and 1740s. They undertook extraordinarily gruelling northern journeys for years at a stretch, prolonged by the annual freezing of the rivers for several months, which made travel impossible. It seems incredible that these miserable and dangerous expeditions could have yielded delicate garden treasures such as delphiniums, gypsophila, lychnis and irises, but these appeared in London gardens, notably the **Chelsea Physic Garden,** during the second half of the 18th century.

TERMS ASSOCIATED WITH RUSSIA

altaicus from the Altai Mountains

amurensis from the area of Heilong Jiang (the Amur River), on the Russian/Chinese border

caucasicus from the Caucasus

russicus from Russia

ruthenicus from Ruthenia, a region of Russia (and used more generally to mean Russian)

sachalinensis from the island of Sakhalin

sarmaticus from Sarmatia, an old name for a region covering part of eastern Poland, Belarus and the Ukraine

sibericus or *sibiricus* from Siberia

tataricus or *tartaricus* from Tatary (Tartary), an old name for a region of central Asia and European Russia

tauricus from the Crimea

R

Sackville-West, Vita (1892–1962)

The intriguing life and inspirational garden of this 20th-century legend have been exhaustively scrutinized and catalogued, but Vita's story, like her garden, has such a romantic magnetism that its widespread appeal seems likely to continue. Her lonely childhood at Knole, the enormous mansion of her stupendously wealthy family, her extraordinary but successful marriage and creative partnership with Harold Nicolson, and her consuming passion for plants and gardening all contributed to the making of **Sissinghurst**, her most famous creation. She loved cottage garden plants, and especially fragrance, and it is fitting that the scented balsam poplar *Populus balsamifera* 'Vita Sackville-West' is named after her, as is *Viola* 'Vita'. She wrote modestly but charmingly and very knowledgeably in her regular *Observer* column between 1946 and 1961, with a large and devoted following. However, for years many of her readers knew comparatively little about her, and she herself considered her reputation as a poet and historian to be at least as important as her garden writing.

Sammons, J.E. (Eric) (1908–1994)

A number of cultivars of cistus and its relatives were bred by this keen amateur plantsman in his garden at Aldridge, near Walsall in the West Midlands. He named *Cistus* × *argenteus* 'Peggy Sammons' after his wife, and the halimium cultivars 'Sarah' and 'Susan' for other family members. His most well-known plants are *Cistus* × *laxus* 'Snow White' and *Cistus* 'Snow Fire'. Cultivar names beginning with his initials 'JES' indicate other plants he bred, such as *Cistus* × *bornetianus* 'Jester', *Cistus* × *rodiaei* 'Jessica' and *Cistus* 'Jessamy Beauty'.

Sargent, Charles Sprague (1841–1927)

The founder of the **Arnold Arboretum**, Sargent was its director for 54 years before appointing as his successor the arboretum's most famous plant hunter, **E.H. Wilson**. Sargent was author of the monumental 14-volume work *The Silva of North America* (1891–1902). His discoveries on his travels in Asia in the 1890s included *Malus toringo* subsp. *sargentii* and *Prunus sargentii,* while the variant of eastern hemlock known in the USA as Sargent hemlock, *Tsuga canadensis* 'Pendula', was found in 1870 in Beacon, New York. Among other plants named after him are *Cedrus libani* 'Sargentii', *Viburnum sargentii* and *Chaenomeles japonica* 'Sargentii'.

Savill and Valley Gardens, Surrey

These mainly woodland gardens in Windsor Great Park belong to the Crown and were begun in 1932 by E.H. (later Sir Eric) Savill, a royal surveyor and gardener, on the site of a small nursery on the estate. More land was added, and more trees and shrubs acquired, many of them gifts to the royal family from great gardens of the time such as **Exbury**. Today the gardens hold National Collections of rhododendrons (632 species), magnolia cultivars, mahonias and ferns. Plants that bear the name of the garden and its creator include *Nyssa sinensis* Savill form, *Clematis* 'Sir Eric Savill',

S

Rheum palmatum 'Savill' and *Magnolia sprengeri* 'Eric Savill'.

Scanlan, Hugh (1851–1928)
Father Hugh was an Irish missionary who spent many years in **China** and is remembered chiefly in the name of an early-flowering yellow rose – *Rosa xanthina* f. *hugonis* – whose seed he collected and sent to **Kew** in 1899.

Schilling, Tony
This distinguished contemporary plantsman has been deputy curator at **Kew**, and from 1963 to 1991 was in charge of **Wakehurst Place**, where the Schilling Asian Heath Garden is named in his honour. He has collected and introduced many plants, including the award-winning ginger lilies *Hedychium densiflorum* 'Stephen' (named after his son) and *Hedychium coccineum* 'Tara' (after his daughter), and *Euphorbia schillingii*, collected in Nepal in 1977. Other plants named for him include a rhododendron, a sarcococca and *Potentilla fruticosa* 'Silver Schilling'. He was awarded the RHS Victoria Medal of Honour in 1989. His wife Vicky, a dendrologist, was instrumental in the founding of the Tree Register with the late **Alan Mitchell**.

Seabrook, Peter
Known first as a familiar face from gardening television, Seabrook was the presenter of *Gardeners' World* from 1976 to 1979 and covered the Chelsea Flower Show for the BBC for 16 years. A former nurseryman, he is also a respected author and journalist, a founder member of the Garden Writers'

Guild and a holder of the RHS Victoria Medal of Honour.

Seemann, Berthold (1825–1871)
Seemann was a **Kew**-trained German plant collector and naturalist who travelled in the Americas and the Arctic. *Hydrangea seemannii* is a well-known plant that carries his name.

Sello or Sellow, Friedrich (1789–1831)
The pampas grass *Cortaderia selloana* is named after this German naturalist and plant collector.

Sequoiah (*c.*1770–1843)
The story of Sequoiah (also spelled Sequoyah), a Cherokee, whose name was actually George Guess, is full of mystery and controversy. He is immortalized in the names of the great American redwoods *Sequoiadendron giganteum* and *Sequoia sempervirens*.

Sharpitor see Overbeck's

Shasta, California
The name of a river, a mountain and a lake in northern California, Shasta is known to gardeners through the Shasta daisy, bred by **Luther Burbank**. The name is used for several other cultivars, for example *Viburnum plicatum* f. *tomentosum* 'Shasta', *Begonia* 'Pink Shasta' and *Papaver* 'Shasta'.

Sheffield Park Garden, East Sussex
Nyssa sylvatica 'Sheffield Park' and *Erica lusitanica* 'Sheffield Park' are named after this woodand garden whose layout and lakes are in the 18th-century

S

landscape idiom. The early 20th century saw much planting of trees and shrubs, particularly rhododendrons and other new arrivals of the period from the Far East, and the garden is especially noted for its autumn colour.

Sherard, William (1659–1728) and James (1666–1738)

The elder of these distinguished plantsman brothers, William Sherard spent several years in the eastern Mediterranean as consul in Smyrna (now Izmir, **Turkey**). He sent plants back from the region to his brother's famous botanic garden at Eltham, in south-east London. Later he founded a chair of botany at Oxford University, and the first professor, Dillenius, wrote an illustrated account of James's garden, *Hortus Elthamensis* (1732).

Sherriff, George (1898–1967)

A key figure among 20th-century plant hunters, Major George Sherriff had got to know India and the North-West Frontier during his military career as a young man, and later made seven expeditions to the Himalayas with **Frank Ludlow**. Between 1933 and 1949 the pair collected several thousand plants, including many rhododendrons and primulas (among them *Primula whitei* 'Sherriff's Variety'), *Euphorbia griffithii,* and the blue poppy now described as *Meconopsis* George Sherriff Group. *Rosa brunonii* 'Betty Sherriff' is named after his wife, who often accompanied him on his travels. The Sherriffs eventually retired to Kirriemuir, Angus, where they made a Himalayan garden.

Shibata, Keita (1877–1949)

The bamboo genus *Shibataea* is named after this Japanese botanist, a specialist in plant physiology who worked in Germany and Java as well as Tokyo.

Siberia see Russia

Sibthorp, John (1758–1796)

Succeeding his father, Humphrey Sibthorp (1713–1797), as professor of botany at Oxford, John Sibthorp had a particular interest in the medicine of the classical world. In 1786 he went to Greece, with the aim of identifying some of the plants described by **Dioscorides** that were still unknown. The botanical artist **Ferdinand Bauer** accompanied him, and they travelled in Italy, Greece and **Turkey** for some two years, returning with many drawings and plant specimens. He was helped by his discovery that shepherds he met were still using the same plant names as the ancient herbals. Plants named after Sibthorp include *Primula vulgaris* subsp. *sibthorpii* and *Helichrysum sibthorpii*. He died of an illness contracted on his second trip to Greece in 1794–1795, but he left money and instructions for the completion and publication of his ten-volume masterpiece *Flora Graeca*, illustrated with Bauer's magnificent plates.

Simon-Louis Frères, France

A well-known plant connected with this long-established nursery in Metz is the free-flowering climber *Clematis* × *jouiniana*, named after Emile Jouin, nursery manager here in the late 19th century. Other plants include

S

Philipp von Siebold (1797–1866)

Siebold's extraordinary life seems to have attracted various colourful and sometimes contradictory stories. The young German from Bavaria followed several members of his family into the medical profession and joined the Dutch East India Company. His lifelong fascination with **Japan** began when he spent six years there in the 1820s. He was captivated by the country and its culture, but was eventually imprisoned and banished from Japan in 1830 following a scandal involving smuggled maps, which were forbidden to foreigners by the secretive Japanese court. He nevertheless managed to set off for The Netherlands with several hundred plants he had collected, and though many were lost, enough survived for him to establish a nursery at Leiden through which he began to introduce into Europe a range of magnificent Japanese plants such as azaleas, camellias and hydrangeas. His stay in Japan also provided him with raw material for his writings, which covered many aspects of Japanese life and included a beautifully illustrated *Flora Japonica* in two volumes, of which he was co-author with the German botanist Josef Zuccarini (1797–1848). It was nearly 30 years before Siebold could return, but he devoted much of his life to studying and writing about Japan and its plants. Among the plants that he introduced from Japan were *Hosta sieboldiana*, *Fatsia japonica*, *Wisteria floribunda* (in 1830), *Lilium speciosum* and *Clematis florida* var. *sieboldiana*, brought to England from his Dutch nursery in 1836. His second trip to Japan, in 1859, produced *Hydrangea paniculata*, *Malus floribunda* and *Spiraea thunbergii*.

Hydrangea paniculata

SIEBOLD'S SECRET

An interesting anecdote about Siebold concerns *Hydrangea macrophylla* 'Otaksa', one of the plants he found on his first trip to Japan. The name that Siebold gave it was a corruption of the name of his young Japanese mistress, Taki Kusumoto, who had been introduced to him, in the Japanese manner, as 'O-Taki-san'. According to some accounts, they married and had a daughter. He had hoped to return to her after his long exile from Japan, but when he eventually went back she was married to someone else. This hydrangea is now lost from commerce (though not, it appears, from cultivation). However, 'Otaksa' was of great value in breeding because its thick, woody stems were strong enough to hold up the heavy flower trusses without support.

S

---

a sycamore, *Acer pseudoplatanus* f. *variegatum* 'Simon-Louis Frères'.

Sinkins, Catherine (1837–1917)

The heavily scented white pink, *Dianthus* 'Mrs Sinkins', named after the wife of its breeder, was launched by Charles Turner of the Royal Nurseries in Slough, where Mr and Mrs Sinkins looked after the workhouse. The flower features in the town's coat of arms.

Sir Harold Hillier Gardens see **Hillier**

Siskiyou Rare Plant Nursery, Oregon

Gaura lindheimeri 'Siskiyou Pink' and *Oenothera speciosa* 'Siskiyou' are the most widely known of several plants selected at Baldassare Mineo's nursery, which is named in turn for a mountain range on the California/Oregon border.

Sissinghurst Castle Garden, Kent

One of the great gardens of the world, Sissinghurst was created by **Vita Sackville-West** and her husband, Harold Nicolson. Their adventure began in 1930 when they bought the derelict land with its Elizabethan tower, two cottages and ruined farm buildings. They spent the next 32 years making an exquisite English garden, with Harold responsible for the layout while Vita took care of the planting. Her planting schemes are legendary, different enclosures in the garden being occupied by the famous White Garden, the Cottage Garden, planted entirely in hot colours, and the Rose Garden, where Vita grew some of her favourite plants. The Lime Walk, renowned for its spectacular displays of spring bulbs, was Harold's own project. In 1967, after Vita's death, the garden passed to the National Trust, who restored much of the infrastructure in order to enable the garden to cope with increasing numbers of visitors. The planting remained for many years under the expert direction of Pamela Schwerdt and Sibylle Kreutzberger, head gardeners from 1959. Several plants bear the Sissinghurst name, among them *Pulmonaria* 'Sissinghurst White', *Rosmarinus officinalis* 'Sissinghurst Blue' and *Verbena* 'Sissinghurst'.

Six Hills Nursery, Hertfordshire

This famous nursery at Stevenage was founded in 1907 by Clarence Elliott (1881–1969), who had trained at **James Backhouse**'s nursery in York. An alpine specialist and a founder member of the Alpine Garden Society, Elliott travelled far and wide, from the Alps to the Falkland Islands, in search of new specimens. A primula and a saxifrage are named after him. Alpine plants were a rather restricted market, and the nursery also had to sell a range of general garden plants for commercial reasons. One of them – the border stalwart *Nepeta* 'Six Hills Giant' – became familiar to generations of gardeners. There is also a *Penstemon* 'Six Hills' and a *Dianthus* 'Six Hills'. The very well-known *Fuchsia* 'Mrs Popple' was also introduced by Elliott, who took cuttings of a hardy fuchsia that had attracted his attention in the garden of his neighbours, Mr and Mrs Popple. It has been a reliable garden favourite ever since Elliott won an Award of Merit with it at an **RHS** show in 1934.

Sloane, Hans (1660–1753)

Sir Hans Sloane was a successful and influential doctor, very much at the centre of the social and horticultural world of early 18th-century London. Born in Ireland, he had trained in France and had already studied botany and developed an interest in plants before he began his climb up the social ladder. He was elected to the Royal Society in 1685, and in 1687 went to Jamaica for a year as personal physician to the Duke and Duchess of

Slieve Donard Nursery, County Down

This influential nursery was founded in 1904, by Thomas Ryan, as the Donard Nursery Company. Subsequent proprietors were James Coey (1863–1921) and then William Slinger (1878–1961), who renamed the nursery around 1928 (after Northern Ireland's highest peak, at 2,796ft, in the nearby Mountains of Mourne). Slinger ran the nursery for nearly 25 years from 1922, helped by his nephew and two sons. One of them, Leslie (1907–1974), took over from his father in 1946.

During its 70-year history, Slieve Donard raised, introduced or named more than 250 plants. Universally known as The Donard, it was famous for its illustrious clientele and for the camaraderie that always prevailed among customers and nurserymen alike. Many Slieve Donard plants remain popular and garden-worthy today, and although the nursery closed down in 1975, after the death of Leslie Slinger, it lives on in the reputation of these plants and in the names of some 20 cultivars.

> **SOME SLIEVE DONARD PLANTS**
>
> Agapanthus 'Slieve Donard'
> Cupressus macrocarpa 'Donard Gold'
> Cytisus 'Donard Gem'
> Eryngium × zabelii 'Donard Variety'
> Escallonia 'Apple Blossom'
> Escallonia 'Pride of Donard'
> Mahonia × media 'Charity'
> Meconopsis 'Slieve Donard'
> Potentilla fruticosa 'Tangerine'
> Viburnum carlesii 'Aurora'
> Dierama pulcherrimum Slieve Donard hybrids
> Mahonia × media 'Winter Sun'

Albemarle. He recorded the plant life of the places he went to, arranging for his finds to be illustrated, and brought back to England a collection of plants and 'curiosities' that attracted much interest: the exotic flora of the tropics was still a great novelty at that time. He settled easily into the life of a London society doctor, much in demand, and by 1722 was wealthy enough to buy and restore the **Chelsea Physic Garden**, leasing it back to the apothecaries. Sloane's collections grew over the years until, reputedly the largest in the world (at some 200,000 items, including not only herbarium specimens but also drawings, manuscripts, antiquities, coins and precious stones) they ultimately became the basis of the British Museum.

Smit, Tim see Eden Project and Heligan

Smith, Eric (1917–1986)

A name long respected by plant connoisseurs, Eric Smith belonged to a select group of plantsmen and nurserymen of his day, a protégé of such respected gardeners as **Margery Fish**, **Amy Doncaster** and **Nancy Lindsay**. He had worked at **Hillier Nurseries** as a propagator of herbaceous plants for some years when he began raising hellebores in his Southampton garden. From 1967 to 1975 he and **Jim Archibald** ran an independent retail nursery called The Plantsmen at Buckshaw Gardens, at Holwell, near Sherborne, in Dorset. Smith later worked with **Penelope Hobhouse** as nurseryman at **Hadspen**. He was particularly associated with hostas and hellebores, raising and naming many varieties. Among plants bearing his name are *Bergenia* 'Eric Smith', *Crocus tommasinianus* 'Eric Smith', *Helleborus* × *ericsmithii*, and *Hosta* 'Eric Smith' and 'Eric Smith Gold'.

Smith, Geoffrey

Superintendent of **Harlow Carr** garden from 1954 to1974, Geoffrey Smith is known mainly for his many television and radio appearances, and for his gardening books. He was a regular contributor to BBC *Gardeners' World* in the 1970s, and was a panellist on Radio 4's *Gardeners' Question Time*. *Fuchsia* 'Geoffrey Smith' is named for him.

Smith, Thomas see Newry

Solander, Daniel (1733–1782)

A Swedish student and assistant of **Linnaeus**, the botanist Solander moved to London and became a friend of **Joseph Banks**, and was invited to join him and Captain Cook on their voyage to **Australia**. Solander later travelled with Banks to Iceland and the Faeroes. He and Banks subsequently worked together at **Kew**, and Solander was also a keeper at the British Museum. Plants bearing his name include *Astelia solandri*, *Carex solandri*, *Olearia solandri* and *Elymus solandri*.

Solly, Richard Horsman (1778–1858)

The award-winning Australian climber *Sollya heterophylla* is named after this 19th-century British plant physiologist.

Soulange-Bodin, Etienne (1774–1846)

Magnolia × *soulangeana* is named for this Frenchman from Tours, who retired after a career in Napoleon's army and devoted himself to his garden and to breeding hybrid magnolias. There are many named forms of his original hybrid.

Soulié, Jean André (1858–1905)

Soulié, a botanist colleague and compatriot of **Delavay**, was also a medical missionary in **China**. While there, he collected thousands of plant specimens to send back to **Paris**, including *Buddleja davidii*, *Cynoglossum amabile*, *Rhododendron tatsienense* and *Rhododendron souliei*. Soulié worked in the remote border country where Sichuan adjoins Tibet, which was hostile to foreigners. Tragically, he fell victim to Tibetan reprisals for attacks by British military in Tibet: he was tortured and shot. He is remembered in *Aster souliei* and *Primula souliei*.

South Africa see Africa

South America see pages 168–169

Späth Nursery, Germany

This historic Berlin nursery business, which features in many plant names, was founded in 1720 by Christoph Späth. It moved to a new site in the 1860s, under the management of Franz Späth (1839–1913), the fifth of six generations of the family to run the nursery. It finally closed in 1944. The property is now part of Humboldt University, including the arboretum that had been the nursery's show garden and trial grounds. Restored

S

in the 1960s and 1970s, it can still be visited. Plants named for the nursery and members of the Späth family include *Syringa vulgaris* 'Andenken an Ludwig Späth', *Clematis* 'Elsa Späth', *Thuja occidentalis* 'Spaethii', *Cornus alba* 'Spaethii', and *Alnus* × *spaethii*.

Spetchley Park, Worcestershire

Many interesting old trees and shrubs form part of the fine mature plant collection that testifies to this 30-acre garden's historic horticultural pedigree. Spetchley had already been in the Berkeley family for nearly three centuries when, in 1891, Robert Berkeley married Rose Willmott, the sister of the great Victorian gardener **Ellen Willmott**. Though somewhat overshadowed by her sister's reputation, Rose was a skilled gardener and plantswoman, and in her 30 years at Spetchley made a wonderful romantic garden that still attracts many visitors. Plants named after it include *Hedera helix* 'Spetchley', *Vitis vinifera* 'Spetchley Red' and *Macleaya microcarpa* 'Spetchley Ruby'.

Spinners, Hampshire

A plantsman's garden near Lymington, Spinners was developed during the 1970s and 1980s, and the adjacent nursery gained international renown for its rare woodland plants. Hydrangeas, camellias, rhododendrons and Japanese maples thrive here, and are underplanted with choice varieties of shade-lovers such as ferns, hostas, trilliums (including a National Collection) and hardy geraniums, including *Geranium* 'Spinners'. A number of other plants are named after the garden including a hosta, a corydalis and a flowering dogwood.

Spooner, Herman (1878–1975)

Clematis spooneri is named after this botanist with the **Veitch** nurseries.

Sprenger, Karl (1846–1917)

Tulipa sprengeri, *Magnolia sprengeri* and the ornamental crab apple *Malus* × *zumi* 'Professor Sprenger' are named after this German botanist who lived in Naples from the age of 30.

Springwood, Stirlingshire

The award-winning winter-flowering heath *Erica carnea* 'Springwood White' was found in the Italian Alps in the 1920s by a Mrs Walker from Stirling, who propagated the plant. It was named after her Scottish home.

Spry, Constance (1886–1960)

Constance Spry considered herself a gardener, but her parents did not allow her to study horticulture. Only when she was in her 40s did she begin professional flower arranging. Very soon she was a household name, opening florist shops in London and New York on the strength of her former hobby. Her talents were much in demand for society weddings, including that of Edward VIII and Mrs Simpson in 1937. She founded the first school of flower arranging, and her demonstrations, lectures and books reached a wide audience. It seems fitting that the first **David Austin** English rose, *Rosa* 'Constance Spry', should have been dedicated to her. Another of her plants is the snowberry *Symphoricarpos albus* 'Constance Spry'.

S

South America

'Flamboyance' might be the word chosen to sum up the contribution that South and Central America have made to our gardens. Much of the area is in the tropics, so many of its plants are too tender for temperate zone winters. Yet South America, on the routes of early explorers, has always been a magnet for northern travellers. Plant hunters who came here, especially in the 19th century, found plants that, though tender, were remarkable for their bold colours or unusual form – ideal to fuel the two Victorian gardening trends of summer bedding and glasshouse gardening. Slightly hardier finds, such as abutilon, embothrium and crinodendron, fed a third passion of the time – for exotic flowering trees and shrubs.

Tropaeolum majus

Interest in the plants of South America was initially for their useful, rather than their ornamental, qualities. The Incas grew and ate potatoes, tomatoes, maize, beans, squashes, peppers and peanuts. Valuable economic products such as rubber, tobacco, chocolate and quinine came from plants that grow in Central and South America. It was mainly to investigate plants of this kind that the botanist Joseph de **Jussieu** travelled to Ecuador and Peru in 1735 on a French scientific expedition led by Charles Marie de la Condamine (who went on

SUMMER BEDDING PLANTS FROM SOUTH AMERICA
Begonia species
Calceolaria species
Heliotropium arborescens
Ipomoea tricolor
Nicotiana sylvestris
Petunia species
Salvia splendens
Tropaeolum majus
Verbena species

THE MAIN AREAS EXPLORED BY THE PRINCIPAL PLANT HUNTERS

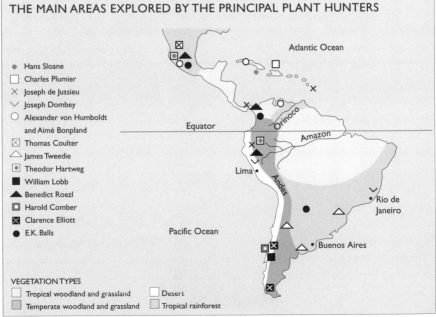

- Hans Sloane
- Charles Plumier
- Joseph de Jussieu
- Joseph Dombey
- Alexander von Humboldt and Aimé Bonpland
- Thomas Coulter
- James Tweedie
- Theodor Hartweg
- William Lobb
- Benedict Roezl
- Harold Comber
- Clarence Elliott
- E.K. Balls

Atlantic Ocean

Equator

Orinoco

Amazon

Andes

Lima

Rio de Janeiro

Pacific Ocean

Buenos Aires

VEGETATION TYPES
- Tropical woodland and grassland
- Temperate woodland and grassland
- Desert
- Tropical rainforest

to travel through Brazil and mapped the Amazon). The heliotrope, which Jussieu found and immediately recognized as something special, was the first of several South American introductions that have survived changing fashions in the gardens of the temperate world, evolving from 'stove plants' or components of extravagant 19th-century parterres to decorations for the conservatories and patios of the 21st century. Others include verbenas and petunias, whose ancestors the Scotsman **James Tweedie** discovered after he emigrated to Argentina in 1825, just at the time when European garden owners were beginning to tire of the landscape tradition and were wanting to enliven their plots with garish 'summer bedding'.

A hardier Tweedie discovery was the pampas grass, *Cortaderia selloana*, native to the more southerly plains of Argentina, where its razor-sharp, silica-edged leaves (*cortar* means 'to cut' in Spanish) make it unappealing to grazing animals. It is a hardy plant, like some of the garden shrubs native to America's southern tip. They include *Fuchsia magellanica*, *Drimys winteri* and *Gaultheria mucronata* (formerly named *Pernettya* after Dom Antoine Pernetty, who recorded it when he travelled to Tierra del Fuego with **Bougainville** in 1763). The diminutive *Gunnera magellanica* is from the same area (its more familiar outsize relative *Gunnera manicata* hails from Brazil and Colombia). Many familiar and fairly hardy garden shrubs come from temperate zones of Chile: *Escallonia* and *Eucryphia* species, *Buddleja globosa*, *Azara microphylla*, *Luma apiculata* and *Berberis darwinii* (identified by the young **Charles Darwin**, and introduced to Britain in 1849 from the island of **Chiloé** by **Veitch** collector **William Lobb**).

South America has never lost its exotic appeal to plant hunters. In the first half of the 20th century, **Harold Comber**, Clarence Elliott of **Six Hills Nursery** and **E.K. Balls** all made collecting expeditions into the Andes, and the tradition continues with contemporary plant hunters such as **Dan Hinkley**.

SOME TERMS ASSOCIATED WITH SOUTH AMERICA

amazonicus from the Amazon
andinus from the Andes
argentinus from Argentina
bolivianus, boliviensis from Bolivia
bonariensis from Buenos Aires
brasiliensis from Brazil
chilensis from Chile
chiloensis from Chiloé
fluminensis from Rio de Janeiro
fuegianus from Tierra del Fuego
magellanicus from the Straits of Magellan
megapotamicus from the Rio Grande
paraguayensis from Paraguay
peruvianus from Peru
uruguayensis from Uruguay

The passion flower story

Several species of *Passiflora* are native to South America. Jesuit missionaries, working here after the Spanish conquest, used the flowers to illustrate the Christian story in their teachings. Each part of the complex flower represents an element in the story. For example, the crucifixion of Jesus is symbolized by the three stigmata (representing the three nails) and the five anthers (representing Christ's wounds), while the ten sepals represent the apostles, excluding Doubting Thomas and Judas Iscariot.

S

Standish, John (1814–1875)

One of the foremost nurserymen of his day, Standish was born in Yorkshire but grew up in Wiltshire, where his father was a forester at Bowood. Having trained there as a gardener, the young John moved to Bagshot, Surrey, as foreman on the Duke of Gloucester's estate. By 1840 he had established his own nursery nearby, breeding rhododendrons (including the lastingly popular *Rhododendron* 'Cynthia'), azaleas, fuchsias and calceolarias. Charles Noble joined him in 1846, and the two men soon acquired **Sunningdale Nursery** and moved the business there. The partnership of Standish & Noble was sufficiently respected in the horticultural world for it to be entrusted with precious new plants and seeds collected by **Robert Fortune** and **Joseph Dalton Hooker** on their travels in the Far East. Rhododendrons were among the stars of Standish & Noble's catalogue, but they launched many other classic garden plants, including *Lonicera fragrantissima* and *Lonicera standishii*. Their partnership, however, was short-lived, lasting barely ten years. Noble stayed at Sunningdale until his retirement in 1898, breeding a number of successful plants including clematis cultivars still popular today, among them *Clematis* 'The President' and 'Daniel Deronda'. Standish moved to new premises, the Royal Nursery at Ascot, where he continued to breed rhododendrons and diversified into growing fruit for another new enterprise, a flower and fruit shop in Knightsbridge. There is an apple variety named after him, and also a slow-growing fastigiate golden yew, *Taxus baccata* 'Standishii', which gained an RHS Award of Garden Merit in 2002.

Stearn, William T. (1911–2001)

A leading 20th-century botanist, Professor Stearn was a prolific author for some 70 years, covering a wide range of subjects ranging from botanical naming to his own special plant interests, which included lilies and the flowers of Greece. His *Botanical Latin* has remained the standard reference work on its subject for over 40 years. He was involved in the **RHS** for much of his life, with several years as its librarian early in his career, and a later spell working on the *RHS Dictionary of Gardening*. He was awarded the RHS Victoria Medal of Honour in 1965. Professor Stearn's later career was spent in the British Museum's botany department. He was awarded the CBE in 1997.

William T. Stearn

Steller, Georg Wilhelm (1709–1746)

This intrepid German botanist and naturalist joined **Gmelin** on a Russian-led expedition to eastern **Russia** in January 1739, and undertook to continue east to the remote peninsula of **Kamchatka**. Here he joined a naval expedition that briefly made landfall in

Alaska, where he collected plants: he may well have been the first white man in Alaska. On the return journey to Russia he stayed to explore Kamchatka for two years, but fell ill and died on his way back west. Many of the plants that he had collected were later described by Gmelin in his *Flora Sibirica*, with a grateful acknowledgement of Steller's invaluable contribution. The herbaceous alpine *Stellera*, *Artemisia stelleriana* and *Allium stellerianum* are named after him.

Stern, Frederick see Highdown

Stokes, Jonathan (1755–1831)
Stokes's aster, *Stokesia laevis*, is named after this distinguished doctor from Chesterfield who had travelled in Europe and had links with the leading botanists of the day. He was particularly interested in the classification of plants and fossils.

Strangman, Elizabeth see Washfield Nursery

Streeter, Fred (1877–1975)
This former nurseryman became head gardener at Petworth House, Sussex, in 1929, later becoming widely known as the leading BBC radio broadcaster on gardening, and one of the first gardeners on television. He was awarded the RHS Victoria Medal of Honour in 1945.

Stuart, John, 3rd Earl of Bute (1713–1792)
A politician and royal adviser who was prime minister for a year under George III, this keen botanist and patron of horticulture had botanic gardens at Luton Hoo, in Bedfordshire, and Highcliffe, in Dorset. He was also instrumental in the early development of the gardens at **Kew**. **Linnaeus** named *Stewartia* after him, but unfortunately misspelled his name.

Sturdza, Princess Greta
Highly respected in gardening circles in many countries, the knowledgeable and inspirational plantswoman Princess Sturdza has a beautiful 17-acre garden at Le Vasterival, near Dieppe, in France, which she has developed since 1957. Sheltering hills, a maritime climate and a woodland setting make a perfect home for dense, informal plantings of a huge range of rarities and choice specimens from all over the world. An award-winning cultivar of *Phlox maculata* is named for the princess, and there was an *Aster* 'Vasterival', but it is no longer in commerce in the UK.

Sunningdale Nursery see page 172

Suttons Seeds, Devon
This well-known family firm has been supplying seeds for more than 200 years. The company was founded as an agricultural seed supplier in 1806, in Reading, by John Sutton (1777–1863). His son, Martin Hope Sutton (1815–1901), put the company on the horticultural map with the introduction of flower and vegetable seeds aimed at the increasing number of small garden owners in Victorian England. Another

S

successful innovation was the introduction of a mail-order service. In 1876 Arthur Sutton (1854–1925) joined the firm. He became a proficient hybridizer, producing improved varieties of vegetables by introducing species from the Near East, and swelling the Suttons catalogue considerably. He was awarded the RHS Victoria Medal of Honour in

Sutton's 'Green Giant' bean

1897, and continued to supply seed during the difficult years of World War I. Suttons moved their operation from Reading to Devon in 1976. The company now belongs to the French-owned international conglomerate **Vilmorin**. Over the years many seed strains have incorporated the Sutton name; perhaps the most familiar today are the foxglove *Digitalis purpurea* 'Sutton's Apricot', and a dwarf broad bean called 'The Sutton'.

Sunningdale Nursery, Berkshire

This iconic nursery had connections with several famous names in horticulture. In the 1850s it was the base of the respected partnership of Standish & Noble, the lucky recipients of many plants collected by great names such as **Fortune** and **Hooker**. After the departure of **John Standish** in 1856, the nursery was run by Charles Noble and then by his manager, Harry White, who worked at the nursery all his life. By the time White died, in 1938, the nursery

SOME SUNNINGDALE PLANTS

Astrantia major 'Sunningdale Variegated'
Bergenia 'Sunningdale'
Cortaderia selloana 'Sunningdale Silver'
Fuchsia 'Sunningdale'
Kniphofia 'Sunningdale Yellow'

had fallen into neglect and its size was much reduced. Only towards the end of World War II did plantsman James Russell come on to the scene. He gradually restored and replanned the nursery, and improvements were well under way by the time the business celebrated its centenary in 1947. In 1956 Russell was joined by **Graham Stuart Thomas**, who also held the post of gardens adviser to the National Trust. He became part-time manager, arriving complete with his collection of shrub roses. With its stock updated and two dedicated experts in charge, the nursery enjoyed a second period of success, which lasted until the late 1960s, when Sunningdale was sold to the Waterer group of nurseries and soon became a garden centre. The plant collections were dispersed: the rhododendrons went with James Russell to his new home at Castle Howard, in Yorkshire, the roses to RHS Garden **Wisley** and to the Royal National Rose Society's gardens in St Albans. Graham Stuart Thomas was able to re-create his collection of old roses at the National Trust property of **Mottisfont**, in Hampshire. Sunningdale's distinguished history continues in the names of a number of plants.

S

Stephen Taffler (1922–2005)

'Taff', in cultivar names, is the hallmark of the knowledgeable amateur plantsman Stephen Taffler, who was an avid collector, for over 40 years, of plants with variegated foliage. His favourite was reputed to be *Tolmiea menziesii* 'Taff's Gold', spotted by chance and hurriedly bought from a New York flower stall while he was rushing to catch a plane. It is now a well-known house and garden plant. He named another of his plants, *Heuchera sanguinea* 'Taff's Joy', after his first wife, Joy. Taffler began a variegated plant group within the Hardy Plant Society, and also founded and chaired the British Ivy Society. He wrote two books: *Ground Cover Plants* and *Climbing Plants and Wall Shrubs*.

SOME TAFFLER PLANTS
Antirrhinum majus 'Taff's White'
Forsythia suspensa 'Taff's Arnold'
Geranium phaeum 'Taff's Jester'
Humulus lupulus 'Taff's Variegated'
Ligustrum ovalifolium 'Taff's Indecision'
Prunus laurocerasus 'Taff's Golden Gleam'
Ribes sanguineum 'Taff's Kim'
Symphoricarpos orbiculatus 'Taff's Silver Edge'

Terra Nova Nurseries, see **Heims, Dan**

Thompson & Morgan, Suffolk
William Thompson (1823–1903) rose to fame as the founder of this world-famous seed company from small beginnings in the little garden behind his father's bakery in Ipswich. His first seed catalogue appeared in 1855, and his reputation as a skilled plantsman grew to such an extent that by 1876 an edition of *Curtis's Botanical Magazine* was published in his honour. In 1897 he was one of the group of outstanding horticulturists honoured by the new RHS award, the Victoria Medal of Honour. After this he took on John

Graham Stuart Thomas (1909–2003)

One of the most respected plantsmen of the 20th century, Graham Stuart Thomas was a gardener, botanist, author, photographer and illustrator. Much of his career was spent in two landmark nurseries: 24 years at **Six Hills Nursery**, at Stevenage, and later a spell at **Sunningdale Nursery** in Berkshire, as manager and then associate director. As gardens adviser to the National Trust for nearly 20 years from 1955, he was involved in many restoration projects, notably at **Mottisfont**, in Hampshire, where he created a famous garden of old roses that became a National Collection. He was the author of more than 20 books, including such classic reference works as *Perennial Garden Plants* and *The Old Shrub Roses*. His long and distinguished career earned him many awards, culminating in the OBE in 1975. Dozens of plants have associations with him, and those named after him include *Rosa* Graham Thomas ('Ausmas'), *Lonicera periclymenum* 'Graham Thomas', *Rhododendron* 'Graham Thomas' and *Eryngium bourgatii* Graham Stuart Thomas's selection.

T

Morgan as his partner, and by the time Thompson died the company was well established as a leading seed supplier.

Thomson, Thomas (1817–1878)
A Glasgow-born surgeon with the East India Company in Calcutta, Thomson became fascinated with the flora of the Himalayas on his visits to Sikkim (with **Joseph Hooker**), **Kashmir** and Afghanistan. He brought many plants back to Britain, including *Rhododendron thomsonii*, *Rhododendron falconeri* and *Rhododendron grande*, and wrote a book on the plant life of India, *Flora Indica* (1855).

Thornhayes Nursery, Devon
Euonymus europaeus 'Thornhayes' and *Malus transitoria* 'Thornhayes Tansy' are named for this specialist tree nursery near Cullompton.

Thorp Perrow Arboretum, North Yorkshire
Trees and shrubs of more than 1,700 kinds make up this fine private collection near Bedale, planted by Colonel Sir Leonard Ropner (1895–1977) and now owned by his son.

Threave Garden, Dumfries & Galloway
The National Trust for Scotland trains its gardeners at Threave, a varied estate near Castle Douglas with a beautifully maintained, stone-walled kitchen garden, a heather collection and an arboretum. Plants named for the garden include *Abies koreana* 'Threave', *Ozothamnus* 'Threave Seedling' and *Penstemon* 'Threave Pink'.

Thrower, Percy (1913–1988)
Britain's first famous television gardener learned his trade from his father, a head gardener in Buckinghamshire. Percy's career as a professional gardener began in the royal gardens at Windsor Castle, then he worked in parks departments, continuing as parks superintendent at Shrewsbury for many years alongside his broadcasting career. His first radio broadcast was in 1948, and by the early 1950s he had found his natural medium as a presenter of television gardening programmes. Percy Thrower attracted ever-increasing audiences, taking on the first presenter's job on a new BBC programme, *Gardeners' World*, in 1968, after the advent of colour television. For the first time, he was able to broadcast from a real outdoor garden instead of a studio mock-up. He remained a successful and popular presenter until 1976, when he was suddenly dropped in a controversy over advertising. He continued to write books, lead tours and run the nursery and garden centre business that he co-owned in Shropshire. *Aster novi-belgii* 'Percy Thrower' is named in his honour.

Thunberg, Carl (1743–1828)
A Swedish doctor who had been a pupil of **Linnaeus**, Thunberg travelled for several years as a ship's surgeon. He visited many distant and exotic destinations including South **Africa**, where he spent three years from 1772. He had gone there to learn Dutch in order to qualify for employment with the Dutch East India Company in **Japan**. In South Africa, he travelled into remote areas, collecting plants

with **Francis Masson**. In 1775 he fulfilled his ambition and went to Japan, travelling in the Far East until 1778. His book *Flora Japonica* was published in 1784. Plants he collected in Japan include *Rosa rugosa*. Thunberg eventually succeeded **Linnaeus** as professor at Uppsala. Plants named after him include the genus *Thunbergia*, *Berberis thunbergii*, *Fritillaria thunbergii*, *Allium thunbergii*, *Astilbe thunbergii* and *Spiraea thunbergii*.

Tien Shan

The name of this botanically important mountain range, on the boundary between **China** and the former Soviet republic of Kazakhstan, means 'heavenly mountains'. Among the horticulturally significant plants that are native to this region is *Malus sieversii*, thought to be the genetic ancestor of the eating apple, which is now believed by some experts to have travelled along the 'silk roads' – ancient (probably prehistoric) trading routes – from the Ili Valley

Apple

in the northern Tien Shan to Europe, the Middle East and India.

Tissington, Derbyshire

Veronica gentianoides 'Tissington White' was introduced into the nursery trade in the early 1980s from this village, where it was believed to have been in gardens for a long time. There is also a monkshood called *Aconitum* 'Tissington Pearl'.

Titchmarsh, Alan

A dianthus and a fuchsia are named after Alan Titchmarsh, probably the most widely known personality in contemporary gardening. He trained at horticultural college and **Kew** before becoming a freelance journalist and then a television presenter. His garden makeover programme *Ground Force*, with Charlie Dimmock and Tommy Walsh, provoked debate in the world of traditional horticulture, but was a hugely successful innovation. For seven years Alan Titchmarsh was the presenter of BBC Television's *Gardeners' World*, from his former garden, Barleywood, in Hampshire. He is also known for his live coverage of the Chelsea Flower Show, and for several other television series. He has also written some 40 books. His many honours include honorary degrees, the MBE in 2000 and the RHS Victoria Medal of Honour in 2004.

Tolmie, William (1812–1886)

Tolmiea menziesii, the 'piggyback plant', is named after this Scottish surgeon who emigrated to take up a post at Fort Vancouver with the Hudson Bay Company in 1832 and later settled on Vancouver Island.

Tommasini, Muzio de' (1794–1879)

Crocus tommasinianus is named for this Italian botanist.

Torrey, John (1796–1873)

The coniferous trees called *Torreya*, yew relatives most familiar in the California nutmeg *Torreya californica*, are named after this American science teacher

T

John Tradescant the Elder (1570–1638) and John Tradescant the Younger (1608–1662)

John Tradescant was an influential gardener and plantsman whose expertise and flair for networking helped him to build contacts throughout the horticultural world, making him one of the most significant names in early garden history. As a professional gardener, he moved in elevated circles, working for various noble families before his reputation ultimately secured him a post with the king himself. Tradescant also had a taste for foreign adventure. His early journeys, in

Liriodendron tulipifera

1609–1611, were to Europe, in search of fine fruit trees and other plants for **Hatfield House**, where he was gardener to Robert **Cecil**, 1st Earl of Salisbury. In 1618, having moved to Kent, Tradescant applied to join a diplomatic mission to northern **Russia** – a rare opportunity to discover Arctic flora. Two years later he headed for north **Africa** on a naval expedition organized in an attempt to control the piracy that was such a threat to trade. This time, Mediterranean plants including cistus and the turpentine tree (*Pistacia terebinthus*) were among his discoveries. Tradescant and his family settled in 1626 at Lambeth, where he filled his house with a huge collection of curiosities gathered on his travels and his garden with interesting plants, later recorded in his valuable *Catalogue of Plants* and also in **John Parkinson**'s *Paradisi in Sole Paradisus Terrestris*.

Meanwhile Tradescant's son of the same name had inherited his father's horticultural interests. He was soon to succeed his father as a royal gardener, but first his longing to travel was fulfilled by the chance to go to **North America**, and he made three trips there between 1637 and 1653. American plant introductions credited to him include the tulip tree, *Liriodendron tulipifera*, the red maple, *Acer rubrum*, and the swamp cypress, *Taxodium distichum*. Another plant brought back by Tradescant the Younger, a member of the genus he subsequently named for his father, was the herbaceous perennial *Tradescantia* Andersoniana Group, previously known as *Tradescantia virginiana* after its place of origin. Yet another was *Aster tradescantii*, the first of many Michaelmas daisies. Today the Tradescants are also commemorated by a **David Austin** rose cultivar, *Rosa* Tradescant ('Ausdir'). A knot garden using some of the plants they introduced has been laid out at the **Museum of Garden History** in London. The museum is housed in the former church of St Mary at Lambeth, where both Tradescants are buried.

and botanist whose career was much occupied with recording the botanical findings of the various government expeditions exploring the United States in the 1840s. Torrey began writing a flora of **North America** in the 1830s, with **Asa Gray** as co-author, but unfortunately it was never completed. He did, however, publish a two volume *Flora of New York* in 1843.

Tournefort, Joseph Pitton de (1656–1708)

A French botanist and doctor, Tournefort explored the Alps and the Pyrenees in search of plants as a young man and was later appointed professor at the Jardin du Roi in **Paris**, where he worked on an early system of classifying plants. In 1700, Louis XIV sent him on an expedition to the botanically rich lands of Greece, **Turkey** and Persia to find new plants and to rediscover useful ones that had been valued in classical times. Tournefort returned after more than two years with over 1,000 species, many beautifully recorded for posterity by his chosen companion, the artist Claude Aubriet. Their adventures are described in Tournefort's posthumously published *Relation d'un Voyage du Levant*. Among his most significant discoveries were *Papaver orientale*, and the wild purple rhododendron (*Rhododendron ponticum*) and yellow azalea (*Rhododendron luteum*). Plants later named to commemorate Tournefort include *Crocus tournefortii*, *Allium tournefortii* and *Scutellaria tournefortii*.

Treasure, John see Burford House

Trebah, Cornwall

One of the great informal tree and shrub gardens of Cornwall, Trebah

Tresco Abbey Gardens, Isles of Scilly

The small island of Tresco, some 30 miles offshore from Cornwall, has for many years attracted visitors eager to see one of Britain's most remarkable gardens. Planting was begun in the 1830s by Augustus Smith, who terraced the south-facing hillside, using the ruined 12th-century monastic buildings as a starting point and taking advantage of the island's unusual climate in his choice of planting. Tempered by the influence of the sea, Abbey Gardens have traditionally been home to a huge range of tender plants that would not normally withstand the British climate. Palms, cacti, agaves, echiums, aeoniums and many others more often associated with the Mediterranean, Australia, South Africa or California are usually safe to grow outdoors here – though in recent years the exotic planting has twice fallen victim to freak weather conditions. In 1987 heavy snow and prolonged frost destroyed 80 per cent of the plants. Their replacements were just becoming established when, three years later, disaster struck again in the form of gales, which felled trees that had sheltered the garden from its earliest days. Since then new shelter belts have been made and the gardens have been much overhauled, with new plantings now established among such survivors as the large Canary Island date palms and other plants that were protected by the priory buildings. Many plants self-sow here, creating a natural effect and testifying to their contentment in their adopted home. The island has given its name to a number of exotics, including *Watsonia* Tresco hybrids and 'Tresco Dwarf Pink', several cultivars of *Lampranthus spectabilis*, *Hedychium spicatum* 'Tresco' and *Eccremocarpus scaber* 'Tresco Cream'.

T

is packed with rare plants that enjoy the favourable site and mild climate. The garden was made in the 19th century but owes its survival to Major and Mrs Tony Hibbert, who came here in 1981, restored the garden and established the Trebah Garden Trust to secure its future. Trebah plants include *Narcissus* 'Trebah', *Salvia* × *jamensis* 'Trebah' and *Rhododendron* 'Trebah Gem'.

Trelissick, Cornwall
Narcissus 'Trelissick' and *Salvia* 'Trelissick' are named for this woodland and parkland estate and garden, in a beautiful setting on the upper Fal estuary. Former owners the Copeland family (of Spode china fame) gave the estate to the National Trust in 1955.

Trengwainton, Cornwall
Cornish gardens were ideal for some of the less hardy finds of the great plant hunters. Many of the exotic shrubs to be seen at Trengwainton enjoy the extra protection of walled enclosures, and would struggle in colder gardens. The garden was made at the time of **Frank Kingdon Ward**, who collected the seeds that produced some of the rhododendrons here. Candelabra primulas, pittosporums, eucryphias and embothriums are among other treasures, and the large magnolia collection includes *Magnolia sargentiana* var. *robusta* 'Trengwainton Glory'.

Tresco Abbey Gardens see page 177

Trewithen, Cornwall
A beautiful garden was laid out around this fine 18th-century house near Truro when it was built, but it was a later owner, George Johnstone, who planted the famous woodland garden with its spectacular collection of trees and flowering shrubs. After he arrived here in the early 20th century, Johnstone planted many new varieties of camellia, rhododendron, magnolia and other sought-after flowering shrubs and trees of his day, and many of these have now made magnificent specimens. Over the years numerous new cultivars of camellia, rhododendron and other plants have been raised and propagated at Trewithen: some are named after the house, and a few after Johnstone and members of his family. The most popular, *Ceanothus arboreus* 'Trewithen Blue', grows in the walled garden, as does *Salvia* 'Trewithen'.

Tschonoski (1841–1925)
Little is known about this 19th-century Japanese plant collector, but he was an invaluable assistant to foreign plant hunters in **Japan**, notably the Russian **Carl Maximowicz**, who trained him, and to whom he continued to send plants at the botanic garden in St Petersburg for many years. It was partly thanks to Tschonoski that Maximowicz became the leading authority of his day on Japanese plants. His name is found in *Trillium tschonoskii*, *Acer tschonoskii* and the ornamental crab-apple *Malus tschonoskii*.

Tulbagh, Rick (1699–1771)
The African bulb genus *Tulbaghia* is named after this Dutch governor of the Cape of Good Hope.

Turczaninov, N.S. (1796–1863)

The Ukrainian Turczaninov spent much of his career in Siberia as a Russian civil servant, later becoming an influential botanist. He built up a herbarium, including Australian collections acquired from **James Drummond** and **Robert Brown**, and became an authority on Australian flora. He is commemorated by the hornbeam *Carpinus turczaninowii*, *Corydalis turtschaninovii*, and *Salix turczaninowii*.

Turkey

Turkey has been a mecca for plant lovers from the West since the days when the floral riches of Constantinople, at the hub of trade routes into Europe, first delighted ambassadors and early travellers like **Belon** and **Busbecq**. The Turks had a long-standing devotion to plants and gardens. In the 16th century, flower markets packed with exquisite cultivated tulips (named from *duliband*, the Turkish word for a turban), hyacinths and crown imperials were an everyday feature of the city of Suleyman the Magnificent. Constantinople gardens brimmed with beautiful flowers, and market gardens kept up the supply.

Some of these plants had travelled from Asia with the Turks on their westward migration, but others may have been, or been bred from, native plants. Wild tulips remain among the chief treasures of Turkey's prodigiously rich flora, and modern botanists, following in the footsteps of the eminent **John Sibthorp**, continue to discover new plant species in the country: more than 1,500 have been identified since 1945.

Turner, William (1508–1568)

Turner was Dean of Wells, in Somerset, and an important early English botanist whose record of Britain's native flora, published in 1538, earned him the unofficial title 'the father of British botany'. His later book, *A New Herball* (1568) resulted from his research into the plants used in Classical medicine by physicians such as **Dioscorides**.

Petunia violacea

Tweedie, James (1775–1862)

This influential Scotsman was head gardener at the **Royal Botanic Garden Edinburgh**. At the age of 50 he emigrated to **South America**, from where he sowed the seeds of a gardening revolution. The showy but tender plants he collected included the first verbenas and petunias, which were soon to lead the Victorian trend for summer bedding. He sent seeds to **William Hooker** and to various Scottish nurserymen he knew, who began to hybridize and propagate the plants and were soon producing their brilliantly coloured offspring in vast numbers for lavish bedding schemes. Seeds of pampas grass, *Cortaderia selloana*, which first flowered in 1842 at **Glasnevin**, in Dublin, were also sent back by Tweedie. A tropical climber, *Tweedia caerulea*, is named after him.

T

Uvedale, Robert (1642–1722)

The Revd Robert Uvedale, a plantsman and scholar who was among the first private gardeners to possess a collection of glasshouses, was headmaster of Enfield Grammar School, in north London. He was an important link in the chain that brought sweet peas (*Lathyrus odoratus*) to our gardens: he conducted a scholarly correspondence with Father **Francesco Cupani**, who discovered the sweet pea's wild ancestor in Sicily, and Cupani sent him some seeds in 1699.

Valley Garden see Savill and Valley Gardens

Deutzia

Van der Deutz, Johan (1743–1788)

Deutzia scabra was discovered by **Carl Thunberg** on his trip to Japan in the 1770s. The new genus was named after this lawyer and councillor from Amsterdam who had been a sponsor of his expedition.

Van Fleet, Walter (1857–1922)

Rosa 'Doctor W. van Fleet' and 'Sarah van Fleet' are two of the cultivars raised by this American doctor who gave up his medical career at the age of 35 to concentrate on rose breeding. Other well-known van Fleet roses include 'American Pillar' and the first (and some say still the best) modern repeat-flowering climber, 'New Dawn'.

Van Houtte, Louis (1810–1876)

When he founded his Ghent nursery at the age of 29, Van Houtte had already worked in the Ministry of Finance, run a seed shop, founded a horticultural magazine, been widowed, spent two years exploring Brazil, and been director of the botanic garden in Brussels. It is perhaps not surprising that this dynamic Belgian's business prospered from the start, soon becoming the largest and most successful nursery in the country. Thousands of plants from all over the

Louis van Houtte

world were grown, from pineapples to peonies and from waterlilies to 1,700 varieties of rose. Van Houtte listed the world-famous Ghent azaleas, though they did not originate in his nursery; he obtained his stock from smaller local nurseries, sometimes acquiring the nurseries themselves. He also sent out plant collectors in search of marketable novelties. The most well-known plant named after Van Houtte is *Spiraea × vanhouttei*. Others commemorating the family include *Campanula* 'Van-Houttei', *Rhododendron* 'Louis Aimée van Houtte', *Clematis* 'Madame van Houtte' and *Rosa* 'Marie van Houtte'.

U
V

Veitch Nurseries, Devon and London

When the Scottish nurseryman John Veitch (1752–1839) travelled to a new landscaping job on Sir Thomas Acland's **Killerton** Estate near Exeter, he could have had little idea that he was on his way to founding the most important family nursery business in the history of gardening. He was in his 50s by the time he ventured into setting up his own nursery, at Budlake near Killerton, in 1808, and 80 when it moved to Mount Radford in Exeter. By then his son James (1772–1863) was in partnership with him, and his grandson, another James (1815–1869), was starting his career in the family business. James spent two years in London learning the nursery trade, gathering new ideas and becoming an orchid expert – one of various specializations in new plants that were to help bring the Veitch nurseries international fame.

By 1840 two other young men who worked for Veitch were about to influence the nursery's fortunes, in the single most significant development in its long history. They were the **Lobb** brothers, who, in 1840 and 1843, became the first of over 20 plant collectors sent abroad by the firm during the next 70 years, including three members of the Veitch family. They returned with countless plants of every kind, which soon found new homes in gardens and glasshouses everywhere. Another major development, in 1853, was the return to London of James Veitch junior to run a new venture, in Chelsea, which became the Royal Exotic Nursery: the birthplace, three years later, of the first orchid hybrid.

The two branches of Veitch subsequently went their separate ways, but the company remained in the family for five generations. James Veitch & Sons, in London, closed in 1914. The Exeter branch, Robert Veitch & Son, was acquired by St Bridget Nurseries, a thriving West Country business founded by Frank Langdon in 1925 and named after one of his first crops, St Bridgid anemones. The Veitch family graves, in the churchyard at Broadclyst, near Killerton, now have a garden planted with Veitch introductions as a tribute to this historic nursery dynasty.

SOME VEITCH PLANTS

Abies veitchii
Corylopsis sinensis var. calvescens f. veitchiana
Echinops ritro 'Veitch's Blue'
Magnolia × veitchii 'Peter Veitch'
Malus 'Veitch's Scarlet'
Rosa 'James Veitch'
Sasa veitchii

SOME VEITCH PLANT COLLECTORS

William Lobb: California, South America, 1840–1857
Thomas Lobb: India, Malaya, 1843–1860
John Gould Veitch: Japan, China, South Pacific, Australia, 1860–1870
Peter Veitch: Australia, Borneo, 1875–1878
Frederick Burbidge: Borneo, 1877–1878
Charles Maries: Japan, China, 1877–1879
Charles Curtis: Madagascar, Java, Sumatra, Borneo, 1878–1884
James Veitch: India, Japan, Australia, New Zealand, 1891–1893
E.H. Wilson: China, Tibet, 1899–1905
William Purdom: China, 1909–1912

U
V

Van Tubergen

This Dutch nursery and bulb firm, founded in Haarlem in 1868, was first known in the 1900s as the breeder of the many popular hybrids known as Dutch iris. The early-flowering spring bulb *Scilla mischtschenkoana* 'Tubergeniana' was found at the nursery in 1931, packed by mistake in a parcel of bulbs from Iran. Other plants that carry the name include *Tulipa clusiana* var. *chrysantha* 'Tubergen's Gem' and *Babiana stricta* 'Tubergen's Blue'. The many plant names that contain 'Zwanenburg' derive from the firm's former estate of that name in Haarlem. Among them are *Crocus chrysanthus* 'Zwanenburg Bronze', *Allium oreophilum* 'Zwanenburg' and *Tradescantia* (Andersoniana Group) 'Zwanenburg Blue'.

Veitch nurseries see page 181

Ventnor Botanic Garden, Isle of Wight

Opened in 1972, this is one of Britain's newer botanic gardens. It enjoys a sunny maritime location, and suitable exotic planting was chosen in the early days, with the help of the late Sir Harold **Hillier**. However, a series of setbacks – some winters in the 1980s, notably that of 1986/87, and then the notorious gales of 1987 and 1990 – damaged or destroyed many plants. Today the results of painstaking replanting have produced a varied and interesting garden, with features ranging from the Japanese terraces and Americas garden to cliffs and grassland where native species are encouraged.

Verey, Rosemary (1918–2001)

Known all over the world for her lectures and books, Rosemary Verey was one of the great English plantswomen and garden designers of the 20th century. She advised on the planting of many distinguished gardens, including that of the Prince of Wales at Highgrove, which is near her own iconic garden at **Barnsley House** in Gloucestershire. One of her many books, *Rosemary Verey's Making of a Garden* (1995), tells how this garden was made; other titles by her include *The Scented Garden* (1981), *The Garden in Winter* (1988), and *Good Planting* (1990). *Geranium* × *oxonianum* 'Rosemary Verey' is named after her.

Vibert, Jean-Pierre (1777–1866)

This French rose breeder rescued plants and breeding notes from the Descemet rose nursery in Paris, which was wrecked and bankrupted in the Napoleonic Wars. Vibert painstakingly built a new rose business, propagating traditional types and developing new varieties. *Rosa* 'Aimée Vibert' is dedicated to his daughter.

Vineyard Nursery, London

Run by **James Lee** and Lewis Kennedy, the Vineyard Nursery in Hammersmith (on the site where Olympia stands today), was described by **John Claudius Loudon** in the late 1820s as the best nursery in the world. It introduced huge numbers of new plants, including some of the first Australian species seen in the European nursery trade. Lee and Kennedy, who had set up in business together around 1745, had many prestigious clients including

Vilmorin, France

This French nursery firm has been in business since 1743, and still has a Paris shop on its original site at 4, quai de la Mégisserie. During its long history, several generations of the Vilmorin family have made their mark on the horticultural world, first serving as royal botanists and seedsmen and later introducing and breeding countless new plants. Latterly the company has moved into overseas markets, becoming the world's largest supplier of packeted seeds, with interests today in over 100 countries.

Seed catalogue from 1911

For many years the company was known as Vilmorin-Andrieux – a partnership established after Victoire de Vilmorin (1746–1840) married the daughter of nurseryman and botanist Pierre d'Andrieux in 1774. In the next generation André de Vilmorin (1776–1862) made his mark by founding the Arboretum des Barres, near Montargis, in 1817. This important tree and shrub collection was expanded in the mid-19th century by Maurice de Vilmorin (1849–1918), who had links with French missionaries collecting in China and elsewhere in the Far East. Plant hunters sometimes preferred to entrust their most precious seeds to professional nurserymen, rather than let them take their chances with the scientists of the botanical institutions in **Paris**, who were inundated with plant material from collectors and could not always give rare seeds the attention they deserved. Thus Vilmorin received seeds from **David**, **Delavay**, **Soulié** and **Farges**. They included *Incarvillea grandiflora*, *Rhododendron augustinii* and 37 seeds of the coveted *Davidia involucrata*, from which Vilmorin famously raised one treasured seedling.

The Arboretum National des Barres has been state-owned for more than 100 years, but the Vilmorin family remained involved until 1935. The 86-acre landscaped park is now one of the key tree and shrub collections of Europe, with over 2,700 species.

SOME VILMORIN PLANTS

Agave vilmoriniana
Cryptomeria japonica 'Vilmorin Gold'
Cryptomeria japonica 'Vilmoriniana'
Cotoneaster vilmorinianus
Davidia involucrata var. *vilmoriniana*
Deutzia longifolia 'Vilmoriniae'
Hosta 'Vilmoriniana'
Potentilla fruticosa 'Vilmoriniana'
Sorbus vilmorinii
Quercus 'Vilmoriniana'

U
V

the royal family, **Thomas Jefferson**, and the wildly extravagant Empress Joséphine at **Malmaison** in France, whom they continued to supply even through the blockades of the Napoleonic Wars. It is said that Kennedy had special passports to allow him safe passage to Malmaison when he was needed there to advise on the making of the garden. Joséphine's artist **Redouté** painted the Australian plant *Kennedia coccinea*, which was named for Kennedy. Lee's son and grandsons ran the nursery after his death.

Wada, Koichiro (1907–1981)

Rhododendron yakushimanum 'Koichiro Wada' and *Saxifraga* 'Wada' *fortunei* are two of many choice plants raised by this dedicated nurseryman from **Japan** whose reputation, like his plants, travelled many thousands of miles from his nursery not far from the foot of Mount Fuji. He bred many fine cultivars of camellia, pieris, maple and tree peony, which found their way via the Trans-Siberian Railway to the gardens of Europe. Many also reached America. It is poignant that *Magnolia salicifolia* 'Wada's Memory' was named during World War II, when it was feared that Wada had been killed because of his association with the British.

Wakehurst Place, West Sussex

The country estate and arboretum of the Royal Botanic Gardens, **Kew**, Wakehurst Place was developed by Lord Wakehurst (Gerald Loder, a member of the distinguished family from **Leonardslee**) after he bought it in 1903. The extensive plantings of hardy trees and shrubs include four National Collections: *Nothofagus*, *Betula*, *Skimmia* and *Hypericum*. An exciting new conservation initiative at Wakehurst is the innovative Millennium Seed Bank, a state-of-the-art storage facility for seed of some 24,000 plant species. Plants named after Wakehurst include *Betula utilis* 'Wakehurst Place Chocolate', *Skimmia japonica* 'Wakehurst White'. *Acer palmatum* 'Wakehurst Pink' and *Pieris formosa* var. *forrestii* 'Wakehurst'. There is a rhododendron named after Gerald Loder.

Wageningen, The Netherlands

Geranium × *oxonianum* 'Wageningen' and *Quercus* × *hispanica* 'Wageningen' are named after this Dutch town whose university specializes in life sciences.

Waldstein-Wartenburg, Franz (1759–1823)

This Austrian botanist and author is remembered in the names of the woodland perennial *Waldsteinia ternata*, as well as in *Cardamine waldsteinii* and *Hieracium waldsteinii*.

Wales: National Botanic Garden see National Botanic Garden of Wales

Ward, Frank Kingdon see Kingdon Ward

Ward, Nathaniel (1791–1868)

A simple but ingenious invention by this east London doctor and amateur naturalist had a profound effect on the transportation of plants. The 'Wardian case', first used in the mid-1830s, was a sealed miniature greenhouse in which plants could travel much more safely on board ship in a controlled environment, recycling their own water through condensation. Before the Wardian case, the shipping of live plants had an extremely poor success rate. Many hard-won specimens failed to reach their destination on long sea voyages – victims of salt spray, wind or drought, or simply of neglect by ships' crews. Dr Ward's innovative solution facilitated the passage around the world not only of garden plants but also of economically important ones like tea, rubber and bananas.

W
X
Y
Z

Nathaniel Wallich (1786–1854)

Gardeners may wonder why so many plants are named after Wallich. It is true that this influential Dane is not a household name, but he played a key role in the introduction of countless plants from the East. Aged 21, he went to India as a surgeon and later joined the East India Company, who put him in charge of Calcutta's developing botanic garden. He soon became its director – a post he held for 30 years. During this time he transformed the garden from a nursery for economic plants to supply to the West, into a place of beauty widely renowned for its collection of ornamental plants. Wallich not only travelled and collected plants himself, but also sent Indian collectors to botanically rich areas of the Himalayas where Westerners were still barred. A string of closed mountain principalities like Sikkim, Nepal and **Kashmir** prevented access from India into the Himalayan heights explored only later by **Joseph Hooker** and, subsequently, by **Frank Kingdon Ward** and his contemporaries. Wallich was also very efficient at sending plants back to England, dispatching to **Kew**, and to friends elsewhere, carefully packed boxes of seeds, bulbs and live plants with almost every departing ship. He is reputed to have sparked the British craze for rhododendron-growing after he sent back some seeds of *Rhododendron arboreum* from Nepal, packed into tins of sugar, in 1815.

Rhododendron arboreum

SOME WALLICH PLANTS

Allium wallichii
Berberis × *interposita* 'Wallich's Purple'
Buxus wallichiana
Dryopteris wallichiana
Euphorbia wallichii
Geranium wallichianum
Lilium wallichianum
Meconopsis wallichii
Ophiopogon wallichianus
Pinus wallichiana
Rhodiola wallichiana
Rhododendron wallichii
Selinum wallichianum

Wargrave Plant Farm, Berkshire

Several plants recall the Wargrave Plant Farm at Twyford, which amalgamated with the Bagshot nursery of Waterer's (see **Knap Hill**) in 1914 to become John Waterer, Sons & Crisp. Examples are *Anthemis tinctoria* 'Wargrave Variety', *Geranium* × *oxonianum* 'Wargrave Pink' and *Trollius pumilus* 'Wargrave'.

Warham, Norfolk

The snowdrop *Galanthus plicatus* 'Warham' is named after this village whose rector the Revd Charles Digby sent **E.A. Bowles** some specimens of this especially good form of snowdrop, which a local soldier had sent back from Sebastopol after the Crimean War.

Warley Place, Essex

Once the home of **John Evelyn**, Warley Place, near Brentwood, later became more famous as the garden of **Ellen Willmott**. Her family moved here in 1875 and she soon set about making the garden. Incurring extravagant nursery bills and sponsoring plant hunters, she sank much of her considerable fortune

W
X
Y
Z

into the garden – especially after the age of 40, when she inherited the property. The leading alpine nursery of the day, **Backhouse** of York, was commissioned to build a huge rock garden, complete with a glass-roofed cave for ferns, and there was a walled garden, an orchid house, a palm garden, trial grounds and of course a rose garden. Gardeners were another essential expense: at one time there were said to be more than 100, reputedly tending 100,000 different plants. Few fortunes could survive such profligacy, and eventually Miss Willmott had to reduce the scale of the garden. After her death it fell into ruin, eventually to be adopted by the Essex Wildlife Trust as a nature reserve. Its other monument is the garden plants named after it: there were once many more than today, but several are still in commerce, including *Campanula* × *haylodgensis* 'Warley White', *Cistus* × *crispatus* 'Warley Rose', *Veronica prostrata* 'Warley Blue' and *Epimedium* × *warleyense*.

Washington DC: National Arboretum

A 446-acre site in north-eastern Washington was set aside in 1927 for this government-run research, conservation and educational institution. Its extensive gardens and collections include both growing plants and herbarium specimens for research. The emphasis is on trees but there are significant displays of other plants, including aquatics and herbs. A long-standing plant-breeding programme has produced many garden plants over the years. One is the fine purple-leaved *Viburnum sargentii* 'Onondaga'; another is the grass *Pennisetum alopecuroides* 'National Arboretum'.

Washington, George (1732–1799)

The palm genus *Washingtonia* honours the first president of the United States. He planned his own 500-acre garden on the banks of the Potomac at Mount Vernon, named in the spruce *Picea orientalis* 'Mount Vernon' and the laurel *Prunus laurocerasus* 'Mount Vernon'.

Waterer family see Knap Hill

Waterperry Gardens, Oxfordshire

An English gardening legend, the Waterperry Horticultural School, near Oxford, was founded by Beatrix Havergal (1901–1980). She was not a wealthy benefactress, but a determined and visionary gardener. She moved here in 1932, with six students and £250 to invest in her venture. It succeeded. School and garden went from strength to strength, supporting each other, and Waterperry acquired a status all of its own, producing illustrious 20th-century women gardeners such as Pamela Schwerdt and Sibylle Kreutzberger, who went on to be head gardeners at **Sissinghurst**, and **Valerie Finnis**. The garden, big and complex with a huge range of plants, was maintained mainly by the students. Beatrix Havergal retired in 1971 and the school closed, but the garden and nursery continue. Among plants with the Waterperry name are *Clematis* 'Waterperry Star', *Aster novi-belgii* 'Waterperry', *Narcissus* 'Waterperry' and *Veronica* 'Waterperry Blue'.

W
X
Y
Z

Washfield Nursery, Kent

Helleborus niger

This nursery near Hawkhurst closed in 1999 after a distinguished career as the birthplace of many widely admired plants, raised by successive owners Hilda Davenport-Jones and Elizabeth Strangman. Hellebores are the plants that connoisseurs associate with the nursery. Hilda Davenport-Jones introduced the most well-known cultivar of the Christmas rose, *Helleborus niger* 'Potter's Wheel', which first occurred as a chance seedling in a Staffordshire garden in the 1940s. Elizabeth Strangman worked for her at the nursery from the early 1960s, after training at **Cambridge University Botanic Garden** and working for **Constance Spry**. She took the helm at Washfield in 1971, by which time she too had become an enthusiastic hellebore breeder. Her breeding and selection work in the following years raised both the quality and the profile of hellebores, helping to dispel their reputation as difficult plants and bringing them into more gardens. Her introductions have included double-flowered hellebores, and many unusual and sought-after strains and cultivars, some with flowers in dark slate-blue, apricot or yellow. She was the co-author, with **Graham Rice**, of *The Gardener's Guide to Growing Hellebores* (1993).

SOME WASHFIELD NURSERY CULTIVARS

Campanula 'Kent Belle'
Geranium clarkei
'Kashmir White'
Heuchera 'Pewter Moon'
Omphalodes cappadocica
'Starry Eyes'
Origanum 'Kent Beauty'

Elizabeth Strangman's unfailing eye for a good plant was not restricted to hellebores. Plants named after Washfield include *Galanthus* 'Washfield Warham' and *Nerine bowdenii* Washfield form, and a number of much more well-known plants have found their way to the gardening public through the nursery, either as chance finds in the wild, as deliberate hybrids, or as plants found or raised by others that were recognized as something special.

Wave Hill, New York

This garden and environmental centre in the Bronx started life as an 1840s house in a historic parkland setting on the Hudson River, in an area of the Bronx called Riverdale. The property was gifted to the City of New York in the 1960s and came under the directorship of the remarkable plantsman and gardener Marco Polo Stufano. For 35 years he ensured that the 28-acre gardens were filled with inspiring planting all year round, using exotic rarities as well as unusual hardy plants to ring the seasonal changes.

Weigel, Christian (1748–1831)

The shrub genus *Weigela* is named for this German doctor and botanist.

Weihenstephan, Germany

Ligularia 'Weihenstephan' and *Hosta* 'Weihenstephan' are named after a contemporary German garden at

W
X
Y
Z

Freising, near Munich. It belongs to the University of Munich's horticultural school, and its perennial borders are planted on sound ecological principles to ensure that plants suit their site and are compatible with each other.

Went, James (1845–1936)
The pretty pink cottage-garden perennial *Linaria purpurea* 'Canon Went' is named after this clergyman who was headmaster of Wigginston boys' school in Leicester.

Westonbirt Arboretum, Gloucestershire
Begun in the 1820s by Robert Holford (1808–1892) and continued by his son George, who died in 1926, this was one of the world's first large tree collections. It remains among the finest today, with over 18,000 trees and shrubs of some 3,700 different kinds in an area of 600 acres. Since 1956 Westonbirt has been owned and managed by the Forestry Commission, who were able to restore the arboretum after a long period of neglect, and eventually opened it to the public for the first time. From 2001 to 2004 it was the venue, each summer, for a festival of contemporary garden design. Trees named for the arboretum include *Pinus sylvestris* 'Westonbirt' and *Magnolia sprengeri* var. *diva* 'Westonbirt'.

Wheatcroft, Harry (1898–1977)
Rosa 'Harry Wheatcroft' is a bicoloured red-and-yellow bush rose named for this Nottingham rose breeder. Other Wheatcroft roses are 'Queen Elizabeth', 'Fragrant Cloud' and 'Super Star'.

Wichura, Max Ernst (1817–1866)
Ancestor of many rambler roses, *Rosa wichurana* is named after this German botanist who found it in **Japan** in 1860.

Wiley, Keith see The Garden House

Wilks, William (1843–1923)
The name of the Revd W. Wilks is perhaps most widely known from the cooking apple that is named after him, but this energetic and dedicated cleric is also remembered for his association with Shirley poppies, named after the parish near Croydon, Greater London, where he was vicar. He selected cornfield poppies that lacked a black eye, and these became the ancestors of the poppies, in a range of sparkling clear colours, that remain popular garden annuals today. Wilks was also a much-respected secretary of the **RHS** from 1888 to 1920, a period during which membership boomed and the famous sites at **Wisley** and Vincent Square were acquired. Having helped put the RHS on a sounder financial footing, he became its first paid secretary, retiring only in 1920, aged 77.

Williams, John Charles (1862–1940)
When the Scottish plant collector **George Forrest** sent seed of *Camellia saluenensis* back from **China** in the early 1920s he could not have suspected that this valuable plant would eventually give rise to more than 100 named cultivars. As one of Forrest's main sponsors, J.C. Williams of **Caerhays Castle** in Cornwall was the first to grow the new plant and raise hybrids from it. The first, and one of the best, was the very free-

W X Y Z

flowering *Camellia* × *williamsii* 'J.C. Williams', which was named only after its breeder's death. Other enduringly successful cultivars raised from the original cross include the award-winning 'Mary Christian', named for Williams's wife, and 'Saint Ewe'.

Willmott, Ellen (1858–1934)

One of the most significant Victorian gardeners, the wealthy and haughty Miss Willmott gardened at **Warley Place** in Essex. She also had gardens in the south of France. A considerable plantaholic, she was a proficient plantswoman, and was active on several committees of the **RHS**. A measure of her standing

Eryngium giganteum

is that she and **Gertrude Jekyll** were the only two women among the 60 original recipients of the RHS Victoria Medal of Honour in 1897. Gertrude Jekyll described her as the greatest of all living women gardeners, and she was the first woman elected to the Linnean Society (see **Linnaeus**). An expert on roses, she financed a lavishly illustrated book, *The Genus Rosa*. She also liked to breed and propagate plants, raising two plants of *Ceratostigma willmottianum* from seed sent to her by **E.H. Wilson**, whom she sponsored. Other plants named for her include *Rosa gymnocarpa* var. *willmottiae*, *Potentilla nepalensis* 'Miss Willmott' and, most famously, *Eryngium giganteum*, the plant known colloquially as 'Miss Willmott's Ghost'.

Ernest Henry Wilson (1876–1930)

One of the most significant of all the great plant hunters, E.H. Wilson was a student at the Royal College of Science, in London, when his first opportunity came. He was asked by the ground-breaking **Veitch** nurseries to go to **China** to find seed of *Davidia involucrata*, the handkerchief tree, first found by **Armand David** in 1866. Wilson was in for a disappointment, for the tree to which he was directed had been felled for timber. However, on this and subsequent trips to China he discovered many new plants – more than 5,000 species according to some estimates. His most famous find was *Lilium regale*, his favourites *Acer griseum* and *Kolkwitzia amabilis*, and he did eventually return with the *Davidia involucrata* that had been his first aim. Wilson ultimately became director of the **Arnold Arboretum**, but was killed three years later in a car accident. The many plants named for him include *Acer wilsonii*, *Corydalis wilsonii*, *Exochorda giraldii* var. *wilsonii*, *Gentiana wilsonii*, *Hypericum wilsonii*, *Magnolia wilsonii*, *Primula wilsonii* and *Trachelospermum jasminoides* 'Wilsonii'. *Sinowilsonia henryi* is a connoisseurs' shrub or compact tree (a relative of *Hamamelis*), first found in China by **Augustine Henry** and later introduced into Western cultivation by Wilson. Its genus name translates his nickname, 'Chinese' Wilson. His daughter Muriel is commemorated by the bamboo *Fargesia murielae*.

W
X
Y
Z

Wilton House, Wiltshire

A bergenia, a rhododendron and a rose are named after this historic house near Salisbury. Period formal gardens around the house have incorporated the work of several contemporary designers, while the broader setting is an 18th-century landscape garden.

Winkworth Arboretum, Surrey

An unspoiled valley near Godalming provides a backdrop of lakes and natural woodland for this sensitively planted collection of trees and shrubs, created from the 1930s and now in the care of the National Trust. There is a National Collection of rowans, and good numbers of Japanese maples, eucryphias and rhododendrons thrive in the neutral to acid soil. A form of birch and a celandine are named for Winkworth.

Winter, William (d.1589)

Captain Winter accompanied Sir Francis Drake, as far as the Straits of Magellan, on his voyage of 1578. In Tierra del Fuego he discovered *Drimys winteri*, an evergreen shrub that later became known as Winter's bark. Rich in vitamin C, it was used by the Fuegan Indians to treat scurvy. Winter brought his valuable find back to Britain – the first recorded introduction of a Chilean plant into cultivation.

RHS Garden Wisley, Surrey

This magnificent garden near Woking is the flagship of the **RHS** and the oldest of its four gardens, acquired in 1903 as the gift of **Sir Thomas Hanbury** and developed continuously ever since. It was in fact the society's fourth garden, at 240 acres much larger, and with scope for far more varied and ambitious development than had been possible at the previous three in west London. Every aspect of the society's activity is represented, with formal, informal and thematic gardens (including model gardens, a walled garden, a large rock garden, borders by **Piet Oudolf**, and a country garden designed by **Penelope Hobhouse**), a range of glasshouses with the huge new Bicentenary Glasshouse, an arboretum, fruit fields, the handsome laboratory building, a horticultural library and an excellent gardening bookshop and plant centre. The Portsmouth Field – overlooked by many visitors – is the main RHS trials ground, where flowers and vegetables old and new are put through their paces and the most successful varieties are awarded the coveted RHS Award of Garden Merit. The numerous expert plantsmen and gardeners who have worked at Wisley have selected or bred countless forms and cultivars, and some 50 commercially available plants are named after the garden.

SOME WISLEY PLANTS

Clematis Wisley ('Evipo001')
Clematis cirrhosa 'Wisley Cream'
Gaultheria × *wisleyensis* 'Wisley Pearl'
Helianthemum 'Wisley Primrose'
Ipheion uniflorum 'Wisley Blue'
Malus 'Wisley Crab'
Nyssa sylvatica 'Wisley Bonfire'
Penstemon pinifolius 'Wisley Flame'
Rosa Wisley ('Ausintense')
Saxifraga 'Wisley'
Sorbus 'Wisley Gold'
Spigelia marilandica 'Wisley Jester'

W
X
Y
Z

Wistar, Caspar (1761–1818)
Thomas Nuttall was responsible for naming *Wisteria* to commemorate this American professor at the University of Pennsylvania. The variation in spelling is explained by Wistar's German origin: his family name, Wüster, had reputedly been anglicized in different versions.

Woking, Surrey
Woking was the hub of an area where many small nurseries mushroomed in the 19th century, rapidly making Surrey the most important county in Britain for the breeding, sale and, increasingly, the export of garden plants. This was partly a result of pressure of space in the old London nurseries. Surrey, within easy reach of London, offered large areas of land that were too poor to farm but easy to work and ideal for the growing number of plants introduced from America and **China**. Famous nursery names from the area include **Knap Hill**, Waterer, **Jackman** and **Goldsworth**, while plants named after the town of their breeding include *Clematis* 'Belle of Woking' and *Rhododendron* 'Star of Woking'.

Wynn-Jones, Bleddyn and Sue see Crûg Farm Plants

Xalapa
The exotic tender perennial *Mirabilis jalapa*, known as the four o'clock flower or marvel of Peru, is named after the town Xalapa, near Veracruz, in Mexico.

Mirabilis jalapa

Yaku-shima
Rhododendron yakushimanum, an important compact species much used in breeding garden hybrids (known to enthusiasts as 'yaks'), is named after this small, mountainous island in **Japan**. Several other plants bear the name, notably *Miscanthus sinensis* 'Yakushima Dwarf' and *Hydrangea anomala* subsp. *petiolaris* 'Yakushima'.

Yinger, Barry
A former curator of Asian plants at the US National Arboretum in **Washington** DC, Yinger is an American plantsman with a special interest in the flora of Asia. He has made many long-distance plant-hunting trips and his specialist nursery, Asiatica, on the farm where he was brought up in Pennsylvania, stocks many rarities. It prides itself on its numerous varieties of *Asarum*, *Arisaema*, *Aspidistra* and *Rohdea*, as well as ferns and hoyas. In operation since 1996, it has links with a number of Asian nurseries and plant collectors. Its owner is named in a cultivar of ground ivy, *Glechoma hederacea* 'Barry Yinger Variegated', and in *Hosta yingeri*.

Zantedeschi, Francesco (1797–1873)
Arum lilies, *Zantedeschia*, are named for this Italian physicist and priest.

Zinn, Johann (1727–1759)
The flamboyant Mexican flowers called zinnias commemorate this German botanist and physicist, a professor at the University of Göttingen.

Zwanenburg see van Tubergen

W
X
Y
Z

ACKNOWLEDGEMENTS

OutHouse Publishing would like to thank the many individuals in nurseries, gardens and horticultural organizations who have assisted in the compilation and checking of information for this book. Thanks also go to Margaret Gregory and the staff of Hampshire County Library, and to the staff of the RHS Lindley Library.

PICTURE CREDITS

David & Charles would like to thank the following for supplying images and granting permission for their use. The Publisher has gone to reasonable lengths to seek any other possible rights holders.

David Austin Roses 21
Adrian Bloom/Bloom Pictures (© Javier Delgado) 34
Beth Chatto Gardens 50
Chelsea Physic Garden 51
Cotswold Garden Flowers 57
Crûg Farm Plants 59
East Lambrook Manor (© Valerie Finnis) 68a
The Guernsey Clematis Nursery Ltd 73
Hillier Nurseries Ltd 5a, 5b, 5c, 94
W.E. Th. Ingwersen Ltd 100
The Board of Trustees of the Royal Botanic Gardens, Kew 109
The Linnean Society 81, 87
National Portrait Gallery 41
Old Court Nurseries 26, 147, 155
Mrs Ruth Stearn 170
RHS, Lindley Library 17, 75, 96, 157, 180, 183